ROUTLEDGE LIBRARY EDITIONS:
MANAGEMENT

Volume 43

ENGINEERS AND MANAGEMENT

ENGINEERS AND MANAGEMENT
International comparisons

Edited by
GLORIA L. LEE AND CHRIS SMITH

LONDON AND NEW YORK

First published in 1992 by Routledge

This edition first published in 2018
by Routledge
2 Park Square, Milton Park, Abingdon, Oxon OX14 4RN

and by Routledge
711 Third Avenue, New York, NY 10017

Routledge is an imprint of the Taylor & Francis Group, an informa business

© 1992 Gloria L. Lee and Chris Smith

All rights reserved. No part of this book may be reprinted or reproduced or utilised in any form or by any electronic, mechanical, or other means, now known or hereafter invented, including photocopying and recording, or in any information storage or retrieval system, without permission in writing from the publishers.

Trademark notice: Product or corporate names may be trademarks or registered trademarks, and are used only for identification and explanation without intent to infringe.

British Library Cataloguing in Publication Data
A catalogue record for this book is available from the British Library

ISBN: 978-1-138-55938-7 (Set)
ISBN: 978-1-351-05538-3 (Set) (ebk)
ISBN: 978-0-8153-6562-4 (Volume 43) (hbk)
ISBN: 978-1-351-26112-8 (Volume 43) (ebk)

Publisher's Note
The publisher has gone to great lengths to ensure the quality of this reprint but points out that some imperfections in the original copies may be apparent.

Disclaimer
The publisher has made every effort to trace copyright holders and would welcome correspondence from those they have been unable to trace.

Engineers and management

International comparisons

Edited by
Gloria L. Lee and Chris Smith

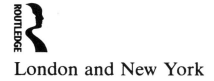

London and New York

First published 1992
by Routledge
11 New Fetter Lane, London EC4P 4EE

Simultaneously published in the USA and Canada
by Routledge
a division of Routledge, Chapman and Hall, Inc.
29 West 35th Street, New York, NY 10001

© 1992 Gloria L. Lee and Chris Smith

Typeset in 10/12pt Times by
Falcon Typographic Art Ltd, Fife, Scotland
Printed and bound in Great Britain
by Mackays of Chatham PLC, Chatham, Kent

All rights reserved. No part of this book may be reprinted
or reproduced or utilized in any form or by any electronic,
mechanical, or other means, now known or hereafter
invented, including photocopying and recording, or in any
information storage or retrieval system, without permission
in writing from the publishers.

British Library Cataloguing in Publication Data
A catalogue record for this book is
available from the British Library.

Library of Congress Cataloging in Publication Data
A catalogue record for this
book is available

ISBN 0-415-06426-0
ISBN 0-415-06427-9 (pbk)

Contents

List of tables vii
Acknowledgements viii

1 **Engineers and management in comparative perspectives** 1
   Gloria L. Lee and Chris Smith

2 **Wheels within wheels: predicting and accounting for fashionable alternatives to engineering** 20
   Ian A. Glover

3 **The engineering dimension and the management education movement** 41
   Peter Armstrong

4 **Japanese engineers and management cultures** 54
   Kevin McCormick

5 **Engineering and management in West Germany: a study in consistency?** 72
   Peter A. Lawrence

6 **The work of engineers in Hungary and their place within management cultures and hierarchies** 100
   Gyula Fülöp

7 **Symbolizing professional pride: the case of Canadian engineers** *Gloria L. Lee*	117
8 **Engineers and trade unions: the American and British cases compared** *Peter Meiksins and Chris Smith*	137
9 **Irish engineers: education for emigration?** *James Wickham*	162
10 **British engineers in context** *Gloria L. Lee and Chris Smith*	184
References	204
Index	220

Tables

9.1 Social origins of engineering students, 1986   165
9.2 Graduate emigration rates, 1984–9   167
9.3 Irish electronics industry employment by sector and ownership, 1985   168
9.4 Engineers and innovation: engineers as percentage of total employment, by industry sector and product innovation   169
9.5 Qualified engineers' function   170
9.6 Engineers' location   171
9.7 Engineers and qualification by functional area   174
9.8 The relevance of degree qualification by functional location (engineers with B.Sc. Electronics Engineering only)   176
9.9 Engineers' evaluation of current job   181

Acknowledgements

The editors would like to thank all the participants in the original Workshop on Management Cultures and the Engineer, for their contributions on the day and for the continuing interest shown by a number of them in the development of the early theme into this book. We also wish to acknowledge the support given to the project by the Centre for the Study of the Professions, Aston Business School Research Institute, and express our special thanks to Julie Ellen for her work in organizing the workshop and in preparing manuscripts for the book.

Chapter 1

Engineers and management in comparative perspectives

Gloria L. Lee and Chris Smith

INTRODUCTION

Growth within capitalist society is dependent upon continual technological renewal and change. Engineers are at the centre of this dynamic process. The organizational form that has come to represent growth is the large corporation. Management, and not owner entrepreneurs, is at the centre of such forms. Engineers and management are therefore central features of contemporary society. Yet how these two groups relate and interact is not straightforward. Assumptions of a simple integration and affinity are not confirmed by experience. Nowhere is this more pronounced than in Britain, where management has become synonymous with decision-making, finance and marketing, and somehow disconnected from making and providing goods and services.

This book examines the relationship between management and engineers through an international perspective. The reason for this is simple. Management as a subject of academic inquiry and a practical set of disciplines and tasks can no longer be understood as simply containing *universal principles* – one best way of organizing and doing things. Ideas of what constituted management conformed to this pattern when American social science and business dominated the world – although there was always considerable discrepancy between this and the actual practices of management. But today, America is no longer the centre of organizational capitalism. Japan, the Pacific Basin and Europe are rival centres of business success. Therefore the possibility of rival models of management has assumed a practical significance. Cross-national organizational research has revealed major differences between societies in their style, structure and practice of management.[1] International management courses are proliferating in business schools, exposing hitherto core principles of management to the microscope of national scrutiny. What was previously considered universal is increasingly seen as only *one* way of managing. We need, then, to see management in a comparative, not a general, light.

The literature on engineers as organizational professionals has also been prone to this comparative myopia. Engineers have been assumed to be technical experts, the translators of industrial design practice, the masters of production control and surveillance, performing similar functions across all advanced societies. And yet, the status of being an engineer varies significantly between countries. Moreover, the association between engineers, managers and other workers demonstrates marked divergences across similar societies. Given the centrality of engineers to modern society, it is important to explain the consequences different patterns of integration into management have for their work and action. This book is an attempt to reach a wider understanding of this relationship between engineers and management. As such it not only sheds a broader view on the British situation, in all its particularities, but also argues that *all* approaches to engineers and managers as *historical* groups require an appreciation of national differences and diversity. Without seeing differences, it is not really possible to begin to see similarities or the emergence of common or 'best' practices across societies.

This chapter will examine some of the differences in the relationship between engineers and managers across divergent economies. It will suggest some models for explaining these differences, relate these to the situation of British engineers and conclude by discussing the possibility and mechanisms for diffusing different ways of integrating these two groups from one society to another.

ENGINEERS AND MANAGEMENT

Management comprises people who bring with them different specialist occupational perspectives, which to a greater or lesser extent continue to shape their thinking about the strategic direction of the organization. Access into management is broadly divided into those who enter as graduate trainees with general and/or professional or specialist knowledge, and those who have worked their way up from the shop-floor or office, acquiring firm-specific competences and experience, and possibly part-time qualifications. There are obvious differences in the *level* of management supplied by these two routes, the graduate route generally facilitating the prospects for higher-level positions, although there are marked national variations in this pattern. In the British context managers are typically people with practical experience of the business, rather than high-level academic qualifications (Handy et al. 1987). Many, particularly among the older managers who survived the two recessions of the past decade, will have spent much of their careers within the same organization, working their way through a particular functional specialism or through general management.

For those who have specialist occupational skills, like engineers, there are two broad alternative career strategies within organizations: to remain in technical work or to move over into more general management. For most engineers their early career is likely to centre around their technical expertise in a particular sphere of work, but their satisfaction from this may diminish, especially if there are limited opportunities for career advancement – in the absence, for instance, of dual career ladders which provide extended career progression through a technical specialism. Also, again particularly in the British and American contexts, they may become increasingly aware of the limitations their role as technical specialist has with regard to events within their organization and therefore wish to take on more responsibility through mainstream management. While some may take this direction through choice, others may feel that it is thrust upon them. Dobson and Stewart (1990), for example, found people in middle management resentful at having to abandon their technical work for which they were highly qualified, in order to take on administration. A more challenging alternative would be to give technical functions more strategic responsibilities without requiring them to abandon engineering.

This latter course has, however, proved problematic, particularly for British engineers. Organizations, especially in the sphere of manufacturing, have traditionally made a distinction between what Dalton (1959) referred to as *staff* and *line* positions. Staff positions, where engineers are usually located, provide specialist support for line functions, but their overall contribution to decision-making is largely unrecognized. Line positions have responsibility for managing the throughput of the organization, which connects them much more closely with the arenas of power and influence.

Functional differentiation has long persisted as the central organizational structure within British companies, and this has reinforced engineers as staff, providing technical expertise in research and development (R & D), design and manufacture. They are concerned with productive activity, which in Britain has less strategic value than marketing, finance or general management. However, as we describe below, this is not the case in other countries. Moreover, over the last decade there has been a major attack on the benefits of functional management, because it reinforces divisions, slows down decision-making and increases bureaucracy. Project management, with integrated teams of specialists united around tasks not functions, has expanded across all developed countries. In many companies, specialist functional structures have been abolished, and 'integrated professional groups' created to facilitate closer integration between design, production, distribution and sales (Smith, Child and Rowlinson 1990). There has also been a tendency to externalize many technical functions to specialist subcontractors, themselves composed of integrated not functional specialist teams (Smith 1989; Whittington 1991). As we discuss in Chapter 10, new information technologies have facilitated organizational reforms of the specialist hierarchy, many of which have implications for the relationship between engineers and managers. The growing technological sophistication of the production environment increasingly necessitates a more technically trained line management, and engineers provide an important source of supply for this area. Old divisions between line and staff appear no longer appropriate to this new situation (Long 1987).

If we look outside the British context, in other management structures, rotation of specialists is more strategic, and the creation of functional occupational identities deliberately minimized. This is the case in Japan. In other words, while the choices available to engineers in managerial hierarchies are not limitless, neither are they confined to what has largely been a British or American practice. In order to explore these comparative differences more fully, we need to examine some of the *reasons* advanced for variety rather than single forms of organizing and integrating engineers into management.

EXPLAINING NATIONAL DIFFERENCES

Before we illustrate the pattern of divergence in the relationship between engineers and managers across the countries covered by this book, it is necessary to discuss some of the various models advanced to explain these differences. First, there is the assumption that each society is unique, and therefore universal or general models of management are not possible. Such a pure *culturalist* view is unsustainable because it cannot explain why societies go through such dramatic changes in their organizational life, why societies *look alike* or, more importantly, learn and borrow from each other's practices (Child 1981). Modified versions of the culturalist approach have studied the character of a country's institutions and how these transmit *differences*. Institutionalism has become the dominant method of explaining differences across societies (Lane 1989). It has proved the most fruitful in terms of research, because, instead of trying to locate and define rather vacuous concepts like 'culture' or 'national identity', it focuses on more concrete and observable entities, like the way management is developed, or how education, skill, training and qualifications transmit different messages and build divergent structures across societies.[2] Within this approach it is possible to suggest that the route a society took to industrialization, or the legacies it brought with it, contributes to explaining national differences (Smith and Meiksins 1991). We are also able to say that the historical structuring of the meanings and boundaries between groups – like management and engineers – is arranged differently between societies because of such issues as the timing and route into industrial capitalism. We can illustrate these points by briefly describing some recent approaches that have borrowed from or used a modified institutionalist explanation of societal difference.

Lane (1989), comparing labour and management in Britain, Germany and France, implicitly divided employment relations into two dichotomous models, and then investigated the manner in which state and civil institutions reproduce these models. Her approach is not truly comparative, but an evaluation of societies against relatively *fixed* criteria. She borrows extensively from institutionalist approaches to achieve this end. The *positive* model is where a society has co-operative industrial relations, secure and segmented employment relations, broad-based, bilateral national training systems, skilled/qualified labour, and technically centred, long-term oriented management practices. The *negative* model is pretty much the opposite of these qualities – adversarial industrial relations, insecure and fragmented employment relations, market-based or *ad hoc* training standards, etc. Her book, therefore, although ostensibly a comparative study of the three countries, is in practice an *evaluation* of each society against these *universal* dualities. Given that the positive model is largely based on one reading of German practices, and the negative model on one reading of British practices, not surprisingly, with some qualifications to the more adulatory attribution to the German model, her book nevertheless concludes by praising the former and bemoaning the latter. Her model has largely defined her narrative, and comparative analysis is relatively weak.

More explicitly on the issue of engineers Meiksins and Smith (1991) have identified four abstract models available for organizing the *production* of engineers in advanced capitalist societies. However, they have not attempted to *evaluate* societies against *fixed* efficiency principles to create a 'pecking order', but rather see the models as abstractions which represent the historical experience of different entry points into industrial capitalism. They suggest that the character of national institutions and work organization can be strongly shaped by the past and timing. Legacies from previous economic systems or state traditions can be *reinforced* by the new mode of production, rather than, as was assumed by Marx and industrial society theory, 'swept away' by the development of the technological forces of the economy.

They distinguish four models for producing and organizing engineers: craft, managerial, estate and corporatist forms of organization (Meiksins and Smith 1991). *Craft* forms are the traditional apprenticeship structure, whereby training and knowledge are acquired under the pupillage of older craftsmen, within the workplace, with little or no formal education away from the workplace. *Managerial* forms, in contra-distinction, are university-based and market-oriented methods of acquiring expertise, qualifications and credentials which are institutionalized through specialist associations. These need not secure closure or licensing for engineers, as in the American case, but they emphasize the integration of engineers into management and away from other workers. Such a form creates occupational associations with an organizational or autonomous character. *Estate* forms are education and training principles sanctioned from above, with state authority, so that statutory controls, a clear hierarchy and fixed correspondence between training and a division of labour occur. *Corporatist* forms are where there is an interaction between state systems and large employers, with the latter creating dependency structures, firm-specific training and reducing market-based occupational identity. Professional associations are weak, and forms of representation are through the firm.

Societies broadly correspond to these different forms, although it is possible, especially for the early industrializers, to develop overlapping forms and therefore display more heterogeneity. Britain, the first industrial nation, alone among capitalist societies developed engineers through craft routes and professionalized them before the development of state education. In Britain, engineers have been unable to differentiate themselves from skilled manual and technical workers, are unionized along occupational lines and are poorly placed within managerial hierarchies. The craft legacy has continued to structure engineers' identities (Smith 1987). In the USA, engineers professionalizing through higher education credentials were at the forefront of organizational capitalism and scientific management, were relatively secure in their managerial status and were unable to form sustainable trade unions. In Germany, Sweden and France, state-led modernization placed the engineer in a well-structured and economically safe position as an estate elite. In Japan, with its giant organizations and weak occupational labour markets, engineers are a stable part of the corporate hierarchy, tied to the firm, with weak professional or external forms of representation.

Another line of cross-national research has focused upon the construction of 'social actors', which involves uncovering the basis of differentiation or boundary formation between classes, groups and occupations. In societies where being an engineer is not clearly constituted, where ambiguity exists with other occupations, social groups or classes, then relations between engineers, management and other employees may be conflictual and unco-operative. Heidenreich (1991), building on the work of Boltanski (1987), has compared the constitution of the white-collar/blue-collar divide in Germany, Italy and France and how this structured the way technical and manual labour utilized information technologies. He concluded that

> The institutional and professional identity of the white-collar worker in Germany shows the greatest stability, as the process of differentiation began very early and can be legitimized as well by reference to specific professional competences – ones necessary for the existence of administrative functions. In Italy the formation of the socially active agent *quadri* has only just begun; the corresponding professional, institutional and cognitive identity is still quite uncertain. In France the identity and extent of the socially active agent *cadre* is continually being called into question by definitional struggles (at least outside the central group of university-educated engineers).
> (Heidenreich 1991: 20–1)

The consequence of these differences for the introduction of computer technology were that in Germany there was consensus over the division of tasks, responsibilities and labour due to the shared technical culture between engineers and manual workers; whereas in France, a rigid divide between mental and manual labour, and ambiguity over the the position of *cadres* encouraged more hierarchy and control. Both societies made 'efficient' use of the technology, but in markedly different ways. In Italy, there was an ill-defined and uncertain relationship between technical and manual groups involved in information technology.

If we apply the same perspective to the British situation, we could argue that British engineers have been experiencing 'definitional' struggles over the boundary relations with technical and manual groups, and attempts by engineering associations to introduce new *elite* categories on a market not a statutory basis have not assisted in clearly delimiting the relationship between white-collar and blue-collar workers. Competition between manual and technical unions over the control of Computer Numerical Control machines, for example, highlights this conflict. The demise of the common craft culture has also undermined the consensual work culture between engineers, technicians and manual workers, and increased hierarchical animosity along the lines experienced in France (Smith 1987, 1989; Crawford 1989).

National diversity is, then, the summation of historical differences in the timing and entry into industrial capitalism, and is reproduced through a society's institutions; but it is not a *fixed* process, but rather one subject to continual change and renewal. Borrowing between societies is normal, and the global nature of the economic systems means there are pressures and contradictions between international and national institutions (Smith and Meiksins 1991). What, then, are some of the differences in the relationship between engineers and management in our country studies?

ENGINEERS AND MANAGEMENT: NATIONAL DIFFERENCES

Britain

The social identity of engineers varies across national boundaries partly because the functional roles they perform in industry and their institutionalization vary. In Britain, 'the line between mental and manual, conception and execution, does not neatly demarcate engineers from craft and production workers' (Whalley 1986: 67). Neither do technical workers possess supervisory responsibility over manual workers, and engineers 'do not routinely engage in supervision' of lower technicians (Whalley 1986: 92). Rather, they work within a division of labour that is relatively fluid and do not monopolize 'mental' labour or conceptualization through educational credentialism that fosters an absolute split between themselves and craft labour. Moreover, employers have not sought to split technical labour into a neatly graded hierarchy determined by educational qualifications, and have generally reinforced the identity of technical workers *as workers*. They 'regard all their technical employees as different grades of the same kind of staff' (quoted in Whalley 1986: 41). It has therefore been logical to see technical workers in Britain as part of a 'staff' or white-collar section of workers. It is consequently harder for engineers to develop a clear *managerial* identity.

Whalley (1986: 192) has noted how the association of engineers with craft apprenticeships 'served to reinforce the general feeling that engineers were not suited to the higher ranks of management'. The growth of managerial hierarchies in Britain has not benefited the engineers, who are under-represented compared with their German, Japanese or American counterparts. Management ideology in Britain lacks a technical heart. Part-time study and apprenticeships remained the dominant method of training engineers until the 1960s. McCormick (1988b: 589) has noted that graduate entrants into engineering accounted for 35 per cent of total engineers in 1945, increasing to 50 per cent in the mid-1960s and over 90 per cent in the 1980s. Graduate engineers are therefore a relatively late development, and exist alongside other sources of entry; and while university training has introduced a new element of segmentation into technical hierarchies, these remain subject to contest and the 'definitional' struggles referred to earlier.

English engineering institutes multiplied in the nineteenth century but entry was only examinable at a late stage, and most technical workers did not belong to these institutes. Early commentators, such as Gerstl and Hutton (1966: 39-40) bemoan the proliferation and fragmentation of engineering institutes and the diversity of entry routes for becoming an engineer. The question this raises is why there was no political strategy to unify the disparate bodies, and, further, how the different interest groups within engineering related to each other and the state. McCormick (1988b: 589) notes that the institutes resisted the offer from university-based engineers to 'provide a complete professional education within the universities'. This offer was 'outvoted by the "practitioners" who insisted on the retention of pupillage and apprenticeship as the means of providing practical training'. We argue in Chapter 10 that the strengthening of the applied elements on engineering degree courses only served to overcrowd them and make them less popular among students. Such efforts reflected the ideas of Finniston (1980) to make engineering education more relevant to the needs of industry, rather than distance university education from industry. At the institutional level, the recent attempts to gain a unified voice through mergers between institutes does not seem likely, of itself, to enhance the national standing of engineers.

British engineers, in comparison with their continental counterparts, are disadvantaged in manufacturing managerial hierarchies, closely identified with manual labour, poorly paid, endowed with an ambiguous social identity, unionized and lacking in credential power. Meiksins and Smith, in Chapter 8 in this volume indicate the different structuring of professionalism in the USA and Britain, and the effect this has had on the propensity to unionize among engineers. The disadvantaged place of British engineers in managerial hierarchies has, they suggest, contributed to this situation.

America

In America, employers structured universities to provide their industries with technical labour already divided into neater segments, and with a clearer integration into managerial careers (Noble 1977). Zussman's (1985: 154) study of American engineers notes that although 'degreed' and 'non-degreed' engineers frequently perform the same jobs, as in Britain, those without qualifications are fewer in number, and 'without a degree, claims to engineering status are not transferable'. Moreover, American engineers are prepared for a managerial career. So, although not management, 'they accommodate themselves to management and adopt a business ethos' (Zussman 1985: 198-9). American engineers enjoy higher status, and a relatively secure, middle-class professional identity; and while they are organizational employees, not fee-based professionals, they are more autonomous from large-firm dependency relative to their Japanese equivalents. American employers have structured managerial hierarchies in ways which integrate engineers, and they therefore have few of the status ambiguities experienced by British engineers. This reflects the nature of American society, which is more market oriented, and the timing of the formation of engineers within American capitalism.

Canada

Engineers in Canada have taken elements from both the US and British cases, although they are distinct from both in having obtained state licensing and occupational closure along classical professional lines. Lee examines these issues in Chapter 7 in this volume. The history of engineers' professional closure in Canada is interesting for the points of contrast with British practice and the effect this has had on engineers' place in management. Millard's (1988) history of the struggle to obtain state licensing for engineers in Canada demonstrates an initial closeness to the British experience, in which at the time an 'engineer', in the public mind, [was] ... still closely identified with tradesmen, [and] stigmatized by negative nineteenth-century British aristocratic attitudes towards manual labour – they were not quite gentlemen like doctors and lawyers' (Millard 1988: 9). Canadian engineers initially followed the British modèl of creating a professional a institute as a learned society to improve the standing for engineers as an elite of independent professionals. But this strategy later changed to one of a struggle towards the state licensing of engineers. Once accepted, licensing was quite quickly pushed through local provincial legislatures – the decentralized nature of the state in Canada assisting this process. This strategy was successful because *all* engineers were represented by a single institute, unlike, say, the highly competitive and fragmented nature of engineering institutes in Britain.

The second contrast is in the decline in number of apprenticeship engineers and the production of engineers through universities, something that only happened in Britain in the 1970s. The late industrialization of Canada meant the levels of engineering expertise necessary to operate in capitalist society could only be obtained through universities not apprenticeships and pupillage along the craft model. Finally, in Britain, engineering institutes have accommodated to unions, as discussed in Chapter 8, perhaps because of their general societal legitimacy, and institute leaderships have not felt threatened, as were the Canadians, into pushing for licensing to block unionization.

Germany

In Germany, management culture is closely informed by engineering concerns and engineers are dominant in management hierarchies in manufacture. As Lawrence describes in Chapter 5, the dominance of engineers within German management has ensured that an engineering perspective on design, production and marketing is the main legitimatory ideology of industry. Manufacturing industry is awarded higher status, which is reinforced by the elites in the society choosing to educate their children in engineering and other production-related pursuits. The legitimacy of manufacturing is thus reinforced. What Lawrence calls a 'congruence' – not conflict – between engineers and management does not mean that engineers, as a group, have always acted in a unified way. The history of the formation of the profession has recently been studied by Gispen (1990), who has uncovered major political battles between competing classes of engineers committed to differing political projects for the place of engineering in capitalist society. The evolution of the profession was not straightforward; neither did it follow the American model of a transition from 'shop culture' to 'school culture'. Rather, the reverse occurred, as an 'industrial-capitalist' faction of the profession broke away and institutionalized itself against the 'academic elite'. Later working-class engineers formed the world's largest technical trade union in order to pursue their interests. What is significant about these struggles is that they received political expression through the different class forces in German society, but produced, as a legacy, a strong position for *all* engineers and legitimacy for technical knowledge across the society. The security of status for technical groups, and the absence of rigid polarization between mental and manual labour, but rather their relative unity through a common *technical* culture, are the enduring strengths of the German situation.

Japan

Engineers in Japan are part of the stable group of lifetime employees, enjoying the same conditions as other core workers. They emerge from a theoretical university education to be trained and retrained with firm-specific skills of the large employers for whom most will work for the rest of their lives. The absence of external professional and managerial labour markets in Japan means the enterprise has considerable control over engineers, who cannot, like their western counterparts, readily exercise their market power by moving to another employer. McCormick, in Chapter 4, following the work of Koike (1988), makes it clear that the logic of employment relations in Japan has been to bring core blue-collar workers up to the status and conditions normally reserved for white-collar workers in the west. Engineers share the same hours, enterprise union and corporate indoctrination into 'company mindedness', socialize out of work together and face similar pressures of regular job rotation and general conditions as core blue-collar workers. This so-called 'white-collarization' has suited employers concerned to maintain control over labour deployment and prevent the formation of strong job properties. The high quality of training and education, the absence of rigid job demarcations and emphasis on mobility and rotation have diffused a shared technical culture within management and the manual workforce, and inhibited the sort of rigid division of labour typical of, say, France and, to some extent, Britain, following the dismantling of apprenticeship systems.

Japanese manufacturing management, like that in Germany, has been dominated by engineers. Far more engineering than science graduates enter large firms. These have tended to be very production-centred, and responsible for the attention to quality and detail we have associated with Japanese manufacturing excellence since the Second World War. But can this position be maintained in a Japanese economy moving into innovation and basic research, no longer able to be dependent upon American and European science and technological development? This shift will require more scientists and engineers and more creative R & D, and may also necessitate organizational structures geared towards encouraging individual initiative. Greater differentiation, dual career tracks, less rotation and a less corporate integration may follow this transition. In other words, Japanese R & D engineers and other technical specialists may come to share the same sorts of conditions as their western counterparts. Just when western firms are adopting certain Japanese practices, the model appears to be changing. Firms like Toyota, the pioneer of 'just-in-time' inventory control, are now abandoning this and building warehouses because of the environmental fall-out of having goods permanently on the roads. In a similar vein, McCormick indicates that creating more room for difference and individualism for innovation among R & D engineers may signal a break with the pressures of conformity within in the corporate community. But how far this will challenge the existing structure remains to be seen. At a more general level, however, this line of analysis suggests that national patterns of training engineers are not immutable, but rather subject to divergent pressures. Hence we must, when describing different national models, be cautious about implying their permanence. They are historically constructed, and as such, remain subject to discontinuity.

Hungary

Our chapter on Hungarian engineers in management (Chapter 6) provides a contrast with other societies, because state socialist regimes impose quite distinct features on to the organization of technical specialists. Gyula Fülöp shows how, prior to the Second World War, Hungarian industry was relatively undeveloped, with engineers few in number. Hungarian development pre-war came under both American and German influence, but it was the

Soviet model of industrialization, and the dominant and particular place of engineers in that process, that chiefly characterizes the Hungarian experience today. Within this model, engineers are treated as technical experts, with little business or organizational training, largely responsible for controlling production, and planning and co-ordinating work within tightly bureaucratic and hierarchical structures. Engineers are in relatively subordinate positions, separated from the managerial hierarchy, although formally the chief engineer and chief accountant share power with company management within the enterprise. Fülöp shows how the experience of being an engineer under this regime was progressively routinized, with most engineers ending up in non-creative, production functions, their technical knowledge under-utilized and their access to research and development circumscribed. Therefore, the post-war experience for Hungarian engineers has been one of degradation, with engineers in subordinate and routine production functions within large, bureaucratically structured Hungarian enterprises. This has resulted in the previous high status for engineers – typical of the German model which was influential in Hungary prior to the war – declining. Despite this, engineers were being produced in large numbers from Hungarian educational institutions, and this over-supply, as with the case in the Soviet Union, reinforced their under-utilization in Hungarian industry.

Reforms in Hungary began from the early 1970s. With the aid of western capital, there was a growth of small-scale industry within the private sector. Engineers, seeking more creative work, did not flood into this informal economy but, as is common in Hungary, retained their state employment and took a second job within the private sector. The 1970s and 1980s witnessed more eclectic borrowings of models of organization – autonomous work groups, brigades, self-management – but not a major structural reform of Hungarian industry and the role of engineers. Only with the radical changes in the late 1980s, and formal democratization and marketization of state socialist societies, has major reform been placed on the political agenda. Despite this, the economic indebtedness of Hungary and increasing competition in global markets mean any transition to a new situation is likely to be slow and painful. For a minority of engineers, more creative, entrepreneurial opportunities in the small-firm sector will be available; but for the majority, without significant capital or support, unemployment or the continued experience of subordination within large organizations seems likely to remain their fate.

Ireland

In general the fit between education and the division of labour within capitalism remains problematic. This is especially true in the case of developing countries. Engineers remain central to industrialization, and not just the management of enterprises. Amsden's (1990) analysis of the spread of industrial capitalism to south-east Asia, for example, argues that production engineers are the only group with the technical knowledge to make imported technology work. In her study of South Korea the expansion of engineers far outstrips that of managers. In Korea economic nationalism and relatively closed internal labour markets within giant firms tie engineers to the economy in a style and pattern of large-firm dependency similar to that already described in Japan. In countries influenced by other models, Ireland for example, the closure of labour markets and relatively 'forced' integration of engineers into the national economy and management structure are much less pronounced. It is often forgotten that when Britain industrialized it too restricted the migration of its craftsmen; the Soviet Union, and all state socialist countries, followed a similar closure of their labour markets in the interests of autonomous national economic development. Autarky or authoritarian state control over the labour market is not unusual within developing countries. Wickham, however, describes in Chapter 9 how in the Irish case, while close co-ordination between state agencies and the universities exists to satisfy the expected demand for engineers, this does not restrict the circulation of this specialist labour. Engineers, moreover, are not the motor for indigenous Irish industrialization, as in the Korean case, but part of a global labour market, working, in the main, for the subsidiaries of foreign multinational companies in Ireland or abroad.

Irish engineers have access to management, and in Ireland the status of an engineer is high compared with Britain, university entrants, for example, needing higher than average entry qualifications. But the dominance of the foreign-owned subsidiary in the economy means management posts are often restricted within the company as a whole. This is particularly the case with Japanese electronics firms, where corporate management is all Japanese and opportunities for Irish engineers to work in Japan do not exist. Moreover, the particular small-scale character of foreign subsidiaries in Ireland means that they do not offer a fast track into corporate managerial hierarchies of multinational companies.

Given the openness of the Irish labour market, and the structure of foreign-firm investment, mainly but not exclusively in production facilities, the reduced opportunities for engineers mean emigration is high – averaging above 40 per cent in recent years. This situation cannot be changed, as Wickham implies, by making engineers' education more practical. It has little to do with what engineers are *taught*, but a lot to do with the structure of the Irish economy – being an open peripheral state on the edge of Europe. Irish managers complain about the absence of practical training among graduate engineers in the same way that British managers complain about their engineering graduates (Whalley 1986). But successful economies, such as Japan and Germany, do not provide their engineering graduates with practical but rather with highly *abstract* skills and knowledge. It is the utilization of this knowledge in the enterprise which is crucial. Paradoxically, given the lack of opportunities at home, Ireland is more integrated into a European-wide labour market for professional skills and Irish engineers may benefit from the creation of European qualifications for engineers.

The Irish case illustrates the importance of considering the entire national environment when analysing the relationship between engineers, work opportunities and management. Nation states, as we discuss in Chapter 10, may still be the main formation agencies for professional labour, but the increasingly global nature of industry means that the pattern of firm-training and socialization into management hierarchies will differ markedly depending upon historical and contextual details of a country's relation to the international economy.

CONCLUSION

This book emphasizes the fruitfulness of studying engineers and management within a comparative context. The engineering profession is everywhere a class- and status-divided entity, its particular national character or representation a reflection of political struggles within distinct national settings and historical periods. The legacies that particular patterns of formation bequeath continue to exercise a powerful influence on existing practices. There is a danger, however, of overplaying the strength of national diversity between societies. Capitalism is, after all, more global today than at any other time. Firms are increasingly transnational, and engineers are part of an international division of labour and in a global labour market. Large firms can create 'best practice' – shared methods, techniques and practices that do not straightforwardly represent *one* country's experience – and this must qualify assumptions about a neat correspondence between institutions and action bounded by *national* practice. Wider developments, such as the regionalization of Europe through the EC, are creating environmental pressures which undercut the autonomy of national institutional standards and practices.

Comparative study, as well as testing the universality of our conception of what an engineer is, also holds up a mirror to one's own society, allowing careful exploration of points of difference, strengths and weaknesses. Reform programmes, such as initiated by the Finniston inquiry (1980), were strongly informed by a comparative perspective, as were the sociological champions of the engineer whose research and comparative national probing partly led to the setting up of the Finniston committee (Glover and Kelly 1991). But changing well-established institutional arrangements is likely to be very slow, and unlikely to remove deeply embedded national cultures. After all, the poor performance of Britain with regard to the provision of technical education and training has long been identified, and the need for change signalled by many government commissions. And yet, reform has been almost non-existent. Reform, especially of a radical nature, cannot be accomplished without representing and mobilizing distinct factions or groups within the society and marshalling these to pressure for change at the level of the state. In Britain, the current prospects for 'revitalizing manufacturing' and 'enhancing the place of the engineer in management' are made problematic by the continuing decline of national manufacturing. Engineering recruitment continues to decline, and a recent survey among engineering graduates found 'two out of three' deciding against a career in engineering (*Guardian* 1989). Without the stimulus of a national crisis or disaster the overhaul of national institutions will only ever be *ad hoc*, sporadic and difficult. The persistence of diverse business and managerial practices, and therefore different patterns, relating to the experience of engineers within management looks likely to continue.

NOTES

1 Cross-national organizational research is too wide an area to review here, but Child (1981) provides a comprehensive summary of the transition from contingency to cultural analysis in organizational theory; Rose (1985) offers a systematic evaluation of the French 'Aix Group' – Maurice, Sellier, Silveste: – Sorge (1991) offers a different interpretation of the same research. Glover and Kelly (1991) look at the consequences of comparative analysis for informing the thinking behind the Finniston inquiry (1980).
2 The Aix Group of institutionalists are connected with a British and German group (including Child) of sociologists interested in Anglo-German comparisons, especially in relation to management and engineers – they include Fores, Glover, Sorge and Lawrence. For an account of their influence on British industrial policy, especially the background to the Finniston report on engineers in Britain, see Glover and Kelly (1991). Rose (1985) has been both a critic and supporter of aspects of institutionalism. Lane (1989) has largely come to institutionalism via Child's work, and is more vocal in her support for German institutions. Gallie (1978, 1983) has been independent of these networks, coming to comparative analysis through a critique of Blauner and contingency theories of technology. His focus has been on Anglo-French comparative analysis through an action frame of reference, and a stress on attitudes and consciousness absent from the Aix school. He nevertheless stresses institutional variations between France and Britain. For a critique of aspects of the British institutionalists' views on engineers see Smith (1990).

Chapter 2

Wheels within wheels: predicting and accounting for fashionable alternatives to engineering

Ian A. Glover

Since the 1970s numerous writers have proposed ways in which 'organizational cultures' might be developed to help make the use of human and material resources more effective. An apparently separate notion which has also enjoyed a considerable amount of popularity among articulate lay people and pundits of several kinds is that of post-industrial society. This chapter argues that each of these notions is highly suspect, that they are interrelated and that they can be most comprehensively understood, in the UK context, as historically contingent and predictable outcomes of British anti-industrialism.

In the first main section of the chapter reasons why the notions are interrelated are spelt out partly by using historical evidence, and it is suggested by way of explanation for them both that they are underpinned by Arcadian assumptions and urges. In the second main section it is argued that concern with culture at the organizational level of analysis and experience might have been predicted from knowledge of a historic lack of concern for task-relevant, sector-specific skills in British systems of education and training. It is argued, further, that attempts to alter organizational culture which are meant to effect improvements in performance necessarily have a shallow, remedial, short-term quality, and that it is very difficult for any improved performance to be sustained over the long term. In the next, third, main section it is suggested that the post-industrial thesis is inaccurate in most of its details, highly misleading in terms of what it is generally understood to imply and most comprehensively appreciated if it is classified as a mainly anti-industrial one.

In the fourth and final main section of the chapter, four

policy-oriented arguments in favour of engineering in general and manufacturing in particular as continuing foci of creativity and sources of wealth are presented. These arguments are used to suggest that in a society in which a dispassionate perception of the role of manufacturing was the norm, the two notions criticised in the earlier sections would probably have either been absent or generally dismissed as being too superficial and ephemeral for serious debate.

FORWARD INTO ARCADIA?

A Veblenian ideal of an industrial society would very probably portray it as one in which producers of wealth were rewarded and respected more than almost everyone else (Veblen 1921). The view that such people are 'human resources' to be 'culturally' manipulated and the apparent desire of the post-industrial theorists to 'outgrow' industrialism are both antithetical to such an idea, and anti-industrial and predictably so.

Britain became an industrial country without experiencing the kinds of socio-political revolution experienced in France, Japan, the USSR, Germany and several other industrial countries. Naval prowess and success in overseas trade and empire-building were important features of the backcloth to the indigenous growth of manufacturing which is often called Britain's industrial revolution (Fores 1981). Commercial interests in the City of London and the landed interest, predominantly in England, often interlinked by marriage and in other ways, underpinned political decision-making through most of the eighteenth and nineteenth centuries. Overseas trade enjoyed more prestige than what took place within the UK and it arguably still does. In the nineteenth century rising manufacturing and commercial interests in the provinces were accommodated and co-opted politically and socially (and educationally). In the process, and with the help of reforms in education, public administration and political organization, they tended to adopt some of the anti-industrial values of those whose social approval they sought.

Industrialization was itself a much slower process than is often assumed, and the relative decline of the British economy that first became apparent around 1870 was partly compensated for by imperial and other overseas activities, political, military and economic, in the century or so after then. Other compensations included the invention and/or spread of numerous 'great', 'British', etc., 'traditions' such as organized sport, popular monarchy, *laissez-faire* economics and adversary politics. These helped to celebrate past success, as well as compensating for, and sometimes exacerbating, contemporary and future difficulties. The harsh truths of the inevitability of the relative economic decline of the last century were largely ignored by politicians, along with the degree to which overseas, especially imperial, entanglements were economic burdens rather than assets (Barnett 1972, 1986).

Attitudes and diplomatic and economic decisions were, however, only important parts of the story of the retreat from reality. Civil service reform, from around 1870 onwards, institutionalized faith in the hopefully well-rounded amateur. Together with state neglect of higher technical and business education, it helped to ensure that in large industrial and commercial undertakings, with few examples outside the civil service to follow, technical, financial and commercial specialists were only too often correctly perceived and employed as subordinates of generalists from more advantaged social and educational backgrounds. The notion that someone might be broadly educated and capable of critical thought, *and* a technical or other specialist, has never taken root in Britain to the extent that it has in western Europe, for example (Glover 1980: 34).

Professional occupations and associations proliferated considerably in the century around 1900, but, as with developments in technical and commercial education, developments were always remedial and usually likely to complicate and obscure the original problems of inadequate education and training and the subordination of technical expertise. Competition between 'organizational professions' for scarce senior managerial positions made for undue complication and inefficiency in managerial hierarchies (Child *et al.* 1983; P. J. Armstrong 1984). Post-experience management education has been offered, with increasing surface success, as a solution for the technical and commercial ignorance of university-educated generalists, as well as for the narrowness of professional specialists. However, as Peter Armstrong (1987a) has emphasized, its content has generally reflected wider British values through its tendency to distance itself from productive activity. Another important weakness of British education and training has been the tendency to misclassify engineering as a subordinate and derivative part of science, with more able school-leavers with relevant qualifications encouraged at least until recently to study science rather than engineering at university level, and also doing so, and in much larger numbers – the opposite of the case in many competitor countries (cf. Finniston 1980; Ahlström 1982).

The organizational culture movement, as noted earlier, represents the activist (and often iatrogenic, whereby an attempted solution for a problem only adds to it) tendency in British culture. The post-industrial thesis has a much more passive quality. The former is ostensibly a 'fight' reaction, the latter a 'flight' one. Thus writings on post-industrial society often exemplify a pronounced lack of concern with reality and detail. For example, Fincham's (1987) otherwise very useful discussion of Lyon's (1986) arguments on the topic deals, among other things, with the changes in occupational structure and the roles of scientific and technical knowledge in economic development which are key topics for post-industrial theorizing. In each case, he skates over details such as what new or relabelled jobs are for, and research evidence on knowledge use, so that some of his arguments on them comprise interesting quibbles (with Lyon's points) rather than new and pointed insights. Fincham refers to Kumar's (1978) criticism of Bell's (1973) and others' assertion that increased research and development (R & D) spending represented the growing economic importance and value of theoretical-scientific knowledge and focuses almost entirely on that part of Kumar's argument concerned with R & D spending, rather than on those concerned with the differences between technical knowledge and scientific knowledge, which are much more pertinent for considering dubious post-industrialist assertions about the supposed primacy of the latter.

Although the organizational culture movement is undoubtedly activist in tone, and although this reflects its North American origins, it also manifests 'flight' beneath its 'fight' tendencies. This is because its underlying concern is with relationships between job holders, with their attitudes towards each other, far more than with their shared tasks (cf. Mant 1983). In this way it is predictably a manifestation of the Anglo-American management ethic which seeks to act as a healing balm for conflicts between job holders which result from unclear priorities and weaknesses in divisions of labour (Fores and Sorge 1981).

The reason why educated English speakers engage in 'fight' or 'flight' behaviour of the above kinds, that is, why they either attack a problem without thought and a plan, or run away from it, is ultimately very simple. They are, as discussed earlier, inappropriately educated and organized, and their reactions include varying elements of ignorance and defensiveness. They have been educated (and trained) to avoid rather than to prioritize and run manufacturing and related activities. Their perceptions of economic life are often arm's-length politicized ones; proffered solutions focus understandably, and in some ways reasonably enough, on the desirability or otherwise of state intervention in education, training and labour and other markets. Yet, although their perceptions are politicized and thus public, they are generally also private in so far as they are infused with individualism or forms of collectivism which are variously part of or reactions against it. Neo-socialist and neo-liberal ideologies compete with no agreed practical or moral philosophy for the role of government and the public sector (Olson 1982; Marquand 1988). The low status of factory work, of making things for the world's markets, and the much higher status of the City of London, of commercial and financial rather than industrial capitalism, of international trade over the domestic variety, conspire with the other factors mentioned above, plus the uncertain long-term benefits of North Sea oil and gas, to produce a situation in which most influential Britons do not know what they want for their nation's economy, except that it should continue to maintain them (Mann 1988). In the absence of some cataclysmic event, something like this situation is likely to continue into the twenty-first century.

ORGANIZATIONAL CULTURES AND DIVISIONS OF LABOUR

Common sense and/or elementary psychology suggest that four conditions need to be met for any form of human co-operation to be effective. First, those involved must be sufficiently motivated. Second, they need to possess relevant skills. Third, they need relevant knowledge, including technical knowledge and any 'theory' needed to help them understand the limits of relevant forms of empiricism. Finally, they need to be deployed in ways which ensure that their efforts, skills and knowledge are logically related to the demands of particular tasks (Glover 1985).

This claim means, in more theoretical language, that the technical and social divisions of labour, respectively those within and outside places of work, and as exemplified in the qualities, actions and deployment of those involved, should fit. Or again, in simpler language, it means that the right kinds of people with the the right sorts of skill and knowledge should do the right kinds of job in the right ways and for the right reasons (Glover and Kelly 1987). The claim is, I would argue, universally valid and relevant, if not by any means always easy to apply in practice. In a broadly successful business context, it is exemplified in Marks & Spencer's 'Gospel According to St Michael', which strongly emphasizes quality in production and of merchandise, service and every kind of relationship, along with 'simple' operating procedures and 'reasonable' prices (Tse 1985).

In his discussion of Marks & Spencer's strengths, Tse argued that they were indistinguishable, not only from those of the most successful Japanese companies, but from those of successful organizations everywhere. However, he also pointed out that because the attributes, attitudes and situations of organizations and labour forces vary so much, success is not a matter of imitating other successful organizations or societies, except in so far as success is understood to be a matter of achieving a suitable balance between focusing on the task and intelligent adaptation to the situation. Thus success could come, for any organization, by simply getting on with its job and by harmonizing with its context; it was not likely to result from the study and imitation of the culture of Marks & Spencer, or that of Japanese or any other companies.

A similar but more forceful attack on what he called the 1980s North American and British 'corporate culture craze' was made by Thackray (1986). For Thackray, the 'culture pedlars' (various human resources/personnel managers, management consultants, journalists and some academics) used the dubious assumption not only that organizational cultures existed but that top managers could positively influence their 'strength, direction, values, myths, symbols, language, mores, etc.' (p. 68). From this they had gone on to argue that corporate strategies could be moulded and altered through *manipulation, by top executives*, of organizational cultures in the forms of rituals, myths, social norms, and so on. Thackray argued that all such assumptions, but especially those implicit in the previous sentence, were facile and indeed dangerous. This was because organizations, rather than 'having' cultures, 'are' cultures, which could not be understood adequately from the top down (p. 69). Further, most organizations contained competing 'multiple . . . sub-cultures, or even counter-cultures', and it was normally impossible for top managers and/or 'consultants and human resources experts' to 'parachute' into them, to 'diagnose only . . . those elements which have strategic relevance' and to change them from the boardroom down (p. 69). A 'football or baseball coach' mentality was being employed in campaigns 'permeated with authoritarianism and bogus pragmatism' (p. 69). It assumed that workers wanted to be freed 'from the drag of weak cultures and to find personal meaning in strong ones' (p. 114). Yet the culture movement had paid virtually no attention whatever to existing 'cultures' at the sectoral and societal levels, nor even to interrelationships between sectoral and organizational ones. Crucial variables such as organizational size, organizational and sectoral structure, technology and the ages of products and services were generally ignored. Thackray concluded his attack using terms like 'banal', 'shallow' and 'irrelevant' in relation to constructive thought and useful action (p. 114).

For Sorge and Warner (1986:ch.2) the common-sensical arguments of Thackray would be supportable by ones which are rooted in physiology, biology, psychology, sociology, philosophy and some of the more heavyweight examples of recent organization studies. They argued that all attempts to differentiate between cultural and other variables in social science are meaningless and that all human action (including organization) is 'cultured', because it always has an emergent, experimental, holistic, unpredictable, pragmatic and non-rational quality, and because it is always '– at least unwittingly – specific to time and place'. This argument drew on the work of Popper and Eccles (1977) concerning the working of the brain, and on one of the authors' own discussions of the 'rational fallacy' (Fores and Sorge 1978; see also Fores, Glover and Lawrence 1991). In the first case human brain function, and human action, had been shown to be non-rational, or arational, in the terms just used to describe it. In the second, Sorge and Warner noted how with 'the waves of increase in mass literacy, education, higher education, and scientific activity, a legitimatory paradigm had been propounded following which the left, articulate brain hemisphere dominates the right one, and rational insight instructs practice'. However, the time had come to outgrow this tendency to exaggerate the formally rational elements of human action, and to 'bring unpredictable ingenuity into its own again' (p. 36).

Sorge and Warner followed these assumptions in going on to stress how, and very much in opposition to managerialist attempts to impose 'culture' top-down on organizations, 'a properly culturalist exploration should be distinctive for a lack of explicit concern about the cultural factor since *this glosses over the essence of culture*' (p. 34, my emphasis). In doing so they point out how the various 'contributions of cultural, contingency, and political-economic factors cannot be separated since they are different sides of the same coin, of non-rational problem-solving' (p. 34–5). This is all very much in tune with the point of Thackray's, noted earlier, about organizations 'being' rather than 'having' cultures.

It has already been suggested that recent concern with culture at the organizational level (of the kind just criticized) might have been predicted from knowledge of a historic lack of concern with task-relevant skills in Britain and of a poor fit there between the technical and social divisions of labour. This means that Thackray's 'corporate culture craze' is best understood as a set of attempts, of a closing-the-stable-door kind, to remedy long-term and fundamental societal-level weaknesses in education and training, occupation-formation, aspirations and expectations, and work organization, with manipulative, rationalistic and inevitably short-term organization-level solutions.

The above points, which are central to this section of the chapter's arguments, can be supported and illustrated by briefly considering some other discussions of the notion of culture. For example, Budde *et al.* (1982) demonstrated the enormous complexity of relationships between national and organizational cultures. They argued that while it ought to be possible to determine which national values and social institutions constrain or facilitate the pursuit of marginal objectives, the sheer range and number of influences and their often very unpredictable ways of interacting were likely to make over-simplification and confusion important features of analysis for a long time to come.

Allaire and Firsirotu (1984) produced a wide-ranging review of theories of organizational cultures and of general notions of culture, juxtaposing and relating together ideas from all the social sciences, with a bias towards anthropology. They described relevant ideas as 'porous' and 'ambiguous' and 'confusing but fascinating' (p. 215–16). Unfortunately the description of organizational culture which emerges has very similar qualities. This was because it was based on 'the symbolic conception of culture', differentiating fairly sharply between organizations' cultural and socio-structural systems, with the former including myths, values and ideologies and the latter structure, strategies, policies and processes (p. 195–9). The authors did little more than elaborate on the traditional distinction in writings on management between formal and informal organization and activity, whereas more comprehensive thinking about management and organization (e.g. Sorge and Warner 1986) regards *all* human artefacts – ideas, social institutions and three-dimensional creations – as 'cultured'. More simply they come close to defining organizational culture as little more than *governing* ideas, instead of as *all* the ideas and *all* the actions and outcomes of action which distinguish or fail to distinguish particular organizations.

This is not to deny that governing ideas are normally more influential than others (cf. Gunz and Whitley 1985). Yet to understand their roles fully, we must also understand the roles of other ideas along with the activities which they penetrate and legitimate, and which are penetrated and legitimated by all relevant ideas. Nor, also, is it to deny the value of studying intra-organizational meanings, values and action, simultaneously using as many relevant perspectives as possible (Meyerson and Martin 1987). Nor, also, is it to deny the practical relevance of variations in management style, in administrative procedures, in staffing practices, in the physical context of work, in the use of status symbols, in attitudes towards expressive behaviour and authority, and so on (Golzen 1987).

Similarly, technical developments in administration and operations are also highly relevant for identifying whatever is distinctive about particular organizations and more generally for understanding change within and across sectors of employment and whole societies (cf. Ettlie 1988). Yet to understand all these things as completely as possible it is also important, not only to try to explain their interrelatedness, but also to locate them – along with academic and managerial concern – historically and psychologically. This might mean acknowledging that the commercial success of books like *In Search of Excellence* and *The One-Minute Manager* may be of more significance to management research than anything that their covers contain.

Implementation of the 1980s thinking about organizational culture is often focused around the notion of human resource management (HRM). The latter's roots were in the American human and neo-human relations movements of the 1930s/1950s and 1950s/1960s, in 1950s advocacy of visionary goal-directed leadership by Peter Drucker and of integrated strategic people-management by Douglas McGregor, in the 1970s organizational development movement, and finally in American interest, following the first so-called 'oil shock' of the mid-1970s, in Japanese management (M. Armstrong 1987). HRM includes – put a little more simply than is usually the case – an approach to the attitudes, experiences and actions of employees which valorizes a visionary approach towards goals and the conscious development of a sense of common purpose. In many ways it is probably best understood as the sophisticated culmination – so far – of the liberal crusade against authoritarian management begun two generations ago by Elton Mayo or perhaps in the first half of the nineteenth century by Robert Owen. In the USA contemporary advocacy of HRM is fairly obviously designed to oppose the practice of traditional 'pay them high, ride them hard' management which Abernathy, Clark and Kantrow (1983) felt placed manufacturing in the USA at such a disadvantage compared with Japan.

Its quasi-religious overtones can be readily appreciated by reading *The Human Resources Revolution* (Kravetz 1988), whose author states on its first page that 'My interest is in the future because I am going to spend the rest of my life there' and offers the unsubstantiatable master assumption that 'the pace of change is accelerating all the time'. In a similar vein the 1960s are designated as the decade when 'the industrial period was at an end' (p. 18). In spite of these and other intoxicating features the book does contain much useful information about patterns of work and employment in the USA. It goes on to promulgate the financial and other benefits of participative management and sophisticated personnel practices. It undoubtedly makes some of the right noises: its main present source of fascination lies in the degree to which the author thinks that his thesis is *new*. A feeling of *déjà vu* results from reading a more specialized American text concerned with 'the clash of cultures' between managers and professionals in which Raelin (1986) applies 1980s style HRM thinking to a debate which first blossomed in the 1950s (cf. Gouldner 1957–8).

In Britain, Tyson (1987) and especially Sisson (1988) have suggested that recession, the need to be more competitive, weakened unions, more assertive managements and more individualized employee attitudes since the 1970s helped to generate somewhat more strategic, sophisticated and integrated employment practices on the part of many employers. However, they felt that full adoption of HRM strategies including full-blown top-down attempts to transform 'organizational cultures' was quite rare. Most relevant changes had probably been externally induced: economic pressures would seem to have been the main force behind the slimming-down of many organizations and tendencies to strengthen line managements at the expense of hitherto proliferating staff specialists.

Given the variety of economic and social arrangements it is not surprising that many doubts have been expressed about the transferability of panaceas from one culture to another. The idea that to succeed like the Japanese it might help to become like them has been widely challenged. Graham (1988) showed how much 'Japanese management' had non-Japanese origins and had long been widely practised elsewhere, arguing, for example, that it only made sense to go on describing techniques like just-in-time as Japanese if the aim was to help change attitudes by publicly equating the terms 'Japanese' and 'competitive'. Similarly, Warner (1987) suggested that while differences and similarities between Japanese and British management might be debated endlessly, the main practical lesson to be learned from Japan was to respect detail.

This point was also made very powerfully by Fukuda (1986: 26). He warned strongly against 'Blind imitation of others, especially from a vastly different culture', advocating 'creative adaptation' after 'the borrowed and the native' had been distinguished. This he felt was 'the most important lesson to learn from Japan' (cf. Sorge 1985 on relevant Anglo-German comparisons). Cool and Lengnick-Hall (1985) made the important and simple point that the easiest Japanese practices to transfer were likely to be those which were the most specific to particular workplaces, with the least transferable being those which depended heavily on nation-specific features of early socialization.

This chapter's contention that serious attempts at organizational change should be informed by understanding of background societal and historical influences can be supported from various angles. The difficulties of the comparative method were emphasized succinctly by Bryant (1970), who pointed out that different institutions in different societies were different institutions *to* them. Jaeger (1984) spelt out a number of difficulties of transporting management philosophies and practices across frontiers in discussing the possibilities for implementing organizational development techniques outside North America. Kempner (1984) attacked Peters and Waterman's *In Search of Excellence* (1982) for suggesting that managerial flair and determined leadership were the major components of competence everywhere. Also Boisot (1986) asked why so many organization theorists and economists so often wrote about culture without realizing it.

Why did the possibility of 'cultural' changes at the organizational level become a concern for growing numbers of English-speaking writers on management in the early 1980s? The deficiencies in education and training and the disjunctions between technical and social divisions of labour referred to earlier are probably most responsible. The tendency of high proportions of the most able members of each generation to eschew industrial (and, to a smaller extent, commercial) careers in Britain has been quite comprehensively studied (cf. Glover 1978, 1985; Sorge 1979; Swords-Isherwood 1979; Locke 1984, 1989; Handy *et al* 1988). Most of these authors record how education and training in the USA, as in Britain, have tended to prioritize the pursuit of knowledge for its own sake and to be subject to less direct state control than in several major competitor countries like France, Germany and Japan. Several of them have depicted Anglo-American attitudes towards manufacturing and various related forms of wealth creation as having complacent arm's-length qualities, with work organization being unduly complicated and top-heavy (cf. Child *et al.* 1983; Bessant and Grunt 1985; Glover 1985; Sorge and Warner 1986).

The onset of recession in the mid-1970s produced more problems for British and American managements than those of, say, West Germany and Japan and generated a fairly dramatic upsurge of interest among British and American management academics in comparative management. The more serious kinds of analysis by English-speaking management academics have included comparative study of the histories and institutions of nations, with varying degrees of focus on technical and social divisions of labour. Less serious analysis in the Peters and Waterman mould has offered quick organizational fixes combined with therapy to harassed managements engaged in slimming down and bootstrap operations. The slightly obsessive notion of excellence is probably attractive to individuals for whom improvisation and crisis management may appear to offer more scope for creative fulfilment than the sort of routine competence exhibited by West

Germans and Scandinavians (cf. Lawrence 1980; Huntford 1983; Lawrence and Spybey 1986).

None of the above points seek to refute those who, like Hickson and McMillan (1981), have used cross-cultural comparisons to show that certain organizational and managerial universals may be usefully applied in most economic sectors and countries. However, questions about where and how to apply them do often remain enormously difficult, demanding highly sophisticated analysis of organizational and national peculiarities, of time and space (Littler 1982; Swidler 1986).

THE POST-INDUSTRIAL CHIMERA

If attempts to change attitudes and behaviour at the organizational level are often well understood as distractions from competent technical work, the notion of post-industrial society often goes further by seeking to sideline and downgrade it.

The more vulgar forms of the post-industrial thesis suggest that the problem of production has been solved, that this is a positive development because manufacturing work is somehow inevitably degrading, and that 'clean' jobs in services, generally assumed to be characterized by intellectual interest and often by 'caring', 'professional' relationships, are increasingly the norm. Industrial society is thereby assumed to be that of the 'smokestack' or 'sunset' industries of the century or so to 1960 or 1970, in which the typical employee is a figure in a Lowry painting or Charlie Chaplin in *Modern Times*. The attractiveness of the post-industrial idea to graduates in the humanities and to many others with intellectual and/or caring political pretensions and without direct experience of manufacturing therefore seems fairly obvious (Barnett 1972: ch. 2).

It may be sensible to assume that the significance of the post-industrial idea lies more in its effects on people educated to regard industrialization as a rather painful process, and on other lay opinion and opinion-formers, than in the writings of such major past proponents of it as Bell (1973) and Touraine (1971). However, we should remember that serious advocacy of post-industrialism does not gainsay the desirability of manufacturing remaining a crucially important activity for the foreseeable future. Instead, such advocacy is more in tune with the 'legitimatory paradigm' described earlier here which exaggerates the formally rational elements of human action and downgrades unpredictable ingenuity (Sorge and Warner 1986: ch. 2).

One important problem connected with the post-industrial notion concerns use of the terms 'technocrat' and 'technocracy'. For Giddens (1973: 258-9), 'Technocracy is not just the application of technical methods to the solution of defined problems, but a pervading ethos, a world-view which subsumes aesthetics, religion and customary thought to the rationalistic mode.' This is virtually identical to the legitimatory paradigm of Sorge and Warner. Yet it is rather different to the sort of technocracy prevalent in (in many ways engineer-dominated) societies like West Germany in which technique, or *Technik*, means engineering conceived as simultaneously controlled and unpredictable ingenuity, and emphatically not the sort of formally rational insight and codified scientific knowledge guiding practice which Giddens (a British critic of post-industrialism), and Bell in the USA and Touraine in France (advocates of it), felt was coming into its own. The significance of this ostensibly mere terminological problem is in fact considerable, because post-industrialists have tended to change the meaning of technocracy from 'rule by engineers' to rule by scientific and economic rationality. Bell and Giddens are inhabitants of English-speaking countries in which science has often enjoyed greater prestige than engineering, and while Touraine's France is arguably the historic home of the 'true' engineer-technocrat, and a country in which natural science is not generally a route to senior executive positions, French engineering higher education and engineering practice do tend to be infused with a belief in scientific rationality and intellectual rigour, and of course Touraine is himself an academic.

The argument will return to the influential idea of post-industrial society as a 'knowledge' one, but it will first address the very central and basic elements of post-industrialism concerned with patterns of employment and of consumption. It is true to say that, in the UK and several other major industrial countries, employment in services has come to include about two-thirds of the labour force, with manufacturing only accounting for around a fifth or a quarter. However, the idea that this means the decline of manufacturing as a source of employment and wealth is a very misleading one indeed. Instead, the relevant changes mean that the significance and weight of manufacturing are *growing*.

This last point is probably the most important one of this chapter.

It relies heavily on the thesis of the self-service economy (Gershuny 1978, 1983; Gershuny and Miles 1983; and on some aspects see also Cohen and Zysman 1987). According to Gershuny, there was an important flaw in the conventional view that fewer people work in manufacturing due to higher productivity and because demand for its outputs is relatively static, and because demand for services is more dynamic, making for more jobs in services. The flaw concerned the idea that demand for goods is relatively static; in fact, it was growing considerably.

Further, many service workers did not ultimately produce services. Service occupations and employment sectors divided into goods-related services and services ones proper. In the former case, services jobs contributed towards, and/or otherwise relied upon, the production of goods. Such jobs included all services ones in manufacturing and most or many in distribution, communications, wholesaling, retailing, banking, finance, insurance, property, technical services, marketing research and advertising, the hiring, maintenance and repair of goods, and so on. Services jobs proper had services, 'social' like health care, government or teaching, or 'personal' like entertainment, catering, dry cleaning, hairdressing, tourism and domestic services, as their 'products'. If goods-related services jobs were added to those in manufacturing (or more broadly defined 'industry'), then industrial/manufacturing jobs remained extremely important, and constituted a half and often considerably more of all jobs in many industrial countries including Britain. Personal services jobs were no more important either numerically or in terms of expenditure than they had ever been, perhaps less.

The main trend which the above represented was that towards the self-service (or 'new service') economy. What was (and is) happening is that people did want more services, but that they obtained and consumed them by substituting goods for services bought on the market. For example, people bought televisions and video cassette recorders instead of live entertainment, domestic appliances instead of domestic and laundry services, and cars and motorcycles instead of public transport. Also, the ongoing division of labour meant that the production of the relevant goods, including DIY equipment, eventually meant that fewer workers were employed in (*more efficient*) factories with more goods-related jobs in 'services'.

Other features, of varying importance, of serious/academic

versions of the post-industrial thesis may be summarized, along with relevant criticisms, as follows. First, it was agreed that the main industrial societies were becoming so affluent that economic scarcity was becoming a non-issue, with class conflict either diminishing greatly in importance or changing its form. Second, Bell, Touraine and others have argued that experts are taking over power from the old owning classes, Bell having regarded the development as benign, and Touraine having regarded it as problematic because he suspected that the experts would rule in their own interest. Thus it is argued that the emerging society is a 'knowledge' one planned by experts, with theoretical knowledge and its owners and/or producers dominating practice, replacing the practical wisdom and experience of the past, and with the university rather than the business firm becoming the dominant institution.

Both of these arguments can be criticized severely. It is not clear whether the industrial countries can sensibly be regarded as having finally outgrown problems of scarcity. Not all of their poorer inhabitants would agree that they have. They face problems in obtaining and using natural resources, which are often linked with fierce and sometimes damaging competition between themselves. On the notion that expert knowledge means expert power, Kumar (1978) criticized the use of educational and R & D expenditure statistics in attempts to substantiate it. Regarding the belief that theoretical/academic/scientific knowledge is the motor of technical change, he used a substantial body of empirical data to argue that it continued to mean the development of practical experience and wisdom, of technical knowledge which often absorbs scientific knowledge but which is not a product of it (see also Fores 1979; and Glover 1987). More generally the degree to which experts are 'on top' rather 'on tap' in the advanced industrial or late capitalist societies has been widely questioned by those who have studied the characteristics of business and political leaders.

Another major strand of post-industrialism concerns an apparently inexorable shift from supposedly 'dehumanizing' employment in manufacturing to hopefully more congenial forms of employment in services. In spite of the widespread use of employment statistics in support, it is none the less misleading. First, large-scale employment in services, in agrarian as well as industrial societies, is far from new. Indeed, Britain was 'post-industrial' in terms of the distribution of employment in 1840, partly because manufacturing jobs had just become numerous enough for the notion of it becoming post-industrial to have meaning (Fores 1981)! Second, the most significant long-term shift of the last century or so in employment patterns in many industrial countries has been from jobs in farming to ones in services, and growth in manufacturing employment has long been exaggerated (Kumar 1978). Third, white-collar jobs are often very routine and other services jobs are often unpleasant and/or menial (e.g. in office cleaning, catering, refuse disposal, with even those of dentists and surgeons being the former), or otherwise stressful in an interpersonal sense (e.g. law enforcement, teaching, social work), whereas manufacturing jobs may be increasingly sophisticated and challenging (cf. Gallagher 1980, who showed that in the late 1970s, and before the early 1980s' shake-out of manufacturing jobs, only about 5 per cent of Britain's labour force was employed on assembly lines in manufacturing, with other manufacturing production being of the craft, batch or process types).

Various other features and criticisms of the post-industrial thesis are worth noticing. It is of course unscientific in so far as it embodies an attempt to predict human behaviour. Also there are significant differences between its North American and continental European versions. The former tend to predict rule by caring professionals and the latter, writing in settings in which technocrats, rather than Anglo-Saxon-style professionals, are prominent top job holders, seem to worry more about unrestrained use of technical expertise.

Some writings of the 1980s, with varied but generally quite speculative concerns and all broadly favourable or not unfavourable towards the post-industrial idea, either expressed serious doubts about its validity, or transparently used it as a convenient metaphor without empirical justification. Thus in *The Post-Industrial Utopians*, Frankel (1987) admitted its catch-all speculative character while explicitly avoiding the issue of whether it was coming into existence. In debating the notion of the information society, which has been variously treated as synonymous with the post-industrial one or identified as its successor, Lyon (1986; 1987) showed how far the two notions are intertwined while admitting that they were so influential and broad in scope that they diverted attention from several issues and trends of much more genuine significance. Veal (1987: 55–8) criticized those who had suggested that 'information workers' were coming to form the dominant group of occupations (in post-industrial society) by pointing out how the (often only apparent) increase in their numbers did nothing to alter the fact that, as ever, the ultimate end products of their efforts were still goods and services. Finally a fairly strong example of the naive use of 'post-industrial society' as a convenient but vapid metaphor for the future was provided by Hirschorn (1984).

Two more hard-nosed discussions of changes in work and employment offered two final criticisms of the post-industrial thesis. Thus Blackburn, Coombs and Green (1985) emphasized how the one common factor in the history of technical change was increasing complexity of mechanization, with the dramatic developments in information technology of the last generation being best understood simply as a very important part of the general trend. In other words, while information technology might have 'revolutionary' effects on many particular aspects of production, employment and consumption, it was neither fundamentally revolutionary in itself, nor likely to revolutionize or otherwise dramatically transform whole societies. Second, Rajan (1987), who studied the recent growth of jobs in services in Britain and its wider economic ramifications in some detail, was unable to offer any real evidence to the effect that jobs in services were replacing manufacturing jobs as sources of wealth. Many services jobs had simply been contracted out from manufacturing. Further, the whole idea that 'information-based' and/or 'service' industries have been replacing older 'traditional', 'low-technology' and/or 'smokestack' ones has been strongly rejected on empirical grounds in recent years by the authors of three texts on American, British and French engineers (respectively Zussman 1985; Whalley 1986; Crawford 1989).

THE ARGUMENTS FOR MANUFACTURING

So far, the chapter's arguments have assumed that competence in manufacturing is desirable, without attempting to support the assumption comprehensively. The few listed points which follow represent a start at making this case. However, three other, preliminary points need making before turning to them.

First, it is assumed, without much explanation or qualification, that wealth generation is a valuable end in itself. This is not, of course, always the case: some products and services are of no value or have negative value to society, and processes of wealth generation often have harmful side-effects like poor treatment of employees and environmental pollution. Nevertheless, the idea that, other things being equal, wealth generation is a benevolent activity is regarded as axiomatic. Second, this chapter is not prejudiced against services, although their status has often suffered because they are intangible and because service-sector employment has often been inefficient and/or menial. Thus it almost goes without saying that the author regards health care and many other services as more socially useful than the production of many goods. Third, the ongoing globalization of the world's economy can be quoted to good effect in support of application of the principle of comparative advantage against the pro-manufacturing case. Thus if country P can prosper more by exporting an exquisitely delectable kind of parsnip which can only grow on a large scale in its unique soil and climate, than by manufacturing and exporting goods, then there would almost certainly be no economic reason why it should try to switch to the latter. Diamond mining or financial services would of course be more likely than parsnips to be profitable in this way.

The four arguments in favour of manufacturing now follow:

1 *The 'strategic reason'.* Most services do not add value as readily as most kinds of manufacturing because they tend to be much less capital intensive, and the scope for expanding exportable services in Britain and many other countries is not great. But, especially in the event of a non-cataclysmic war, or in that of a major recession, an economy which lacks the ability to make a wide range of things including producer goods is particularly vulnerable. In 'normal' times (and in any case) attempts to encourage growth of production are much more likely to succeed in countries which retain basic capacities such as those for steel-making, machine-tool manufacture, and so on. More generally, the ability to produce equals national power, for use for good or ill (Pollard 1982: 18; Kennedy 1987).

2 *The rise of the self-service economy.* This was covered in the previous section of the Chapter. It was argued there that living standards and employment are increasingly, not less, dependent on manufacturing as households replace services with goods and because a high proportion of jobs in services are goods-related or goods-dependent rather than 'pure' services jobs. Britain's growing dependence on manufacturing was discussed graphically by Godley (1986), who noted how from 1981 to 1986 spending

on goods was rising about twice as fast as spending on other things, and how a rapidly rising proportion of this spending was on imported goods. The dependence of services jobs on manufacturing has been thoroughly explained for the USA by Cohen and Zysman (1987), who noted, for example, that 'manufacturing plus services sold to manufacturing firms equals half the [US] economy' (p. 22; see also Aldington 1986 on Britain). The chairman of Sony put the last point a little differently by arguing that 'only manufacturing creates something new ... products ... of more value than the raw materials they are made from' and that (in Japan anyway) 'the service elements of our economy are subsidiary and dependent on manufacturing' (Morita 1988: 51–2).

3 *'Fascinating fabrication is preferable to boring bureaucracy or aggro in handling customers.'* This statement comes from a student's essay of some years ago, and (on 'aggro') a newspaper television reviewer's description of *Fawlty Towers* as 'great comedy' because it depicted 'a single great truth', in this instance that many service-sector jobs of the type which 'process people' are conflict-ridden due to the relative absence of a shared focus or task such as the making of a tangible end product. The serious point being made here is *not* that it is desirable for as high a proportion of the labour force as possible to work in factories (cf. Alford 1988: 51). The opposite may almost be the case, at least as far as large-scale production is concerned, because capital-intensiveness normally implies superior levels of output and efficiency. The point is that, as Harvey-Jones (1986) and Evans (1986) have argued, engineering is a highly creative, inherently exciting activity, and human beings are engineers by definition (see Glover and Kelly 1987). Thus, man is *homo faber*, the maker and doer, and it is no accident that historical epochs or periods are named after materials, artefacts or energy sources (e.g. the Bronze Age, the Computer Age, the Atomic Age). For Morita (1988) the idea that services jobs were somehow more 'advanced', because they are generally cleaner, quieter, and so on, than manufacturing ones, was misleading. On average, manufacturing work was technically more complex than work in services, and it was facile to think of it as less advanced simply because the numbers directly engaged in it were declining.

4 *Third World Keynesianism versus the Arcadian post-industrial*

cop-out. Here the argument is that in an increasingly interdependent world economy, it is selfish for a people to opt out of its development in order to indulge itself in the genteel poverty of post-industrial navel-gazing. Harvey-Jones (1986: 86) thus suggested that to

> say that we are looking backwards if we try to reverse the decline of UK manufacturing overlooks the fact that for millions of people around the globe, the benefits of manufacturing haven't yet arrived. There is an immense future for manufacturing when much of the world's population still spends its time weeding.

Or, from a slightly different angle, Alford (1988: 102) argued that the invisible earnings obtained in the City of London represented 'an outstanding case of private gain achieved at the expense of considerable social loss', because it was in the nation's long-term interest for some of the effort and ingenuity that went into running financial institutions to go into manufacturing.

Summarized, these arguments for manufacturing suggest that it is generally necessary for maintaining or improving a place in the world (1), that is the core economic activity around which most others revolve, and increasingly needed for enhancing life (2), that it can offer employment that is at least as satisfying as that to be found elsewhere (3), and finally to look down upon and to opt out of it is to be illogical in terms of pursuit of one's own interests, *and* selfish (4).

The validity of this case for manufacturing *is* undermined, at least up to a point, by the principle of comparative advantage discussed near the start of this section of the chapter. What this principle means here is that manufacturing prowess is not crucial for the prosperity of every collectivity, region or nation. It qualifies the above case without damaging it severely. It does very little indeed to threaten a modified and more moderate version of it, namely the view that technically more sophisticated people will usually be more prosperous and powerful than technically less sophisticated ones. Nor does it alter the fact that for nearly two centuries, at least, the world's most powerful nations have invariably been manufacturing success stories.

Chapter 3

The engineering dimension and the management education movement

Peter Armstrong

THE ENGINEERING DIMENSION – THE NATURE AND DIMENSIONS OF THE OPPOSITION

The premise of the Finniston report (1980) was that all industrial management, in whatever function, and at whatever level, has an 'engineering dimension'. Its diagnosis of British industry was that the relative absence of professional engineers in senior management positions was leading to a neglect of this 'engineering dimension'. A consequence was the persistence of uncompetitive designs and production methods. The report's conclusion was that this could best be remedied by changes in the professional 'formation' of engineers to be carried out under a statutory engineering authority. In order to tackle the associated problem of the 'low status' of engineering in Britain, this authority would also have had the duty of awakening British employers and the public to the importance of engineering expertise in management.

Shortly after the publication of his report, Sir Monty Finniston declared himself pessimistic. 'What I wanted was an engine for change,' he told Anthony Sampson (1981:224). 'Instead we have got a shunter moving along disjointed lines.' The idea of a statutory engineering authority was torpedoed by Sir Keith Joseph, determined, in the cause of rolling back the frontiers of government, to avoid the creation of another quango. In this effort, he was aided by the engineering institutions, reluctant to hand over their traditional control of the profession, and prepared to outflank the majority opinion of their own membership in order to avoid doing so. Although masters' courses in engineering, on the lines advocated by Finniston, have appeared in some universities, and although steps have been taken to improve the quality of industrial training received by engineers, there is as yet no evidence that these actions have increased the flow of engineers into senior management positions.

One object of this chapter is to point out a possible reason for this. In essence, the argument is that the Finniston diagnosis of the ills of British management was insufficiently fundamental, in that it failed to consider the nature of the competition which faces professional engineers in their efforts to attain senior management positions. In particular, it neglected the impact, competitive and ideological, of Britain's massive and expanding management education programme.

The fundamental point is that the Finniston premise, that of the importance of the 'engineering dimension', is *not* accepted by the management education movement (MEM) – a term I shall use for the loosely defined group of eminent educationalists and converted senior industrialists which is now energetically sponsoring the expansion of British management education. According to the major programmatic document of the MEM – the Handy report (1987) – it is accepted that the traditional mix of 'management subjects' (roughly speaking, business strategy, marketing, financial control and behavioural science) is broadly correct (Handy 1987: 17), and that the only item now on the agenda is how to achieve an urgent expansion of the scale of provision. For example, Forrester (1986), taking as a premise that the Master of Business Administration (MBA) should become the normal qualification for about half of Britain's departmental or works managers, and for all managers above these levels, points out that this would lead to an annual replacement need of about 10,000, as against the 1986 output of about 1,200.

In addition to the MBAs, then, the current situation is that there are about 70,000 students studying the traditional mix of management subjects on various lower-level courses (Handy 1987: 12) and there is every prospect of a considerable expansion. Apart from those post-experience students recruited on to MBA or Diploma in Management Studies (DMS) courses who happen to be engineers (and who appear to be more interested in getting out of engineering altogether than in importing engineering expertise into senior managerial positions – (Ascher 1984: 33), virtually none of this very large number of students will possess an operational expertise of any description. Production management options in MBA courses, where offered, are not very popular with students

(Whitley, Thomas and Marceau 1981), even though they may be gutted of technological content in an effort to make them so.[1] Moreover, a cursory comparison of A-level entry grades suggests that the graduates from first-degree business studies and equivalent programmes may be rather more capable in a general sense than their engineering equivalents. Their ability, plus the transparent ambition which recruited them on to these courses in the first place, means that they represent formidable competition for engineering graduates.

There are two ways in which this situation affects the prospects for an adequate recognition of the 'engineering dimension' within British management. Most obviously, the competition from business and management graduates is likely to keep at least some engineers out of senior positions. More subtly, these students are the carriers of a peculiarly British view of management, which regards it as something quite distinct from technical expertise; which, indeed, in its more virulent versions, actually regards technical expertise as a *disqualification* for managerial positions (e.g. Platt 1963). The success of business and management graduates further reinforces a managerial culture which does not accept Finniston's belief that an 'engineering dimension' should permeate managerial decision-making and which, in addition, fails to recognize the managerial credibility of engineering qualifications.

The chapter now proceeds to outline the conception of management which is promulgated by the British MEM, to indicate how the mainstream of thinking and research on management has been distorted (not necessarily intentionally) so as to perpetuate that conception, and to show how that particular view of management is locked into the interests of those involved in management education and consultancy.

WHAT DO MANAGERS DO? THE VIEW OF THE MANAGEMENT EDUCATION MOVEMENT

An intelligent observer from Mars might approach the problem of defining management by observing what managers actually do. Indeed, some intelligent non-Martians have taken this approach, with results that we shall discuss shortly. Meanwhile our observer might note with Berthoud and Smith (1980) that the work of many managers includes a substantial amount of engineering, or conversely, with Gerstl and Hutton (1966), that the work of many engineers includes a substantial amount of management. They might then conclude, with Sir Monty Finniston, that a good proportion of managerial work does indeed contain an engineering dimension.

That, according to a very widely used text on general management (Koontz and O'Donnell 1968: 55), would be a mistake: 'The failure to distinguish executive functions from nonmanagerial technical skills is [a] source of confusion . . . The manager . . . may or may not possess such technical skills. In his managerial capacity, he certainly is not using such operating expertness [sic].' It appears that the manager who has acquired a measure of technical expertise, through education or experience, has wasted her time: 'if he [sic] can rely upon, and successfully use, the technical skills of others, he need not possess a nonmanagerial skill at all'.

To F. W. Taylor (1947), one of the twin founding fathers of management theory, such sentiments would have been unthinkable. In his view the *core* of managerial expertise was the knowledge of productive processes which enabled the industrial engineer to redesign them so as to eliminate 'waste' effort. Indeed, Taylor considered the possession of such knowledge to be the sole legitimate basis on which management could claim authority over the workforce.

However, a distinction between technical expertise and management *does* occur in the thought of the other founding father of managerial thought, Henri Fayol (1949). Concerned, unlike Taylor, with drawing up guidelines for directing the enterprise as a whole, Fayol observed that the proportion of managerial to non-managerial work increases at higher levels of the 'scalar chain of command'. Taken in isolation from the mass of Fayol's writing, this assertion implies that technical expertise may become more or less irrelevant at very senior levels of management. In the modern multi-divisional corporation, of course, headquarters management is *intentionally* divorced from operational matters, a principle which flatly contradicts Finniston's concept of the 'engineering dimension'. However, a certain disillusion is setting in with the economic consequences of this form of organization (e.g. Williams, Williams and Thomas 1983). Certainly the 'excellence' literature (e.g. Goldsmith and Clutterbuck 1984) indicates that some companies are achieving success by partially dismantling the cumbersome apparatus of headquarters financial monitoring and strategic control and allowing substantial autonomy to managers of operating subsidiaries – often engineers by background. Writing in an earlier era, of simpler organizational forms, Fayol himself took it for granted that even the most senior managers would have *some* knowledge of the processes being managed – possibly because he was writing from his own experience as a mining engineer, in charge of mines.

The process whereby the usage of the term 'management' in the English-speaking world has changed over time, so that it now signifies a controlling and directing activity *separable* from expertise in the process being managed, is complex and beyond the scope of this chapter (see P.J. Armstrong 1987a for a preliminary historical analysis). Certainly a self-consciously abstracted conception of management informs the work of Fayol's great popularizer in the English-speaking world – Lydall Urwick, a figure who dominated the British MEM until the massive expansion of management education during the 1960s. In Urwick's view (1963), the Taylorite idea that engineering training was a prerequisite for management was a sign of 'immature thinking'. In an anticipatory contradiction of Finniston, Urwick argued that, in order to establish management as a profession in its own right, with its own distinct knowledge base, it was necessary to *detach* it from its historical entanglement with engineering.

The end result – a conception of management as an activity quite distinct from engineering and other operational expertise – has already been illustrated from the Koontz and O'Donnell text. A further consequence is that, once management has been conceptually separated from the particularities of operational technologies, it also becomes possible to believe that:

> managers perform the same function regardless of their place in the organizational structure or the type of enterprise in which they are engaged. . . . The implications of this principle are several. In the first place, it means that anything significant that is said about the functions of one manager applies to all managers. . . . In the second place, the principle implies that managerial knowledge and experience are transferable from department to department and from enterprise to enterprise.
> (Koontz and O'Donnell 1968: 54)

And again, from the most famous management guru of them all:

> Every manager does many things that are not managing. He

may spend most of his time on them. A sales manager makes a statistical analysis or placates an important customer. A foreman repairs a tool or fills in a production report. A manufacturing manager designs a new plant layout or tests new materials. A company president works through the details of a bank loan or negotiates a big contract – or spends dreary hours presiding at a dinner in honor of long-service employees. All these things pertain to a particular function. All are necessary and have to be done well. But they are apart from that work which every manager does whatever his function or activity, whatever his rank and position, work which is common to all managers and which is peculiar to them.

(Drucker 1955: 343; also quoted, with disapproval, in Mintzberg 1973: 57)

In other words, the apparent similarity of all managerial work is actually the product of a systematic dumping of all the differences – principally concerning operational expertise – in a bin marked 'non-managerial'.

Though there may be pockets of dissent here and there (notably in management education for the catering industry), the abstracted view of management sketched above is entirely characteristic of the modern British MEM. Certainly such beliefs have convenient consequences for those involved in furthering the cause of managerial professionalism and education. As far as the latter is concerned, the divorce of management from industry-specific technical knowledge has consequences analogous to the standardization of engineering components: it enables the same course to be offered as suitable for actual and would-be managers across the entire spectrum of industrial settings. Similarly, the belief that management is essentially the same activity at all levels means that forepersons and senior executives can be catered for with only minor adjustments to the syllabus (and possibly less minor adjustments to the price tag). In Urwick's own educational practice of the 1940s, for example, virtually the same course was offered to foremen and to top executives. The advantages in marketing and economy of intellectual effort are obvious.

For students, this conception of management fosters the encouraging belief that management education offers them a wide choice of career and that the techniques they learn on undergraduate, Higher National Diploma (HND) or even National Examinations

Board for Supervisory Studies (NEBSS) courses are also relevant to corporate leadership. The same beliefs enable management consultants, like fortune-tellers, to offer essentially the same service to whomsoever is willing to pay, (the standardized nature of the reorganization packages offered to British industry by McKinsey and Co. during the 1960s is a case in point). Finally, a belief in 'management' as a relatively self-contained set of abilities enables senior managers to hop from industry to industry, secure in the knowledge that their innocence of the actual processes being managed is irrelevant to the success of their endeavours. In summary, both the providers and consumers of management education as well as those who live by providing 'professional' management services have a strong vested interest in perpetuating and defending a conception of management which is quite at odds with the 'engineering dimension' of the Finniston report.

EMPIRICAL RESEARCH ON MANAGEMENT AND ITS PRECONCEPTIONS

But if Finniston was correct, surely an 'engineering dimension' to management should have been revealed in those well-known empirical studies which have set out to challenge traditional prescriptive formulas. In fact, these studies, despite their apparent lack of theory, have been conducted from within the MEM frame of reference, and thus tacitly exclude the possibility that operational expertise might be integral to the practice of management. The best-known example is the work of Mintzberg (1973).

This begins, promisingly enough, by attacking the earlier quotation from Drucker (see p. 46) on the grounds that it is arbitrary and illegitimate to disregard as non-managerial parts of the work which managers actually do. On the positive side, Mintzberg claims to have established by direct observation (a) that managers' jobs are remarkably similar and (b) that they essentially *consist* of ten roles. These are the interpersonal roles of figurehead, leader and liaison, the informational roles of monitor, disseminator and spokesperson, and the decisional roles of entrepreneur, disturbance handler, resource allocator and negotiator.

Despite its wide influence, Mintzberg's study is deeply flawed. It is elementary sociology that roles are established, not by an actor's behaviour, but by other people's expectations of that behaviour. In observing managerial behaviour, therefore, Mintzberg did *not* observe roles, as he claimed, but inferred them. This is not just an academic quibble: by claiming merely to have observed, Mintzberg obscured the part played by his own theoretical preconceptions in his construction of managerial roles. Mintzberg's actual procedure was to abstract the elements of interpersonal behaviour from real-life situations and to categorize these behaviours as a representation of managerial work. Despite his strictures against Drucker's exclusion of the 'non-managerial' (quoted above), this amounts to a tacit selection principle whereby operational expertise (and much else) is disregarded as irrelevant. Of course this kind of abstraction is inevitable in any empirical enquiry, and there is no difficulty so long as reader and researcher are aware of the consequent limitations of the evidence presented. The problem in Mintzberg's case is that this awareness was lacking. Instead, the work was presented, and is read, as evidence that managerial work really does consist essentially of a number of interpersonal roles, when this representation was actually assumed in the research procedure. As a corollary, Mintzberg's supposed empirical confirmation that the work of managers is 'remarkably similar' across functions and levels (a key article of faith for the MEM) is actually a product of that same process of abstraction whereby the characteristic differences by level and function are disregarded.

The danger with Mintzberg's research – and with other studies in the same genre, such as those of Stewart (1982) and Kotter (1982) – is that a reader already inclined towards the half-truth that management is essentially about 'handling people' rather than knowledge of processes (e.g. Urwick 1964) can easily read Mintzberg's study as empirical confirmation. In reality, a crucial component of 'handling people' may be the offer of expert advice or guidance – which takes us back to Finniston's 'engineering dimension' and, indeed, to F. W. Taylor. This important feature of real-life management will always be obscured by any empirical 'management research' conducted from within the conceptual framework of the MEM, just as it is from its texts and courses.

THE MANAGEMENT EDUCATION MOVEMENT AND THE CONTAINMENT OF CONTRA-INDICATIONS

The production and dissemination of management knowledge, and the managerial careers based upon the particular conception

The management education movement 49

of management which underlies it, now constitute a massive bandwagon. It would be surprising if this had not evolved ways of containing criticism and neutralizing evidence that all is not well with its characteristic approach to management. Criticism there certainly has been, in considerable volume, and most importantly from industrialists disillusioned with graduates of the MBA programme (e.g. Ascher 1984). In this brief chapter, the manufacturing director of Lucas will have to speak for this entire body of opinion: 'There has been a whole generation of MBA students who will not go near a manufacturing strategy. . . . They want to be in at the gin-and-tonic end with the financial strategy' (Parnaby 1985:45).

Less prominently, but persistently and cogently over the years, a group of academics, of whom Ian Glover has been a leading member, have established the cultural particularity of the British approach to management and raised many questions concerning its economic consequences (e.g. Fores and Sorge 1981). Finally, from the engineering profession itself, both the Finniston and Fielden (1963) reports contain what amount to critiques of presently existing British management, though both avoided confronting the issue head-on.

For the most part, the response from the MEM has been silence: the Fores/Glover/Mant/Sorg school of thought has never been engaged in public debate. To be fair, this may be because the output of mainstream management thought is now so vast that its protagonists are able to establish academic reputations without venturing beyond its conventional assumptions, and so may remain unaware that there exists a well-developed dissenting position. Possibly for similar reasons, neither the Finniston report nor the Fielden report is so much as mentioned in the recent crop of major reports on management education by Handy (1987), Mangham and Silver (1986), Constable and McCormick (1987) and Forrester (1986). Engineering, it appears once more, is irrelevant to the business of management education.

Because of its source and volume, criticism from industry has to be taken more seriously. This has been met by a mixture of distortion and bluster. The latter is well illustrated by breathless wording of the foreword to the Handy report: 'We cannot afford the luxury of lengthy debate. Action is needed now' (Handy 1987: v).

This technique of smothering opposition by appealing to the

urgency of affirmative action has something of a tradition in the history of the MEM. The Franks report of 1963, which led to the foundation of the London and Manchester business schools, scarcely troubled to argue the merits of the case for doing so. It simply asserted that this was universally agreed (which it was not), that the matter was urgent, and proceded with the question of how the deed might be done.

The Handy Report also illustrates the manner in which the reasoned reservations of industrialists concerning the present *content* of management education are distorted by representing them as nothing more than a Neanderthal mistrust of education for managers *per se*:

> For no other important role in life, other than parenting, is there no proficiency test, no preparatory education or early apprenticeship. Managers in Britain have, for the most part, been exempted from such requirements perhaps because so many used to believe that managing was like parenting, something which you picked up as you went along.
>
> (Handy *et al.* 1987: 16)

Thus, the well-established fact that some senior managements have seen little of relevance to the actual work of their middle managers, in the present offerings of business schools, is first dismissed as an atavistic grunt, then conjured into non-existence with a patronizing and airy 'perhaps'. In such a manner, by a combination of ignoring and discrediting dissent, the MEM has largely avoided the irksome task of arguing the case for its preferred pattern of management education.

In fact, that case is shaky in at least three important respects. It is instructive to examine the manner in which the MEM deals with the evidence that this is so.

In accordance with the characteristic MEM belief that management is essentially the same activity at all hierarchical levels, business and management courses, from HND upwards, typically include a substantial element of strategic management, often taught through corporate-level case studies. The major policy documents from the MEM contain no hint that this emphasis on corporate strategy is now under attack from within Harvard Business School itself, once the high temple of the strategic orthodoxy (Hayes and Abernathy 1980), and that industrial enterprises in the USA are finding that an over-concern with the strategic options for capital investment deflects attention from the business of achieving the manufacturing improvements necessary to combat imports from the Far East (Hurst 1986). This, of course, was more or less Finniston's point. Similarly, the heavy emphasis on management accounting and financial strategy in current management education remains unquestioned, despite a substantial body of work which throws doubts on the wisdom of leaving policy-making to financially trained senior executives (e.g. Kaplan 1984).

There is also a large body of evidence from comparative studies, some of it produced by Ian Glover and Peter Lawrence, that the education and development of managers in the most successful capitalist economies in the world – West Germany and Japan – differ substantially in content from what is advocated by the MEM. Albeit in different ways, the development of potential managers in both countries ensures that they have a grasp of relevant technologies and there is less emphasis on control through accounting procedures and the nostrums of behavioural science. Interestingly, the Handy report itself reviews some of this evidence, and even half-raises a question on the number of qualified accountants involved in British management. However, instead of going on to question the wisdom of persisting with the present orthodox mix of 'management subjects', as it terms them, the report uses the evidence from international comparisons only to point to the much higher *level* of qualifications of managers in other economies. Differences in the *content* of the qualifications, though recognized in the report, are attributed to a process of adjustment whereby each society has evolved a form of management education which suits its own culture. According to this logic, of course, there *cannot* be anything wrong with the content of British management education – or with anything else, for that matter. Thus evidence that there are better ways of educating managers is stood on its head and used to argue for an expansion of the present pattern of provision.

Finally, despite the millions of words spent on the question of evaluating management training, there is no evidence that the present form of management education is of any economic benefit whatsoever – and there is some evidence that it is not. Mangham and Silver (1986) found no correlation at all between company performance and expenditure on management education. Yet the same report unblushingly calls for an urgent expansion of the latter! With the possible exceptions of the military and the sexual, it is difficult to think of another field of human endeavour in which such clear evidence of futility could be used to justify calls for more of the same. By contrast, the Fielden report of 1963 referred to a study which showed that manufacturing companies which had professional engineers on their boards of directors outperformed those which did not. However, British companies, or at least the 'Charter Group' among them, appear to be willing to act on the Handy report but not the Fielden report.

IMPLICATIONS

The idea that engineers have been losing out in the competition for senior management positions to variously qualified specialists in finance and administration has been current for most of this century, as has the belief that the solution lies in importing some form of education in these matters into engineering curricula (P. J. Armstrong 1987b). Part of the intent of this chapter has been to cast doubt on this apparently natural assumption.

In the first place, the terms on which 'management' is currently offered to engineers by the MEM imply that it comprises a body of knowledge, a set of skills, techniques or qualities to which engineering or other operational expertise is basically irrelevant. As long as this is accepted, it places engineers in the position of dabblers competing with specialists who have studied the subject full-time. There are, however, reasons why such a view of management should *not* be accepted.

If the thesis of the Finniston report is to be taken seriously, it amounts to a challenge to the notion that 'management specialists' *can* successfully run industrial enterprises. Though it is naturally ignored by the current MEM, the research base from which such a challenge might be mounted is beginning to accumulate, and some of it has been indicated in this chapter.

It also needs to be recognized that the conception of 'management' behind current management education implicitly denies the managerial relevance of engineering itself. Yet, in the real world, management, as Taylor and Fayol conceived of it, is *integral* to engineering. Technological work means precisely nothing until the engineer has also organized the labour force to put it into practice. This is recognized explicitly in the Conference of Engineering Societies of Western Europe and the U.S.A. (EUSEC) definition of a professional engineer and implicitly in the insistence by the engineering institutions on a period of *responsible* professional experience before chartered status is awarded. In effect, engineering is the *only* major profession which insists on practical experience of management as a condition of qualification. Finally, it is evident that the problem of the missing 'engineering dimension' in British management is as much a problem of management education as of the professional 'formation' of engineers. As long as business and management schools can prosper on the basis of offering students courses which promise access to senior management positions in whatever industry the student chooses, as long as sufficient of Britain's current generation (largely non-engineering) senior managers accept the relevance of such courses, and as long as the government keeps faith with 'market forces' as a determinant of the provision of management education – as is stridently advocated by Griffiths and Murray (1985) – nothing is going to change. On the other hand, the growth of in-house management development schemes, possibly in reaction to the MBA syndrome, offers at least the possibility of importing an engineering dimension into senior management, though there remain many problems which cannot be explored further in this chapter.

NOTE

1 This chapter is based on work carried out during a two-year secondment at the Industrial Relations Research Unit at the University of Warwick. The author is grateful for the help and criticism freely offered by members of the unit.

Chapter 4

Japanese engineers and management cultures

Kevin McCormick

INTRODUCTION

In the 1870s the Japanese government sent missions to Britain to study the engineers and engineering of the world's then most advanced industrial nation. A century later the roles appeared reversed. In the 1970s the British government-sponsored enquiry into the engineering profession sent a mission to Japan. By the 1970s there was a widespread belief that the ills of the British economy had much to do with the way in which engineers in Britain were educated and trained and engineering skills managed in manufacturing industry. On the other side of the coin there was a belief that the success of the Japanese economy had a good deal to to do with the way in which Japanese engineers were educated and trained and engineering skills managed in Japanese manufacturing industry.

The central argument of this chapter is that the institutional features of Japanese large corporations and their management have been important in securing the effective deployment of engineering skills in the past. However, their contribution in the future is more problematic. It cannot be assumed that employment policies and organizational forms highly suited to promoting incremental innovations and their diffusion through mass production industries will be equally effective in promoting radical innovation, the management of research and development (R & D), centres and the development of high-technology companies. And large Japanese corporations are now increasingly concerned to advance pioneer technologies. In order to gauge the efforts of Japanese corporations to adapt their managerial cultures to cope with the scientific and engineering manpower resources in R & D, the chapter will draw on a comparative study of careers and R & D management in Britain and Japan.

In their examination of international engineering practice the Finniston committee drew attention to several features of the organization of Japanese engineering which contributed to corporate and national economic success, including the high standard of education, the quality of education, the large numerical supply of engineers, the culture of Japanese industry and the collaboration between corporations and government in industrial development and planning (Finniston 1980: 209–14). In citing the culture of Japanese industry the Finniston committee pointed to the roles of employee participation and consultation in decision-making, consensus decision-making, lifelong employment, seniority, enterprise unionism and flexibility in work roles. All these factors were alleged to shape a close identification among engineers with their companies and a strong commitment to enterprise goals: 'In our view the successful record of Japanese engineering cannot be dissociated from the Japanese ability to develop a cultural system at the level of the firm commanding universal loyalty throughout the workforce' (Finniston 1980: 211).

There can be little doubt about the relative success of the post-1945 Japanese economy, whether it is measured in terms of GDP per capita, share of world trade, unemployment rates, balance of payments or rate of inflation. (Boltho and Hardie 1985; McCormick 1985). Boltho and Hardie (1985: 527) neatly summed up the contrasting relative economic experiences of Britain and Japan:

> while in the early 1950's Britain accounted for nearly 8 per cent of the OECD area's GDP and Japan barely 2.5 per cent, thirty years later these shares had changed to 6.5 per cent and 14.5 per cent respectively. Japan's per capita income, from being some 20 per cent of Britain's level in 1950–1, had edged ahead by 1980–1.

A phenomenon as complex and as elusive to political control as economic growth could hardly have excited the attentions of politicians and social scientists over the two hundred years since Adam Smith if it had monocausal or even simple explanations. Therefore full accounts of national economic growth must deal with world markets, home and foreign government monetary and fiscal policies, trade policies, industrial and market structures, savings rates and capital investment levels, the state of industrial relations, and so on. Yet there is a strong case for giving particular attention to the scientific and technological labour force and its education, training and utilization. And in utilization particular attention must be given to the way in which companies generate management cultures to elicit effective engineering contributions to enterprise goals.

Freeman (1987), who stresses the importance of technological innovation to national economic competitiveness, gives especial emphasis to social innovations too. In particular he stresses the search for new ways of organizing the education, training and work activities of graduate engineers and scientists. Thus in coining the concept of a 'national system of innovation' to distinguish and analyse national differences in the inter-institutional relations of companies, governments and universities, Freeman draws attention to the distinctive features of Japanese enterprise organization, employment systems and management style which aided the rapid development of mass production industries in the years following the Second World War (Freeman 1987: 45–9).

In developing the argument about the perceived need to adapt a successful system of personnel management for engineering manpower for new tasks and challenges, I will trace the historical outlines of the development of Japanese industrial organization to underline the links between Japanese company structures, management cultures and engineers in the second section of this chapter. The third section will examine some propositions about the characteristics of Japanese engineers (or more properly Japanese R & D personnel drawn from the comparative and collaborative study) and the extent to which these characteristics aid Japanese companies in their R & D effort. While there are differences between companies in both countries in their policies and practices, I will concentrate here on distinguishing broadly national patterns, on a 'Japanese' and a 'British' pattern. The fourth section will examine some of the ways in which Japanese companies are endeavouring to adapt 'traditional' human resource development policies and practices to the management of the rapidly expanding R & D staffs.

JAPANESE CORPORATIONS, MANAGEMENT CULTURES AND THE MAKING OF JAPANESE ENGINEERS

From the Meiji Restoration in 1868 and the start of Japan's determined bid to build the technological strength to defend itself against potential western encroachment, Japan created a distinctive variant of capitalism. In the early twentieth century the Japanese enterprise developed in a form which emphasized the need for graduate engineering skills and stimulated the development of the educational system to meet those needs. Moreover, the development of the Japanese enterprise stimulated the development of career structures for engineers to senior management levels and promoted a 'productivist ideology' which sustained and legitimated the importance of engineering skills. These developments stood in marked contrast to Britain, where the course of developments in the capitalist enterprise have restricted the career structures of engineers and restricted the growth of a 'productivist ideology', that is, an ideology of management which legitimates managerial activity in terms of managerial understanding and competence in directing the technology and productive capacity of the enterprise (P. J. Armstrong 1987: 430–1). Without a strong demand for engineers as functional specialists in areas such as R & D or a demand for engineers to be groomed for technological and business leadership, there was only a weak stimulus to the educational system to provide engineering manpower.

One of the more significant promotional efforts of the Meiji government was that of the joint stock company system (Nakagawa 1977). In a span of forty years after its introduction, the joint stock company system had penetrated all the main sectors of the Japanese economy at a much faster rate than that achieved in England. One factor in this rapid diffusion was the close association between the introduction of the newest western industrial technology with the newest social technology of business organization. Nakagawa cites a further factor in the preferences of the educated sons of ex-samurai for employment in joint stock enterprises rather than traditional family businesses (Nakagawa 1977: 22). Large joint stock enterprises became prominent in the growth of the cotton industry in the late 1890s, but these companies remained single-product and single-function enterprises, for they were dependent on the general trading companies (*sogo shosa*) for their marketing functions. With the trading companies concentrating on the creation of a worldwide, efficient marketing system and the development of links with companies which could supply better-quality products at competitive prices, the industrial companies concentrated on production. Management in the industrial companies became the management of the (imported) technology rather than the management of marketing or even finance (Iwata 1977; Yonekawa 1984). It enabled the development of a conception of management as the management of productive technology.

By 1910 Japan was hardly 'modern' or 'industrial': agricultural labour constituted almost 60 per cent of the labour force; agricultural output made up 40 per cent and manufacturing less than 10 per cent of net national product (Rosovsky 1972: 230). Male factory workers did not outnumber female factory workers until the 1920s, reflecting the character of rural industrialization in small workshops and the preponderance of the textile industries. Yet Japan was attempting to adapt feudal institutions to modern purpose. Initially the Meiji government controlled a range of technological developments closely linked to the development of national military and economic strength, such as mining, military arsenals, chemical industries, shipbuilding and machine manufacture. The early managers tended to be lower samurai who had lost their stipends but gained a little technological knowledge. Often they made mistakes, and the heavily bureaucratic structure of the government 'model factories' was a hindrance. Yet after the financial crises of 1881 and the sale of the 'model factories' the way was clear for the recuitment of graduates in engineering, commerce and social studies in the 1880s and 1890s for management posts. By the 1890s increasing attention was being given to heavy industries after the stimulus of the Sino-Japanese War (1894–5). In these years the private companies associated with mining, electrical machinery and shipbuilding began to establish research laboratories. Although the scale and intensity of effort were limited, it was a portent of future more systematic industrial research and a reminder that the starting point of developments was not so far behind initiatives in the west.

With direct and indirect support the major *zaibatsu* groups, such as Mitsui, Mitsubishi and Sumitomo, extended their dominance of the major industrial enterprises. In the 1920s they extended their recruitment of graduates for managerial careers, built on intra-firm skill training and developed those measures to encourage employee loyalty – long-term employment and seniority wages – which have come to be termed the 'Japanese employment system' in the post-war period (Okayama 1987). Although the *zaibatsu* were based on family interests, were organized around the *ie* (household principle) and fostered a paternalistic management style, they were not run as directly controlled family businesses, for executive activities devolved to university graduates recruited for professional management. Meanwhile the technological levels in cotton textiles and in the *zaibatsu*-controlled companies were changing from the 1920s to the 1930s such that Chokki can depict the passage of an era, from that of the 'old engineer' without formal technological education to that of the 'new engineer' graduated from the university (Chokki 1977: 173–4).

By 1945 the Japanese economy was in ruins. Shorn of empire, it had a further six million repatriate mouths to feed. Meanwhile the American occupation ushered in a determined effort to refashion Japanese institutions into the American mould of democracy involving reforms in the constitution and political institutions, land reform, the break-up of the *zaibatsu*, the encouragement of labour unions and the democratization of education. After the bitterly fought struggles of industrial relations between nascent unions and the purged managements, Japanese corporations emerged to further consolidate the triple foundations of the 'Japanese employment system' of lifetime employment, seniority wages and enterprise unionism (Okayama 1987). They were seen as vital elements to tie employees into careers in the large corporations and to head off class-based unionism. The negotiation of reform was a complex process negotiated between the occupying forces and the Japanese administration and its course was much influenced by perceptions of developments in the cold war. The outbreak of the Korean War with the boost of 'special procurements', and rising exports to south-east Asia from 1950 were very important factors in boosting industrial production up to pre-war levels. By 1952 independence had been granted and the Japanese administration had more freedom to shape its own economic and industrial policy. Instead of continuing the logic of comparative advantage in 'low-quality textiles' and 'gadgetry', based on abundant supplies of cheap labour, the Ministry of International Trade and Industry (MITI) determined that Japan needed capital – intensive industries if it were to raise living standards for a population of 85 million people on a limited land space with few natural resources (Scott,

Rosenblum and Sproat 1980). In the 1950s most of these industries – steel, automobiles, petrochemicals, industrial machinery, electronics – were under protection as 'infant industries', but they emerged as vigorous competitors for their share of growing world markets in the 1960s.

The growth of Japan's domestic market after the Korean War boost meant that advantage could be taken of mass production and increased mechanization. The astute adaptation of western technology and production methods in Japanese industry developed pace under the watchful eye and 'administrative guidance' of MITI. The enthusiasm in Japan for American production engineers who appeared to be lost prophets in their own country is becoming a legend (Halberstam 1987: 311–18). Japan has proved a fertile ground for the germination of ideas from American engineers such as J. Edwards Deming and his emphasis on quality standards. The company groupings based around the reconstituted *zaibatsu* remained a significant element in the export efforts of Japanese companies given the elaborate communication networks for co-ordinating intelligence, marketing and distribution in the trading companies. However, with the increased importance of product-specific skills, services and facilities associated with high-technology industries and growing markets, the manufacturers of automobiles and electrical goods began to develop extensive marketing operations and the more extensive managerial hierarchies of managerial capitalism (Chandler 1984). In turn the growth of these companies in the 1960s stimulated the further expansion of engineering education in the universities and colleges in order to supply the technical specialists and managerial cadre of the companies.

During the 1950s and 1960s the Japanese companies in steel, autos and electrical goods reaped the benefits of mass production through policies of technology licensing, 'reverse engineering' and continuous product and process engineering (Freeman 1987). 'Reverse engineering', or attempting to manufacture a product similar to one already on the market without direct foreign investment or the purchase of blueprints for product or process design, had some beneficial side-effects according to Freeman. Freeman suggests that, first, it encouraged engineers, managers and workers to think in a holistic way about product and process design; second, it fostered the concept of 'the factory as a laboratory', with R & D engineers intimately involved in the production area; third, it encouraged the links between assembler and supplier companies; and fourth, attempts to overcome the early defects evident in first attempts stimulated the concern with quality standards at each stage of production (Freeman 1987: 40-3). The success of the innovation-based strategies rested on the ability of the companies to recruit employees with the general knowledge and learning skills to cope with changing technologies and tasks, on their ability to combine them in systems of work organization which maximized productivity gains and flexibility, and on their ability to develop systems of developing necessary knowledge and skills through the employees' working careers (Wersky 1987).

Aoki has emphasized the importance of the 'semi-autonomous problem-solving capability (information processing capacity) of workers' and the horizontal communication flows in the Japanese work organization, since these factors rendered distinctions between control and operating tasks less explicit and blurred the emphasis on professional control evident in the west (Aoki 1988: 4). This system of work organization is buttressed by aspects of the 'Japanese employment system' in the large corporations, including long-term employment for regular workers, rotation and a commitment to systematic 'learning by doing' by employees who have high standards of formal schooling. In addition, it depends on a high concentration of engineers in the production areas, with relatively low social distance between the engineers and blue-collar operators, all carefully cultivated by employers with their emphasis on the common status of company members (Okuda 1983: 23-6).

The corporation emphases on building corporate loyalties, on devising a quid pro quo of corporate beneficence for employee loyalty, have had their parallels in the relative distancing of shareholders from the corporation. Drawing their funds from bank loans rather than equity capital and having a high proportion of their equity capital held by other allied corporations, the Japanese corporations have been relatively insulated from short-term financial considerations, and relatively free to respond to the aspirations of employees for growth and the correlates of growth in career opportunities. As Dore observed (1985: 10): 'Japan's is a managerial, production-oriented capitalism, not a shareholder-dominated form of capitalism.'

SOME PROPOSITIONS ABOUT JAPANESE ENGINEERS

Some of the beneficial effects of the development of these institutional arrangements can be seen in comparison with engineers from other national systems. For example, we can look at the snapshot of contemporary Japanese industrial R & D derived from our survey of over 1,000 engineers and scientists in thirteen companies in Japan and Britain. (See the appendix for further details of the samples and the survey methods.) In so doing we shall follow Japanese practice in looking at the 'technically qualified staff member' or *gijutsha*, which provides the closest Japanese equivalent to the English term 'engineer'. However, the Japanese term is broader than the English equivalent, which reflects something of the breadth in education and flexibility in functional roles.

'Japanese engineers are well educated'

For most Japanese the educational system can be characterised as a '6-3-3 system', comprising nine years of compulsory education with six years of elementary education and three years of junior high school, and topped for 95 per cent of the age group by voluntary attendance in the fee-paying senior high-school system. For graduate engineers the route to graduation is through four years of university. Now, however, the large corporations are seeking three-quarters of their new annual graduate recruitment from the graduates of the two-year masters' courses. Over 60 per cent of the Japanese R & D staff in our sample held masters' degrees, whereas the typical qualification among the British sample was a bachelors' degree. At the very least Japanese engineers are well educated in the sense of years of education completed. There are several other senses in which Japanese engineers can be said to be well educated too.

Japanese engineers are broadly and reliably educated. The existence of a national curriculum means not only that engineers experience a broad curriculum in both school and university, but that employers recruit a fairly standard and reliably known product.

Japanese engineers are educated to high standards. The high standards in cognitive abilities in maths and physics encouraged by the mixture of comprehensive schooling, extra-curricular cram-school attendance and the fierce competition of university entrance exams are widely recognized in international comparisons (McCormick 1988a: 43–5). It is sometimes suggested that Japanese students use their period at university as a recuperation period away from the rigours of the competitive university entrance examination system (Rawle 1985: 32–3). While there may be a grain of truth in these comments for arts and social studies students, they seem to be tenuously based on casual observation when applied to science and engineering students. Moreover, they neglect the fact that entry to the graduate school is competitively based on undergraduate grades or entrance exam. A more measured judgement was made by the US government's Office of Educational Research and Improvement, which suggested that the popular image of indolent Japanese students was more likely to be derived from casual observation of arts students rather than engineers. For example, OERI pointed to the better integration of specialist and general education, the better faculty/student ratios and the greater likelihood of more serious study through the four undergraduate years in the faculties of engineering, science, agriculture and medicine (Office of Educational Research and Improvement 1987: 51).

The net implication of these comments on education is that Japanese engineers have a broad base on which to build later employer-specific training and retraining, and employers have fairly readily accepted the division of labour between universities and employers on education and training (McCormick 1988a). However, it must be conceded that the Japanese educational system has not been geared to educating and training the doctorate-level research manpower in large proportions. For example, only 7 per cent of the Japanese sample held doctorates compared to over a quarter of the British sample. In terms of disciplinary balance, engineering enrolments in the four-year undergraduate programmes heavily outweigh the science enrolments; for example, in the 1988 School Survey 27.8 per cent of all students were in engineering compared to only 6.3 per cent in science (Muta 1990: 73). While British (engineering) observers might applaud the bias towards engineering, some Japanese observers argue that the science proportion should be expanded to meet the need for more indigenous research (Dore 1986).

'Japanese engineers are well trained'

One corollary of the expectation of lifelong employment for graduate engineering staff is that companies are keenly interested in the training of a labour force to whom they are committed. Further contrasts with a more market-oriented system are that training is conceived in different ways – in its locus, mode, agency and purpose. For the Japanese engineers, training is much more likely to be in-house, on-the-job training, carried out through supervisors or senior engineers, with the aim of improving technical skills for the current or future job. For the British engineer, training tends to be conceived as an off-the-job course, requested or initiated by the individual in order to advance managerial promotion prospects.

Rotation through other departments can arise in relatively spontaneous fashion from discussions with a supervisor or from more deliberate career planning. Rotation serves in the short run by providing an extra pair of hands and meeting the exigencies of organizational life from the pool of flexible labour, but in the longer run it serves to build a shared corporate-wide perspective on the company. Rotation is part of the process of building and diffusing an engineering culture through the company.

Considerable prominence has been given to production in the training of future managers irrespective of likely future assignments. For example, Tanaka (1980: 30) cites Mitsubishi Electric as one example of a common pattern among manufacturing companies:

> The focus of Mitsubishi Electric's on-the-job training is the recognition that production depends on the coordination of many departments and the co-operation of many employees, including those who receive the order, design the system, assemble the parts, inspect and adjust the product and ship it to its destination. No matter what type of managerial job the new employees may be assigned to in the future, Mitsubishi Electric requires that they not lose sight of the importance and difficulty of production.

'Japanese engineers are hard-working employees'

At the very least Japanese engineers put in long hours of work; the typical working week is estimated as 53 hours by the Japanese sample compared to the 41 hours of the British sample. Moreover, these Japanese engineers put a good deal of further time and energy into out-of-work-hours socializing, which is thought to have work-related benefits.

To some extent these long hours put at the disposal of the company are the 'dark side' of the lifetime employment systems. Individuals, groups and corporations have a vested interest in policing the potential 'free rider'. A great deal of managerial and colleague effort is put into monitoring 'correct attitudes'. Bhasanavich, an American Westinghouse engineer on an internship at Mitsubishi Electric, gives a vivid account of the first year of company life in the company dormitory as indoctrination, of training activities and friendship opportunities 'planned and staged by managers', even of the very difficulty of finding oneself alone (Bhasavanich 1985: 73). While this system may have fostered a great sensitivity to co-operation and teamworking, some doubt the extent to which it is tolerant of nonconformity and conducive to radical innovation. Therefore there is some attempt to expand the variety of background and experience of R & D recruits.

'Japanese engineers participate'

Japanese engineers are more likely to feel that their interests have been considered in planning their projects (87.2 per cent in Japan compared to 57.2 per cent in Britain), and are more likely to participate in the membership of professional study associations (67.7 per cent in Japan compared to 53.5 per cent in Britain) and in labour unions (60.5 per cent in Japan compared to 27.6 per cent in Britain) than their British counterparts. The reported feelings on project planning are consistent with the much-reported 'bottom-up' style of management in Japanese corporations in which there is a considerable management investment of effort in informal, pre-decision processes of discussion and mutual accommodation (Smith and Peterson 1988: 148-52). The professional societies serve a study function only, and do not carry any role in qualification. They are valued for the opportunities which they provide for the diffusion of technical information and the presentation of research results. On the other hand, labour unions are enterprise-based and membership follows almost automatically on joining the company until arrival in the managerial grades. It is another factor which links white-collar and blue-collar workers in a common enterprise-based activity.

'Japanese engineers have long time horizons'

Japanese R & D engineers in large corporations are more likely to have have had more years of formal schooling than their British counterparts. They are more likely to enter their first employment aged 24 or 25, after the master's course, compared to the British engineer who embarks on his first job aged 21 or 22 after a three-year bachelor's degree. By age 24 or 25, over 30 per cent of British engineers will have joined their second employer.

Having arrived at their first employer, whom the majority anticipate will be their only employer, the Japanese graduate engineers settle to learn the skills of engineering, which they anticipate will take much longer than the time scale anticipated by their British counterparts. The 'career milestone' for regarding oneself as a 'fully fledged engineer' is typically estimated at age 28.7 by the Japanese engineers and at age 23.6 by the British engineers. Similarly, the career milestones of 'project leader' and 'manager' are reached at later ages by the Japanese sample (33.2 and 33.0 years respectively) compared to the British sample (27.7 and 29.8 years respectively).

The differing time orientations of Japanese and British have implications for attitudes to training and skill development, where British R & D staff seem determined on moving out of technical roles and into managerial roles as quickly as possible. While Japanese R & D staff might eventually move out of labs and into the corporate managerial cadre, they are prepared to do so at a slower pace and they acquire skills and the corporate vision on the way.

'Japanese engineers do a lot of engineering'

While engineers in R & D in both countries expect their managers to be technically competent, Japanese engineers and their companies lay more stress on the role of manager as co-ordinator and carrier of the administrative burden. Therefore the division of labour in technical and administrative tasks between the main grade engineer and the manager is sharper in Japan than Britain. The net consequence is that, given the proportion of time spent on technical activities in the working day, the length of the working week and the longer time spent as an engineer in the working career, relatively speaking, Japanese engineers do a lot of engineering for their companies over the course of their careers.

ADAPTING HUMAN RESOURCE DEVELOPMENT SYSTEMS FOR THE R & D LAB

Japanese corporate cultures can be seen to have had a relatively 'good fit' with the perceived tasks of the main industries from 1945 to the mid-1970s. Corporate cultures which emphasized the making of organizational members, which drew from relatively similar educational backgrounds, which granted broad equality of status, which emphasized local organizational knowledge and skill development, which promoted lifetime employment and career routes through internal labour markets, and which rewarded in a system of seniority wages and relatively narrow differentials, can be seen to have been related to the pre-eminence of the processing and machinery industries, and their major preoccupation with productivity improvement and cost reduction through incremental change on the shop-floor. Now, however, the economy is changing; many corporations are hoping to achieve radical innovation through the laboratory as well as incremental innovation on the shop-floor.

For Koike the past success of Japanese corporations rested on securing the commitment and loyalty of the blue-collar labour force in the large corporations by extending to them the career experiences of employment previously reserved for white-collar workers, the 'white-collarization' of blue-collar workers (Koike 1988). But now the question arises of 'what is happening to white-collar workers?' as corporations boost their reliance on scientists, engineers and other technical specialists. Do the new targets imply increasing differentiation in recruitment, organization, training and reward? And what would such changes imply for the corporate culture and moral order of the Japanese corporation?

(1) The expansion of the central R & D lab facility in the large corporations has stimulated a growing sophistication in the recruitment of new graduates, a search for greater diversity in the backgrounds and experience of R & D personnel and a greater interest in mid-career recruitment, even head-hunting and poaching.

Where companies might have relied in the past on the reputation of the university as a hallmark of quality in their recruitment of bachelor-level graduates, they are paying much closer attention to their knowledge of courses and professors in their recruitment of master-level graduates.

The justification for recruiting graduates from a relatively narrow range of elite universities and with relatively homogeneous social and educational background in terms of the support which it lent to a sense of common purpose seems less strong for R & D if the aim becomes the promotion of radical innovation. Therefore companies are being urged to grant more autonomy and discretion to the central labs in their search for greater heterogeneity among talented recruits. Some companies are providing fellowships for foreign researchers, although as yet this is on a very small scale.

Companies attempting to break into new technological fields are among those taking closer interest in head-hunting and poaching. Yet while companies are being encouraged to be more positive in this field, they remain very circumspect (Sato, Imano and Yahata 1987). Mid-career recruits carry the disadvantage that they lack the local knowledge and immersion in corporate culture enjoyed by lifetime employees. They cause headaches in fitting them into payment systems which still carry a heavy weight towards seniority.

(2) With a growing sense that Japanese industry must undertake more basic research, corporations are being urged to adopt distinctive organizational structures and personnel administration systems for basic research in central labs, without jeopardizing the traditional strong links between R & D and production or creating new tensions between the research sections and the development sections. They are being encouraged to adopt patterns of work organization which encourage the freshness and vitality of researchers, for example, the use of 'free time' for more autonomous research, conference attendance and more deliberate rotations.

(3) Corporations which appear to have always taken the prime initiative in career development are now being urged to adapt their career structures to provide for more diversity in career routes, to provide routes to 'advanced researcher' in ways reminiscent of the 1960s debates on 'dual career ladders', to provide for faster promotion and to make more provision for more formal off-the-job training.

(4) The pay systems of the Japanese corporations, which have

appeared formidably complex to outsiders, with various elements of base pay, seniority, family allowances, housing allowances and bonuses, are coming under pressure to provide distinctive rewards for researchers. Surveys suggest that R & D staff are dissatisfied with their present pay systems (Japan Productivity Centre 1985, 1987).

In each of these four areas of corporate structure and personnel administration, the net effect of proposed reforms is the call for increased differentiation in order to cater for the 'needs' of R & D engineers and scientists. Yet managements are circumspect about wholesale change, as the Japan Productivity Centre surveys demonstrated by showing contrasting responses from researchers and managers on matched items. This reserve is understandable given the widespread belief among managements that the past emphasis in corporate cultures on homogeneity has sustained corporate structures that have been proved successful. In essence there are fears that change might breach the moral order of the Japanese corporations. Emphasizing common membership of the corporation, aiming for equal opportunities and fair criteria in promotion and determined efforts to avoid or mitigate conflicts of interest among groups and departments have been intended to produce tightly cohesive communities committed to aggressive competition with outsiders. Differential statuses and rewards might imply differential loyalties; and while a process of differentiation might imply simply differences, there is a fear that it might imply antagonistic hostility too. Therefore there is understandable caution in shaping institutions towards new purposes. When Japanese lab managers are said to be introducing for their staff new measures such as 'free time' to do 'under-the-counter' research and encourage their vitality and creativity, it should be remembered that they do this in the context of a 53-hour working week! Japanese corporations still strike a very exacting effort-bargain with their engineers and scientists.

CONCLUSIONS

The development of a reasonably broad consensus on the appropriate division of labour between universities and industry has enabled the large corporations to recruit well-educated graduates for their R & D laboratories. The corporations have been able to grow a managerial culture in which the technically qualified labour force could develop strong commitments to their companies. Thus structural and cultural features of Japanese companies have been closely examined by many visiting delegations for links to economic performance.

The nature and timing of Japanese industrialization influenced the role which engineers and engineering played in companies. And a variety of foreign examples were absorbed and adapted from the late nineteenth century. The Japanese case provides some interesting contrasts and parallels with the German model. For example, the German case suggests the need to boost engineers' pay and prestige, that is, to enhance social differentiation in the workplace, in order to enhance company manufacturing performance, whereas the Japanese case suggests the need to de-emphasize social distance in the workplace.

As the British Finniston committee delegation arrived in Japan in the late 1970s to study the organization of manufacturing technology in Japan, more Japanese attention was coming to be focused on the organization of R & D. Over the past decade there has been increasing debate on the extent to which Japanese corporations could, should or even must strive to adapt their personnel policies and practices for new challenges. For the contemporary observer these debates must prompt the question whether 'looking at Japan' runs the risk of 'looking at yesterday's model'. The answer here is a guarded 'no'. The answer is 'no' because the sense in which it was useful to characterize a 'Japanese employment system' remains valid as an analytical tool in contemporary large corporations, and the changes evident in the large corporations are more usefully described as adaptations of the model rather than heralds of wholesale change. The answer is 'guarded' because the question is far too simplistic and neglectful of the variety and dynamic of organizational life for Japanese engineers in both the past and the present.

ACKNOWLEDGEMENTS

I am grateful for the stimulating collaboration of the 'Japanese team' (Hiroki Sato, Koichiro Imano, Shigemi Yahata and Scott Davis) during our case studies and survey planning. Material help in travel and survey costs was provided on the British side by the Great Britain–Sasakawa Foundation and the University of Sussex–Institute of Manpower Studies Joint Research Fund. Of course the research would have been impossible without the very willing and full co-operation of companies and their staffs in the two countries.

APPENDIX ON METHOD

The data are drawn largely from interviews and questionnaires with R & D staff in the R & D labs of six Japanese and seven British companies, operating in the electronics industry (three Japanese and three British companies), the chemical industry (two Japanese and three British companies) and the food-and-drink industry (one Japanese and one British company). In Japan the main case studies and questionnaire distribution were undertaken by the Japanese collaborating team supplemented by my interviews with R & D and personnel management. In Britain I undertook the main case studies and questionnaire distribution, supplemented by interviews with R & D and personnel management by the Japanese team. Questionnaires were directed to graduate engineers and scientists aged 25-45 and working in R & D labs. The random samples of staff were devised by managements, and 555 Japanese and 449 British questionnaires were returned with response rates varying between 60 and 92 per cent across British companies and between 85 and 100 per cent in the Japanese companies. In terms of educational disciplines the division between science and engineering was approximately 50:50 in both the British and Japanese samples. The terms 'engineers' and 'scientist' sometimes excite controversy in Britain as occupational groups stake their claims to identities, job territories, recognition and reward. In these companies the R & D staff tended to be called 'engineers' in the electronics companies and 'scientists' in the chemical companies, irrespective of whether degrees were held in science or engineering. A larger proportion of the Japanese respondents were gathered in areas which they recognized as being at the 'research' rather than the development end of the R & D spectrum (66 per cent versus 29 per cent). In Britain a larger proportion of British respondents were at the 'development' end of the R & D spectrum (38 per cent versus 40 per cent).

Chapter 5

Engineering and management in West Germany: a study in consistency?

Peter A. Lawrence

INTRODUCTION

In Anglo-Saxon societies the tendency is to see engineering and management as distinct, and at some points as antithetical. Certainly some managers are engineers (qualified in engineering) but only some, and they are the ones who have in some sense given up engineering for management. Engineering is felt to be about technical perfectionism; management is about profits, planning, controls and the big picture. Engineers glory in technical excellence; managers subordinate it to organizational objectives. No one starts out a manager and aims to end up an engineer. But many young engineers hope eventually to get into management (Gerstl and Hutton 1966). Engineering has a contribution to make to the achievements of management. Management knows how to control and harness this contribution of the engineers.

So the two are related in the Anglo-Saxon view, but as specialist to generalist, as contributor to controller, as inputter to extractor. To cross the line from engineer to manager is to effect a transition from self-driven to system-driven.

But Germany is not Anglo-Saxon, and its interest lies precisely in the fact that these taken-for-granted understandings appear less valid there. Not only is engineering the object of more traditional esteem in Germany, but the German understanding of management is also somewhat different, the difference facilitating a more harmonious integration of the engineering dimension with industry.

Indeed, Germany departs so strongly from our accepted understandings that it is necessary to lay some foundations. To this end, and to build up a picture of the essential character of engineering and management in Germany, we will outline the German education system and range of qualifications, present in a summary way a series of surveys of German management and its background and qualifications, and also engage in an exploration of the German notion of *Technik*. These are all important for an understanding of how and where engineering fits in German society.

There is also a special circumstance that readers are invited to note. This is that all the research studies and surveys discussed in this chapter, as well as the broad institutional arrangements, refer to the German Federal Republic as it existed from 21 September 1949 until 3 October 1990, that is, until reunification. It is not that reunification invalidates the interpretation offered, simply that the studies cited derive from the pre-unification time and place: hence the many references to West Germany that may now sound a little odd.

A CONGRUENCE OF STATUS

A key feature of Germany as industrial society is that the status of engineering is high, the status of industry is traditionally high, and the two statuses are mutually sustaining.

With regard to the status of industry in Germany it is important to emphasize that it has always enjoyed high standing, in contrast to some other societies, for example Britain and the Netherlands, where industry management has only received a boost in the 1980s. The traditional English view that industry was no place for a gentleman, or an intellectual, seems never to have existed in Germany even if German industry achieved a special élan in the post-war period as the vehicle of reconstruction and national economic achievement. In this post-war period a variety of studies show industry in Germany to be a strong career choice (Hutton and Lawrence 1981; Lawrence 1981), and show that salaries in industry tend to be superior to those in the public sector for similarly qualified people (Kogon 1976; Hutton, Lawrence and Smith 1977).

This particular point concerning salary may be broadened. In an earlier survey of mechanical engineers in Germany we cross-tabulated a variety of work-role features and professional achievements on the one hand with whether the subjects work in industry or the public sector (Hutton, Lawrence and Smith 1977).

From this exercise it emerged that those German engineers based in industry had more of everything. Not only did they enjoy higher average levels of remuneration, they also had more subordinates and more extensive authority, and were more likely to have a secretary, more likely to engage in business travel and more likely to speak English. Again these industry-based engineers had higher degree or engineering college grades, and were more likely to have given professional papers, more likely to have published, more likely to have a doctor's degree and much more likely to have patented inventions to their credit. It seems reasonable to interpret these systematic differences as indicative of the status of industry in Germany.

There are a number of reasons for believing engineers in Germany to enjoy a higher standing than is the case for their professional colleagues in Britain, but we will focus on three of these considerations. Remuneration is the first. Comparable late-1970s salary data showed German engineers to be substantially better remunerated than their British colleagues, even after allowing for the higher cost of living in West Germany (Hutton, Lawrence and Smith 1977). It may be objected that most German salaries are higher than British ones, so that this finding is not of itself very telling. There is also, however, some salary relativity evidence for the two countries, which does suggest that the German engineer is relatively favoured (Fores 1972). This particular study assembled salary data for engineers, senior civil servants and university professors for both Britain and West Germany. Engineers in Germany were shown to out-earn both the higher civil servant and the university professor, whereas engineers were in third place in Britain in salary terms.

The second consideration is access to (higher) management posts. All the available studies tend to suggest that engineering is the most important route to industrial management in Germany (Hutton et al 1975). But before discussing the literature on the educational background and qualifications of German managers it may be helpful to indicate what the range of possible qualifications is and where they are located in the national system of education.

GERMAN EDUCATION AND THE RANGE OF QUALIFICATIONS

Primary education in Germany runs from the ages of 6 to 10 (though it is 6 to 12 in West Berlin) and secondary education from

10 to 16 (legal minimum). There are a few comprehensive schools, but they are not numerous except in the state of Hessen. What is basically in operation in West Germany is a tripartite system of secondary education roughly similar to what existed in Britain in pre-comprehensive-school days. There is the *Hauptschule* (secondary modern school), the *Realschule* (technical school) and the *Gymnasium* (grammar school). The proportions attending these three types would be approximately 45:20:25 (with some 5 per cent at comprehensive schools and another 5 per cent at special schools), in marked contrast with pre-comprehensive Britain where only a tiny proportion attended the technical schools. Since the role of private education is negligible it is fair to say that the overwhelming majority of German managers senior enough to figure in surveys of background and qualifications have attended the *Gymnasium*.

There is an examination known as *mittlere Reife* which is taken at the age of 16 and approximates to GCSE level in England. And there is a further examination, *Abitur*, which is taken at 19 and which corresponds to GCE A-level in England. In fact, the *Abitur* usually consists of a larger number of subjects than the customary three at English A-level, some of these being the subject of written examination, others being examined on a continuous assessment basis. Or to put it another way, there is less dropping of subjects in the *Gymnasium* than in the old English grammar school. *Abitur* admits to university, in principle to any faculty of any university without more ado, though in practice this freedom of student choice has been modified by a *numerus clausus* (limited entry) for overcrowded subjects, usually subjects involving equipment or laboratory facilities – medicine is the notorious example.

The *mittlere Reife* is usually taken by pupils at the *Realschule*, and by pupils leaving the *Gymnasium* early (i.e. not staying on to take *Abitur*). Thus in Germany people tend to have either *mittlere Reife* or *Abitur*, depending on the type of secondary school they attended, or when they left; it is not usual to have both as it is for those who reach university in England. Again, managers senior enough to figure in (most of) the background and qualification surveys discussed subsequently will generally have *Abitur*.

University courses tend to be somewhat longer in West Germany than in England, the official minimum length being four years and actual average time taken to graduate being longer. Anyone who successfully completes an undergraduate course in the minimum four years can quote this as an achievement in itself in much the same way that one might cite one's double first with pride in England. Degrees, and *Abitur* results for that matter, are also graded in West Germany, the top grade being 10.

A general difference between West Germany and Britain is that the relationship between the subject studied at university and subsequent employment and career is much tighter in the German case. Or to put it another way, German graduates have much less freedom of choice than their British opposite numbers; the Germans to a much greater extent chose their career when they decided what to study. To give a practical example, the history graduate in Britain might do research or become a schoolteacher. He or she might enter the higher civil service or the liberal professions. Posts in the media are possible and graduate traineeships in industry eminently possible. The German history graduate can become a schoolteacher and pretty well nothing else. This does not mean that Germany is littered with thousands of unemployed history graduates, since everyone knows 'the way it is' and this is reflected in low enrolments (proportionally) in subjects with limited occupational outlets.

The subject which does, of course, pre-eminently lead somewhere occupationally is engineering. Engineering, however, is not taught at the ordinary universities (except for Bochum and Erlangen) but at the *technische Hochschulen* or *technische Universitäten*. These specialized technical universities were mostly established in the nineteenth century; they enjoy parity of esteem with the ordinary universities, and admission to them is also via the *Abitur* examination.

A first degree in Germany is usually called a *Diplom*, and graduates in particular subjects are designated by a *Diplom*-plus-subject compound noun. A *Diplom Volkswirt*, for example, is an economics graduate; a *Diplom Kaufmann* or *Diplom Betriebswirt* is a graduate in business economics, and a *Diplom Ingenieur* (standard abbreviation *Dipl.Ing.*) is an engineering graduate. The three recurrent subjects studied by graduate managers who figure in surveys are law, economics and engineering. Graduates in natural science subjects are not very numerous among the ranks of industrial managers, except in the chemical industry. It is also the case that students of the natural science subjects constitute a relatively small proportion of the total undergraduate population in West Germany compared with Britain. Frequently, in the analyses of survey data, scientists are bracketed with engineers; it is important to note that in the German context 'scientists and engineers' means battalions of engineers and a handful of scientists. It is the reverse in Britain.

Another distinctive feature of the German university scene is that, strictly speaking, there are no undergraduate courses in management or business studies. The nearest approach to management or business administration at undergraduate level in Germany is courses in *Betriebswirtschaftslehre*, or business economics. To be fair, the curriculum for these business economics courses is somewhat similar to that of business administration courses in Britain, and enrolments grew massively in the 1980s. But they are 'coming from' a particular disciplinary base, and are not called 'management'.

Management teaching *per se* is not as developed in West Germany as it is in Britain or the USA. In Germany courses for managers are invariably post-experience, not undergraduate or immediate postgraduate. They also differ from many American and British courses in that they are more specialized as to content and as to the level and more particularly the function of the executives attending them. Germans have also been criticized in the past for not showing as much interest as managers from other countries in the international management education centres such as IMEDE and INSEAD.

There are no masters' degrees in West Germany, in the British and American sense of a degree falling between the bachelor's and doctor's degree, though to confuse the issue some German universities use 'MA' to designate the first degree. Above the first degree (*Diplom*) in Germany comes the doctor's degree. Many senior managers in fact have a doctorate, the most common subjects being law (*Dr.Jur.*), business economics (*Dr.rer.pol.*) and engineering (*Dr.Ing.*). Managers with the doctor's degree in chemistry are also very prevalent in the chemical industry. To complete the picture of the hierarchy of university qualifications in West Germany there is yet another called *Habilitation*, a super-Ph.D. qualification attained by research and thesis. The *Habilitation* is not a qualification available to anyone who happens to fancy something superior to the doctor's degree: it is a qualification for professional academics, officially a prerequisite for appointment to a full professorship. As such it is not, of course, a qualification that German managers in general are likely to have, though there are a few managers in West Germany who are ex-professors (in the chemical industry, for instance) and who therefore have the *Habilitation*.

This fact does not, unfortunately, come out very clearly in surveys of managers' qualifications in West Germany, but there are also a range of non-school, non-university qualifications. First, there is of course the apprenticeship (apprenticeship is discussed in more detail later). On the craft-technical side there is the *Industrielehre* and the *Handwerkslehre* (industrial apprenticeship and craft apprenticeship). The *Industrielehre* is the dominant one now, though the *Handwerkslehre* carries an added element of prestige. It is not unusual for the engineering graduate (*Dipl.Ing.*) to have done an apprenticeship and it is quite normal for the non-graduate engineer (*Ing.Grad.*; see p. 79) to start their working life by doing an apprenticeship. In consequence there are many German managers who have done an apprenticeship and who hold the *Facharbeiterbrief* (skilled worker's certificate) obtained by passing the examination at the end of the apprenticeship. The possession of this qualification (the *Facharbeiterbrief*) tends not to show up in the surveys but it is quite common; it is, however, becoming less common because of both increasing academicization in general and changes in the recruitment to the *Ing.Grad.* course (see p. 79) in particular.

There is also the *kaufmännische Lehre* (commercial apprenticeship), which is even more important as an original qualification for at any rate the older generation of German managers. Formal qualifications equivalent to the *Ing.Grad.* and *Dipl.Ing.* in the technical functions tend to be less common on the commercial side of German companies, so that the *kaufmännische Lehre* is more prominent in the qualification set on the commercial side. Qualification levels are going up all the time, of course, and this applies to the commercial side as well, but there is still a difference. It is unusual to meet a manager on the technical side who has *only* a successfully completed apprenticeship behind him, but it is not unusual to meet a quite senior and demonstrably able *Industrie-Kaufmann* (as the ex-commercial apprentice is known) in finance, sales, administration or personnel.

On the technical side again there are often qualifications which managers may have, not usually in the sense of a terminal qualification such as a university degree, but in the sense of more junior qualifications obtained earlier in their career. There is the *Technikerprüfung* (technician's examination), usually obtained by part-time attendance at a junior technical college. There are certificates in work study, known as *Refa Qualifikationen*, and there is a formal qualification for foremen known as the *Meisterbrief*. But perhaps the most distinctive feature of the German further education system is the existence of an important sub-university qualification. The courses leading to this qualification are offered in senior technical colleges called *Fachhochschulen*. The qualification is offered in a very wide variety of mostly vocational subjects, of which the two most important as management qualifications are business economics and engineering (all branches). The courses are full-time and last a minimum of three years. Students usually begin these courses at the age of 18. Although *Abitur* (the German equivalent of A-level) is not required for entry to the *Fachhochschule*, it is normal for *Fachhochschule* entrants to have had twelve years of full-time education and to have obtained an entry qualification known as *Fachhochschulreife* (literally, readiness to attend a *Fachhochschule*) at a junior technical college. The level of this *Fachhochschule* examination in British terms would be somewhere between GCSE and A-level, probably closer to A-level. All the lecturers at the *Fachhochschule* are themselves university graduates and they are required by law to have a minimum of five years' relevant occupational experience. In the case of lecturers in business economics or engineering, this means, of course, five years' experience in commerce or industry. Students who successfully complete courses at a *Fachhochschule* are described as *graduiert*; so someone who has studied business economics becomes a *graduierter Betriebswirt*, someone who has studied engineering a *graduierter Ingenieur* or, to use the standard abbreviation, an *Ing.Grad.*

Qualifications at this level are important in West Germany, where vocational education is taken more seriously than in Britain or France. Particularly important is the *Ing.Grad.*, a qualification which is very common among German middle managers. Although there is a general trend towards recruiting and promoting university graduates, the *Ing.Grad.* is still to be found at all levels in the German management hierarchy. The *Ing.Grad.* is also the dominant qualification in design and production functions.

It should, however, be added that the *Ing.Grad.* qualification, and the younger generation of engineers who are so qualified, will probably figure less in the ranks of German management in the future than is the case at present. This is not only because of a general trend towards the recruitment of graduates; it also reflects changes in the way students are recruited to the *Ing.Grad.* course and industry's unfavourable view of the changes. The system of admission to the *Fachhochschule* described above has only existed since about 1970 (the changes were implemented at different times in different federal states). Previously, a $3^{1}/_{2}$ year apprenticeship or two years' supervised practical experience in industry was the standard route for admission to the *Ing.Grad.* course at the *Ingenieurschule* (engineering school, the old name for the present *Fachhochschule*). The point is that under the old system the *Ing.Grad.*, the day they left the *Ingenieurschule*, could already claim years of practical experience on the shop-floor by virtue of their earlier apprenticeship. The new style *Ing.Grad.* does not have this claim to practical prowess and in consequence has not been so sought after by industry.

THE EDUCATIONAL BACKGROUND OF GERMAN MANAGERS

If we turn next to the educational background and qualifications which German managers actually have as demonstrated by the survey evidence, some introductory remarks may be helpful. As with surveys of managers' social backgrounds there is, arguably, too much concentration on the higher ranks. When it comes to the educational profile of the *Vorstand* (executive committee of a German public company), the surveys have achieved overkill, but we know relatively little from this source about the qualifications of the typical salesman and production superintendent. Furthermore, many of the samples tend to be treated in an elitist way as though the only qualification worth mentioning were a university degree. This is a pity for two reasons. First, one of the strengths of the German system is the fact that there are substantial non-university vocational courses – those leading to the *graduiert* qualifications. Second, it is one of German industry's distinctive features that a significant minority of its managers do combine the humbler qualifications listed earlier with the higher *graduiert* and university qualifications.

In discussing some of the extant surveys of the educational background of German managers it becomes clear that the only consistent finding is the primacy of three subjects of study – law, economics and engineering. In one study 70 per cent of the managers will be graduates, in the next only 30 per cent. This does not mean that the whole exercise is nonsense. It is simply a manifestation of the fact that all surveys are only as good as their samples. In this context it matters a lot whether one surveys *Vorstand* chairmen or *Vorstand* members; owner-managers or employed executives; all managers in North Rhine Westphalia or *Aufsichtsrat* (supervisory board of a German public company) members for the top 100 companies; and so on.

In the same connection, readers who would like to know how German managers compare with those in other countries have to be satisfied with scientifically second-best answers. That is to say, the only wholly satisfactory answer is one based on a simultaneous survey in the two or more countries concerned and one which uses the same sampling frame selecting members of the two or more national samples evenly in terms of company size, executive rank and branch of the economy. Such studies are very rare, so the best one can usually do is make rough comparisons between unlike samples surveyed at different times.

One of the earliest post-war studies was made by Heinz Hartmann (1956) using executive registers and address books as the information source. The survey is of senior managers – members of the *Vorstand* and of the *Geschäftsführung* (top management of the *GmbH* and *KG* type of companies) and of other senior ranks – and the size of the sample was 6,578. Of these, some 31 per cent were university graduates, though this figure is probably an underestimate since academic qualifications were not always given in the sources used. Among the graduates the largest single group were the engineers (36 per cent), with law graduates in second place (19 per cent) and economics graduates third (17 per cent). Hartmann notes that lawyers tended to be promoted at a relatively early age and were favoured for appointments to the *Aufsichtsrat* (supervisory board). Yet engineers were the dominant group; one out of four graduate *Vorstand* (executive committee) chairmen was an engineer and the *Dr.Ing.* (Ph.D. in engineering) was the most favoured qualification for the chairmanship of the *Vorstand*.

Moving to the early 1960s the business magazine *Capital* published the results of its own survey of the educational background of some 377 managers. As with Hartmann's survey the sample is very much a top management one – *Vorstand* members, *Geschäftsführer* and *Prokuristen* (a *Prokurist* is a senior manager empowered to represent the firm legally). Of the sample 62.9 per cent were university graduates. Educational details were not given for the other third, though it is reasonable to suppose that these other managers had some of the non-university qualifications discussed in the previous section. Again, engineers constituted the largest proportion of the graduates (42.6 per cent); lawyers were in second place (21.5 per cent), and economics graduates in third (19.8 per cent). Graduates in natural science subjects and arts subjects, taken together, accounted for only a small proportion (9.7 per cent) of the graduate sample.

This *Capital* survey is also of interest in presenting graduate rates for different branches of industry. Taking companies rather than individual managers as the units of analysis the sample is modest, comprising eighty companies. This sample size constraint can lead to distortion, as in the finding that top management in the construction industry is 100 per cent graduate (two companies, represented by five managers, all of them engineering graduates!). Setting aside this chance entity, the order was that 77 per cent of the top managers in the electrical industry were graduates, 76.8 per cent of those in the chemical industry, 72.3 per cent of those in the iron, steel and metal industry, but only 48.8 per cent in the mechanical engineering and motor car industries. In five out of the eighty companies, none of the top managers was a graduate, while in another eleven companies the whole *Vorstand* was graduate.

A similar small-sample top manager survey was made in the mid-1960s by Wolfgang Zapf (1965). Zapf's sample, in fact, is even more homogeneous, constituting 318 *Vorstand* (executive committee) members drawn from the fifty largest companies by turnover. Of this sample 95 per cent had attended a *Gymnasium* (grammar school) and had *Abitur* (A-level). Graduates comprised 89 per cent of the sample. Of the 11 per cent of non-graduates, 8 per cent were *Industrie-Kaufmann*, that is, had begun their career by doing a commercial apprenticeship; 1 per cent had served an apprenticeship and gone on to higher (non-graduate) qualifications, and the final 2 per cent were (former) skilled workers (with the *Facharbeiterbrief*). A small new finding was that one in ten of the university graduates had done apprenticeships before going to university. This is very German in its humility and insistent practicality.

Among the graduates the engineers as usual are in first place; in fact, the engineers and scientists together constituted 57 per cent; lawyers and economics graduates both accounted for 21 per cent of the graduate sample. This survey is the most striking illustration of the fact that engineering, law and economics are *the* subjects of study for prospective German managers.

Zapf has also checked the proportion of graduates for different age groups. For those managers in the sample who were over 65, some 88 per cent were graduates; the proportion was lower for the middle age groups (45–65), but for the youngest age group (remember that we are concerned here with *Vorstand* members), those managers under 45 were all university graduates. This is a piece of tangible evidence for the frequently made assertion that German management is becoming increasingly graduate dominated. Incidentally, not only were 89 per cent of the sample graduates, but 61 per cent of these also had Ph.Ds.

A study with a very large sample, dating again from the mid-1960s, is that of Hartmann and Wienold (1967). The sample was made up of the 21,707 top managers and owner-managers listed in a directory of leading figures in West German economic life. This enormous sample was a *mélange* of *Vorstand* members, *Geschäftsführer*, managing partners and owner-managers (heads of *GmbH* and *KG* type companies).

This time 27 per cent of the sample were university graduates. It will be noted that this is less than the proportion (31 per cent) in Hartmann's earlier 1956 study. This almost certainly represents a difference in sampling, since the earlier study concentrated on large joint stock companies whereas this study, with its enormous sample, has sizeable proportions of owner-managers and managing partners with whom educational standards tend to be lower. Of the graduates, 36 per cent had studied engineering and science, 21 per cent economics and 13 per cent law. The employed executives were more likely than the owner-managers to be graduates. For the prize position of chairman of the *Vorstand*, graduates with either a legal training or a Ph.D. seemed to be most favoured. Again law graduates, with or without a Ph.D., seemed to be favoured for *Vorstand* appointments generally, relative to their numbers, and were particularly strong in banking and insurance. The owner-managers, though less likely to be university educated, were most likely to have studied engineering if they had been to university. Like the authors of the *Capital* survey, Hartmann and Wienold checked which branches of industry had the highest proportion of graduates and found the 'winners' to be banking and insurance, the power and coal industries and chemicals.

Max Kruk (1967) conducted a survey similar to that of Hartmann and Wienold using the same directory of leading figures in the West German economy, though in fact the 1965 edition of the directory (Hartmann and Wienold had used the 1964 edition). This yielded another enormous sample of 31,427, a more heterogeneous sample than that of Hartmann and Wienold, including *Aufsichtsrat* (supervisory board) members and non-managing partners as well as the usual categories of senior managers and owner-managers. In fact all types of owner-manager included constituted 59.6 per cent of the whole sample. This again had the effect of depressing the educational profile, with 31.6 per cent of the whole sample being graduates, though the graduate proportion rises to 60 per cent for *Vorstand* members. Over half the graduates also held Ph.Ds. The subjects studied were as always engineering, economics and law, in decreasing order of importance, with other subjects playing only a minor role. Kruk concluded that engineering studies were still the best route into higher management, though law studies conferred an advantage for appointments to the *Aufsichtsrat* and to the *Vorstand* of banks.

Moving now into the 1970s, Pross and Boetticher (1971) surveyed a sample of some 538 *Vorstand* members and other senior managers from thirteen large joint stock companies. These researchers also found that the majority of managers at this level had attended a selective secondary school, 89 per cent of them having been to a *Gymnasium* (grammar school). The majority were graduates, and Pross and Boetticher documented the fact that graduate dominance increases with hierarchic rank. In their sample 58 per cent of the *Prokuristen* (managers with a power of attorney) were graduates, and 77 per cent of the *Vorstand* members were. The proportion of *Vorstand* members who were graduates is low compared with the figure which emerges from some other studies; this is probably because Pross and Boetticher chose their companies on the basis of personal connections – the companies did not represent the largest thirteen in West Germany nor thirteen from among the top fifty as in some other studies already discussed. Incidentally, about half the university graduates also had Ph.Ds.

The distribution of graduates among the various subjects was quite consistent with the results of all the other surveys: 60.6

per cent engineering and science, 22.1 per cent economics, 13.5 per cent law. Pross and Boetticher argue that the proportion of lawyers has declined and that the number of engineers in top management has been declining as well, though engineers are still the dominant group. The corresponding gains have been made by graduates in business economics. The authors regard these changes as indicative of a change from production orientation towards a marketing orientation. It should be added that there are other studies which do not show this rise of business economics graduate and a decline in the dominance of engineers. In relation to their overall numbers the engineers' chance of getting to the top (e.g. *Aufsichtsrat* or supervisory board posts, chairman of the *Vorstand*) is not especially good, and not as good as the lawyers'. On the other hand, the engineers are the most numerous group and by sheer weight of numbers remain the dominant group at the top (and for that matter in the middle).

Kruk (1972) conducted a second survey of the background of German managers. Kruk's later study comprised a sample of 2,053 managers of the 381 largest companies. As in earlier studies it emerged that the great majority, some 88.3 per cent, had attended a *Gymnasium*. Kruk noted here a change over time in that older managers in the sample tended to come from the *humanistisches Gymnasium* with its emphasis on Latin, Greek and Hebrew, while the younger ones were more likely to have been to the *neusprachliches Gymnasium*, favouring modern languages and science.

Some 75 per cent of Kruk's sample were graduates, with engineers and scientists, economics graduates and lawyers comprising three approximately equal groups, though engineers were the dominant group in manufacturing industry considered separately. Graduates in other disciplines accounted for a mere 1.6 per cent. Some two-thirds of Kruk's graduate sample also had Ph.Ds. Kruk also characterized the subject groups socially, viewing the lawyers as the social elite among top managers (this is consistent with the fact that most surveys show them to be favoured for *Aufsichtsrat* posts), the engineers as lower-middle-class and the business economics graduates as lower-class and also on average younger (cf. Pross and Boetticher). Kruk noted too that work experience abroad appeared to be significant for a successful career. It is also claimed by Kruk that although the *Praktiker* (practical man, in this context one lacking university qualifications) was generally losing ground to the graduate manager, he is still holding his own in some particular functions including sales and purchasing.

If we attempt to sum up on the basis of this mountain of survey evidence on the educational backgrounds and qualifications of German managers, then the simple fact is that among graduate managers in Germany more, as we have seen, have degrees in engineering than in any other subject. It is possible to construct an argument to the effect that people qualified in other subjects, in the German case law and economics, may have better promotion *chances* (relative to their numbers), but by sheer weight of numbers the engineers have dominated. The same picture emerges with the sub-degree-level qualification pattern.

There is a further twist to the predominance of the qualified engineer in German industry, highlighted by a study not so far mentioned. This study with a sample of something like 20,000 (Brinkmann 1967) demonstrated that:

- qualification levels are higher on the technical side of German firms than on the commercial side;
- the technical functions – development, design, engineering, production, production planning, quality control, testing – are dominated by qualified engineers;
- the commercial functions are not similarly dominated by people qualified in economics or business economics; in fact, engineers 'overspill' into the commercial functions, but the reverse does not hold; i.e. non-engineers do not 'overspill' into technical management posts.

It is unfortunate that Brinkmann's study has not been replicated at a later date. With a qualification about the lapse of time in the completion of this study, its findings are a powerful testimony to the dominance of engineers in German industry.

EDUCATIONAL FACTORS

The third consideration we would urge in support of the claim that engineers enjoy a higher standing in Germany is educational, or rather a package of educational considerations:

- Engineering students constitute a higher proportion of the total university population in Germany than in Britain (Bayer and Lawrence 1977).

- Engineers constitute a higher proportion of the QSE (qualified scientists and engineers) group in Germany than in Britain.
- There is no evidence that engineering students in Germany ever had an inferior school attainment, though they clearly did have in Britain (Bayer and Lawrence 1977), even if there appears to be some improvement.
- There is no evidence that some German engineering students are failed applicants to science courses, though this phenomenon has been common in Britain.
- Contacts between engineering educational establishments on the one hand and industry on the other are on the whole good in Germany and there is some substance to these relations.
- Engineering courses in Germany are simply longer and arguably more substantial, both at degree level (*Dipl.Ing.*) and the next level down (*Ing.Grad.*), than in Britain.

We have not attempted an exhaustive treatment of the proposition that engineers enjoy higher status in Germany than in Britain, though such a treatment is given elsewhere (Hutton, Lawrence and Smith 1977) but instead focused on the issues of remuneration, access to management posts and educational considerations.

AN UNDERSTANDING OF KNOWLEDGE

Departing for the moment from these tangible considerations – salary, education system factors and the qualifications of managers – it may be helpful to discuss the German notion of *Technik*. This is a word and concept which has equivalents in some other languages, for instance *teknik* in Swedish and *techniek* in Dutch, but not in the English language. The starting point is that there are differences in the ways in which societies perceive and evaluate skill and knowledge; differences in the way in which they group and label branches of knowledge.

In Britain we distinguish between arts and sciences. The distinction is there in common speech and assumptions, is reflected in school timetables and college brochures and is actually thought to connote something. The distinction was formalized, publicized and given a further thrust by Sir Charles Snow's famous 'Two Cultures' lecture at Cambridge over thirty years ago. The key question here is: what is the role of engineering in the two cultures scheme, or the art-versus-sciences distinction? C. P. Snow solved the problem by fitting in engineering as 'applied science', and this is a common, if not invariable, convention in the English-speaking world.

This 'applied science' label is, however, rather damaging to engineering. It tends to accord engineering a junior, dependent and subordinate status under the aegis of science. This has been unfortunate for the status of engineering in Britain. It is also misleading since it tends to suggest that any advance in engineering is dependent on a prior advance in science and this is simply not true. Sometimes the relationship and dependency exist, sometimes they do not. The 'applied science' label also implies some misconception of engineering work. It suggests, that is, that engineering work consists of the application of knowledge and principles derived from science, and again this is only partly and sometimes true. The 'applied science' formula also suggests a similarity between science and engineering, albeit with engineering as the junior partner. This is totally false. The output of science is knowledge; the output of engineering is three dimensional artefacts. Much scientific work takes place in laboratory conditions where the influence of undesirable variables has been controlled; most engineering work is conducted 'on site', and is subject to environmental influences. Scientists, who study things, seek ideal solutions and universally valid laws. Engineers, who make things, seek workable solutions which do not cost too much. In short the 'applied science' label is damaging and misleading. And it does not exist in Germany.

It is indeed linguistically and culturally difficult to represent the 'two cultures' thesis in German. This is not because the Germans do not make distinctions, but because they make different distinctions. Engagingly, they use the same word for arts and sciences. The German term *Wissenschaft* covers all formal knowledge subjects, whether arts, natural sciences or social sciences in the British scheme of things. And particular subjects are often designated by compound nouns based on *Wissenschaft*: economics, for instance, is *Wirtschaftswissenschaft*; literature, as a university subject, is *Literaturwissenschaft*. The Germans employ a second term, *Kunst*, to refer to art. Not to 'the arts' in the British sense of the humanities, but to the end products of art – the paintings and statues and symphonies. And third, the Germans use the term *Technik* to refer to manufacture and the knowledge and skills relevant to it. That is, of course, to engineering knowledge and engineering and craft skills. In short, the existence in German culture of the concept of *Technik* not only avoids the demotion and misconception of engineering implicit in 'applied science', it also tends to dignify and even glamorize engineering under its distinctive rubric.

It is also fair to add that the word *Technik* is actually used in German, and used in quite homely ways. It is not a term for the exclusive use of those who write books on the philosophy of science. In conversations with German managers the present writer has come across such gems as: 'Die Technik ist sauber' ('*Technik* is wholesome' – a manager denouncing the American practice of using pretty girls in machinery advertisements) and 'Ich bin eigentlich Technik Liebhaber' ('Actually I'm a *Technik* lover' – a production manager expounding on his job satisfaction). A standard German phrase is 'technisch gesteuert', meaning technically guided, or directed in terms of *Technik*. One hears of advertising departments which are 'technisch gesteuert', or sales departments, or whole companies.

Thus *Technik* exerts a pervasive influence in German firms and on German managerial thinking. It tends to account for the uncomplicated view taken by top managers of company goals and the means to achieve them. The goals are in the German view 'technicized'; to the German manager they are self-evident and there is no need to have a seminar on it. *Technik* similarly accounts for the relative lack of interest in techniques of planning, control and decision-taking noted in the Booz, Allen and Hamilton report, discussed on pp.93–7. The German is more likely to feel that *Technik* is in the foreground and managerial techniques and corporate strategy take second place. The standing of *Technik* again supplies the clue to the traditional German apathy on foreign investments, mergers and take-overs. These measures are outside *Technik*; they are not the way in which German firms have usually expected to make money.

Technik is also, *ceteris paribus*, a force for integration. The German company is *Technik* in organizational form. The skilled worker, the foreman, the superintendent, the technical director are all participants in *Technik*. Of course, there are many things which they do not have in common, but *Technik* is something which transcends hierarchy. It may also transcend particular functions in the company. This is most obviously true for the various technical functions – research and development (R & D), design, production, production control, maintenance and quality control.

Qualificational homogeneity in these functions (nearly everyone has one of two different qualifications, *Dipl.Ing* or *Ing.Grad.*; they are all of course engineers) tends to integrate these functions, and *Technik* provides them with a cultural umbrella. It is also conceivable, though the point should not be exaggerated, that *Technik* is sufficiently pervasive to have some integrating effect as between technical and commercial functions. The first occasion on which the present writer heard the word *Technik* used by a German manager was in the observation of a public relations manager in a commercial vehicle company that 'Die Firma lebt schliesslich von der Technik' ('After all, the firm lives from *Technik*').

There is a separate but overlapping German tendency to valorize sapiential rather than structural authority, to use the terms from Barnard's classic typology of authority (Barnard 1938). The German reaction against the Third Reich encompassed a rejection of rank or office-based authority, and a modern predilection for the authority of knowledge, experience or expertise. In practice this often turns out to be technical knowledge/expertise. As we have seen, German thinking avoids subordinating the engineer to the scientist, while preferring the authority of knowledge to the authority of rank.

To take one simple manifestation of these trends, German industry is unusual in demanding for the most part qualified foremen (foremen who have the *Meisterbrief*). There is a standard route to the position of foreman in German industry. After leaving secondary school, one does a $3^{1}/_{2}$-year apprenticeship (this may be shortened for those who have the German equivalents of GCSE and A-level GCE described in a previous section). This apprenticeship is completed by passing both a practical and a written exam, and then one becomes a *Facharbeiter*, or skilled worker. *Facharbeiter* is a legally protected status, and being a skilled worker is coterminous with the completion of an apprenticeship.

Some years of experience as a skilled worker will follow, and then the ambitious worker will enrol on the foreman's course, leading to the award of the *Meisterbrief*. There are various ways of going about this, but most commonly this course is pursued part-time over a $3^{1}/_{2}$-year period; and as with the apprenticeship, there is a written exam at the end. At this stage, one is qualified to be appointed to the position of foreman.

All this immediately marks off the typical German foreman from the typical British one, who usually lacks both general educational and specialist technical qualifications. But perhaps more indicative is the content of the German *Meisterbrief* course. This is primarily craft and technical, not organizational, managerial or supervisory skills-related. Our purpose in underlining this point is not to say that the Germans have necessarily got it right, but to suggest that the conviction that the supervisor's need is for more craft skill and technical knowledge, rather than for 'management of human resources' know-how, is distinctively German and at odds with Anglo-Saxon orthodoxy.

APPRENTICESHIP: A GERMAN INSTITUTION

The two forces discussed, *Technik* and an unpretentious predilection for relevant and specialist knowledge, cross in the institution of apprenticeship in Germany. Apprenticeship in Germany is different in all sorts of ways from apprenticeship in Britain.

While the apprenticeship systems in both countries have their origin in the Middle Ages, they have developed differently in the two cases. In Britain apprenticeship acquired a somewhat old-fashioned aura, and was thought to be associated with the stable engineering industries of the nineteenth century such as boilermaking and shipbuilding. In Germany the newer industries of the twentieth century embraced apprenticeship as the obvious way to sustain the input of necessary knowledge and skill.

In Britain apprenticeship was associated with maintenance rather than with production; in Germany it is associated with both. In Britain apprenticeship exists for (some) blue-collar jobs; in Germany apprenticeship serves both blue-collar and white-collar occupations (the *Banklehre* or banking apprenticeship, for example, is much sought after in Germany, and those accepted will usually have *Abitur*, the equivalent of A-level). Or again, apprenticeship in Britain has become something of an industrial relations football, with 'them' wanting to use non 'time-served' people in skilled jobs (dilution) because it is cheaper, and 'us' resisting this dirty move by capitalist employers! This confrontational set-piece does not seem to have arisen in Germany either, where both 'sides of industry' are likely to agree on the importance of a trained and skilled workforce. Indeed, individual German employers often claim when times are bad that they have taken on more apprentices than the company really needs, as a contribution to fighting recession and unemployment.

More generally, apprenticeship is held in higher esteem in Germany. A higher proportion of the age group engage in apprentice training than is the case in Britain, and there are more occupations in Germany, getting on for 500, for which a recognized apprenticeship exists. Interestingly, there is a word in German, *Lernberuf*, that denotes an occupation with required apprenticeship training, and it has a thoroughly laudatory ring.

Finally, apprenticeship locks into *Technik* and the German system in a variety of tangible ways, some of which have already been mentioned. First, apprenticeship is the *sine qua non* for achieving *Facharbeiter* or skilled worker status. Second, as we have seen in the previous section, apprenticeship is the starting point for anyone who would be an eventual candidate for the *Meisterbrief* and the post of foreman. Then, until around 1970 an apprenticeship was typically a prerequisite for admission to the old-style *Ingenieurschule* from which the *Ing.Grad.* qualification was obtained. And lastly, it is not uncommon for university graduates, especially in engineering, to have done an apprenticeship at an early stage; one even meets Ph.Ds in Germany with apprenticeships. All this testifies in the German case to an emphasis on the vocational, specific and mostly technical.

A MANAGEMENT ACCOMMODATION

German management is qualitatively different in various ways that facilitate the accommodation of engineering. First of all, the Germans have a weak concept of management. There is not really an indigenous word for management in German. The idea of the professional manager, as opposed to the *Unternehmer* (= entrepreneur), the responsible, proactive business owner, was slow to develop in Germany. Germans do not take readily to the idea that there is something called management that is separate from the more specific things that are done within manufacturing companies, or that such a management entity can be extrapolated and made the subject of generalization. As individuals German managers tend to prefer functionally specific titles – production controller, designer, industrial salesman – rather than the general title of manager.

German management tends to be a bit old-fashioned. It is 'hands-on' rather than 'arm's-length'; weak on delegation, marketing and strategy, but strong on personal responsibility, the organization of production and operational detail. A major review of German management, commissioned by the federal government, was horrified to discover how un-American it was (Booz, Allen and Hamilton 1973). Indeed, the genesis of this study is both fascinating and ironical.

The *Bundeswirtschaftsministerium* (Federal Economics Ministry) commissioned a report on German management from the Düsseldorf office of the American consultancy firm Booz, Allen and Hamilton. The report was presented in German, but an English translation has been published accompanied by a critical assessment. The *Bundeswirtschaftsministerium* chose Booz, Allen and Hamilton precisely because the ministry was keen to have a non-German (objective) evaluation of German management, and cut through any German tendency towards executive insularity: the ministry got more than it bargained for.

The report is highly critical. Its criticisms, however, should not be taken too seriously since the whole operation is somewhat vitiated by two (untenable) assumptions:

1 If it happens in the USA it must be good.
2 The American way is the only good way.

What, in fact, the authors do is work their way through a check-list of American executive concerns, assumptions, practices and developments and look to see them reflected or represented in German companies. For the most part they do not find them and to this extent German management stands condemned in the report as old-fashioned and unsophisticated. There is another weakness, to which the commentary also draws attention. The report is not empirically documented; it is never really clear on what the report's findings are based. There are no references to a sample, to data-gathering methods, to numbers of firms investigated or managers interviewed. Although there are some references to medium-sized firms, one suspects that the report is based primarily on contact with large firms, which is to be condemned on the grounds that small and medium-sized companies constitute a higher proportion of all manufacturing establishments in West Germany than in the USA. This is a fair point and the same difference exists as between West Germany and Great Britain, though to a lesser degree.

BOOZ, ALLEN AND HAMILTON REPORT ON GERMAN MANAGEMENT

German companies are criticized for being person-oriented rather than system-oriented; that is, being oriented to the practices and predilections of top managers as individuals, rather than to an impersonal management system with its own dynamics. The top managers are not good at formulating company goals, and medium-sized companies generally lack formal (written) statements of goals. A lot of the top managers are 'operators' first and foremost, that is, they are concerned with the conduct of daily affairs. The report says of the typical top manager:

> As a rule he does not advance to his top management position from the staff departments of the enterprise. Thus, it is very hard for him to 'put his feet on the table' and to consider how the company should develop in the next five to ten years. He tends instead to delegate this assignment to a staff position.

It follows, of course, from this contention that corporate planning in German companies is not very satisfactory either. Overall planning is vitiated by 'a strong penchant for detail and lack of uniform criteria'. Financial planning tends to be done well in big companies (though not as well as in the USA), but not in medium-sized companies. Large firms use the concept of return on investment, but 'on the other hand, there are still many companies of medium size which have hardly heard of return on investment'. And no one appears to use the concept of discounted cash flow.

German thinking on diversification and expansion is also criticized. R & D activity and the acquisition of other existing companies are just two different forms of diversification, but the Germans tend to treat them as separate activities. But they are, the report asserts, just alternative routes to higher profit and lower risk. Indeed, the Germans are just not aggressive enough. They are lukewarm, it is suggested, in their search for merger partners and take-over victims. Neither has Germany invested enough abroad, certainly much less than the USA has done. Relatively few German firms have subsidiaries abroad, and the Germans have even failed to exploit the Common Market countries in this connection.

German firms are held to be weak on delegation, in both personal and organizational ways. Only recently, it is argued in the report, have big companies started subdividing into units. In many medium-sized companies

the principle of delegation of authority has hardly been introduced. A good example for this contention can be found in the large spans of control in many of these companies, and cases are far from rare where top management executives find themselves in charge of ten to fifteen heads of departments.

The Germans are also weak on the 'specification of objectives' as a prerequisite for effective delegation of authority.

The report assesses German collegial management in the form of the *Vorstand* (executive committee) and manages to say a few 'nice things' about it. The basic orientation, however, is again critical. The *Vorstand* is invested with all the putative ills of committee government: slowness, compromise, reciprocal back-scratching, avoidance of individual responsibility and the emergence of complicated interpersonal relationships. It is fair to add that not a scrap of evidence is offered in the report for this view.

The report moves on to some particular American management devices which are held to be neglected in Germany. The Germans make little use of the project team or task force: that is, a group of managers probably drawn from different functions and levels who come together to accomplish some particular major purpose and disband afterwards. The Germans are said to be weak on control (except financial control), not realizing that control should correspond to planning and organization and reveal deviations from the plan. The German conception of operations research is primitive, and the supply of operations research specialists is limited. It is suggested that the Germans are rather vague on simulation, linear programming, decision theory, PERT (programme evaluation and review technique) and risk analysis. Similarly, the potential of management information systems has not been generally appreciated (apart from their application to accounting systems), but then management information systems require managers schooled in OR with a ready appreciation of what computers can do, and the Germans are not in this happy position. German use of the concept of cost-benefit analysis is also limited. (Readers should keep in mind that this is an evaluation of German management in the 1970s.)

The report claims that marketing is, or soon will be, the most important management function. By marketing as opposed to sales is meant a series of interrelated decisions and activities concerning pricing policy, choice of distribution channels, advertising arrangements, sales promotion, and so on. It is suggested that the Germans do not fully appreciate this, tending to emphasize sales rather than marketing, with the marketing functions being discharged by a staff group in sales.

The Germans are praised for their handling of cost control, though the report makes some criticisms of the way in which overhead and secondary costs are allocated. Cost reduction, however, is another German weakness, in the very basic sense that cost reduction is not regarded as a continuous objective in German companies. Cost reduction programmes tend to be introduced only during recessions, without the real support of top management and with inadequate preparation.

A section of the report discusses German managers *per se*, and explicitly compares them with American managers. It is argued that the things they have in common are a similar age structure, a similar and rather high proportion of managers of lowly social origin, a high proportion with university education and comparable levels of inter-company mobility.

But it is the differences between German and American managers which the writers of the report perceive are of more interest. The Germans, it is declared, have been educated: the Americans have been trained. The German managers are more specialized; they are willing to change company but do not like to change industry. By American lights the Germans are more conservative, the older German managers having been shaped by economic stagnation between the wars. The Germans, it is argued, are more cautious and more prone to compromise. German managers feel their achievements are not recognized by the general public and they do not seek the limelight. They have a bad conscience about earning so much. They are industrious, typically working 10–12 hours a day, but 'this industriousness often seems to be compensation for knowledge about modern management'.

The report ends with some strictures on training. It is maintained that the Germans do not take management training seriously enough, do less of it than the Americans, make insufficient use of the European business schools like INSEAD and IMEDE and furthermore do not like having their performance subjected to objective assessment.

Now it is getting on for twenty years since the Booz, Allen and Hamilton report was published, and factually much of the substantive detail will have changed. Yet the report remains a fascinating document. It describes, albeit for the 1970s, a society with very un-American, indeed one might say unmanagerial, management. And this in a country every bit as successful economically as was the USA at this time if not more so. Yet more interesting for us are the 'negative clues' in the report to Germany's attachment to the practical, unpretentious, product-driven and engineering-related.

Above all, German management has been specialist rather than generalist in its orientation. People are picked, placed and advanced on the grounds of their specialist knowledge, experience and skills. This is, of course, particularly true on the technical side, and the technical functions have enjoyed higher standing than in Britain. Germans will often name design or development as prima-donna functions (and never finance). The production function has more standing than in Britain. It has even been argued in a comparative study of the nature of managerial control across companies in Britain, France and Germany that German companies are differently structured (Horovitz 1980). This view sees the typical German company as structured predominantly in functional terms, with few levels of general management. Thus one can 'go a long way' in a German company without losing functional (specialist) purity, and this still tends to be welcomed by Germans. In short, the standing and contribution of engineering are predicated on a different and more accommodating understanding of management.

NO COUNTRY IS AN ISLAND

It would be wrong to end without relativizing a little the picture presented in this chapter in terms of the passage of time. The 1980s, like no previous decade, were an assertion of the claims of the management. Entrepreneurs, managers and company affairs and performance caught the public imagination as never before. In countries as traditionally un-obsessed with management as Britain and the Netherlands, undergraduate provision for management education expanded massively, demand rose spectacularly, and so did entry standards. In France, for the first time since the end of the Second World War, the *patronat* (employers) was forgiven its supposed sins, from collaboration with the Nazis, to sluggishness in performance, and the public demanded business heroes, of whom Bernard Tapis is perhaps the most eye-catching (Barsoux and Lawrence 1990). Even in stalwart, socialist Sweden, change was afoot. A cult of the proactive and imaginative manager was launched with Jan Carlson's early success with SAS, and the 1980s decade ended with tough managers winning respect by taking unpopular decisions. In the spring of 1990 Saab cars were acquired by General Motors, and the new Stockholm-based president is an American national from the Harvard Law School. This was a decade of heady excitement throughout Western Europe, and Germany was not immune. So what changed in Germany in the 1980s?

First, management has blossomed as an undergraduate subject. Or to be precise, as in the earlier discussion of German qualifications, the subject that is the nearest German approach to management or business administration as taught in the Anglo-Saxon countries, namely *Betriebswirtschaftslehre* or business economics, has enjoyed a new lease of life. At the beginning of the 1980s *Betriebswirtschaftslehre* was seen as something of a poor relation to *Volkswirtschaft* or political economy. Better students would do *Volkswirtschaft*, and companies having a choice would probably choose these graduates rather than those in *Betriebswirtschaftslehre*. But by the beginning of the 1990s the position has been reversed: *Betriebswirtschaftslehre* is riding high with booming enrolments and higher standards.

The second thing is much less tangible, but deserves to be mentioned. Germany-watchers and business commentators tend to think that German management changed somewhat in the 1980s, becoming more professional in the textbook American sense. Or to put it another way, there has been some movement away from the rather patriarchal style presented in the Booz, Allen and Hamilton report discussed above. In practice, this means more systems, more delegation and more emphasis on marketing and strategy. Another interesting development is that there are German companies making their mark which are outside the areas of Germany's traditional strength – chemicals, mechanical engineering, electrical engineering and automobiles. Hugo Boss, Deutsche Bank, Aldi, Adidas and for that matter Lufthansa are all obvious examples.

Finally, there has been some restructuring of the West German economy in the 1980s and this in a country where merger and acquisition have been the exception rather than the rule. And with reunification a new restructuring vista has opened up, and so has new territory for (West) German retailers and banks.

Do these changes mean that the contrast explored in the main body of this chapter is now a thing of historic interest only? No, they do not – the changes sketched above are accretional not revolutionary. They are 'bolt-ons' in a different society, where engineering and management never followed the Anglo-Saxon model. Germany remains the land of *Technik*, specialization and vocational training.

CONCLUSION

Our purpose is not so much to pass judgement on German interpretations (or achievements) but to draw attention to the differences from an Anglo-Saxon viewpoint.

Distinctive attitudes to management, entrepreneurialism, specialism–generalism, control, competitive advantage and the structuring of company organization tend to make German companies qualitatively different. At the same time they are rendered more hospitable to engineers and more disposed to value the technical competencies of the engineer.

Not only is the Anglo-Saxon understanding of management not universal, but certain questions are raised by the German practice and understanding. Let us conclude by formulating two of these questions.

Are we right to compartmentalize engineering and management? And are the Germans right in their implicit suggestion that management is not a separate job but a part of all jobs?

Chapter 6

The work of engineers in Hungary and their place within management cultures and hierarchies

Gyula Fülöp

To get a picture of the position of Hungarian engineers and their place in management cultures and hierarchies today, an overview is needed of the main features of engineering work in the Hungarian context in relation to the socio-economic processes which have led to the present situation.

Here the development of Hungarian organizational structures and approaches to management practice will be discussed, together with the present system of engineering education and training. These issues, together and in relationship to each other, define the role and position of engineers in organizational cultures and hierarchies.

HISTORY OF ENGINEERING IN HUNGARY

The roots of the formation of Hungarian engineering reach back to the early period of capitalism in the country in the eighteenth century. At that time, the first technical institutions were established to meet the demands of capitalism. The diplomas which were awarded to mining engineers from the 1740s onwards carried with them certain privileges for the holder.

Engineers as a significant group within the social structure appeared at the end of the last century by gaining a certain independent role and establishing their own institutions (Harsányi 1961; Huszár 1978). By the beginning of the twentieth century there were 2,500 to 2,600 technical staff employed in Hungarian manufacturing industry, some of whom had graduated from higher technical education schools. In addition, there were some 4,000 works managers, who together with the technical staff constituted 2.5 to 3 per cent of employees in manufacturing industry.

International comparisons indicate that in this respect Hungary could be considered an underdeveloped country at that time. The number of engineers, representing technical development and a technical culture, was low in absolute and relative terms. Total stagnation characterized Hungarian manufacturing industry in the period between the First World War and preparations for the Second World War.

This economic stagnation had an effect on the life, research and development work of Hungarian engineers. Although there were some exceptions, the period was mainly characterized by inertia and a falling behind in general technical progress. The education and training of engineers did not keep up with the requirements of the time. There were no new educational institutions established, for example, for training electrical engineers or engineers in manufacturing technology for heavy industry, production management or industrial engineering. These developments had to wait until 1945.

After 1945 rapid developments began in Hungary. This was shown in the increased education of engineers and technicians, in the establishment of new research and development (R & D) institutes, in the formation of new branches of engineering and in changes in the social composition of engineers. Development between 1949 and 1958 was so rapid that there was an average annual increase of 10 per cent in engineering training. As a result, within ten years more than 21,000 engineering diplomas were awarded.

After 1945 not only had the number of qualified engineers doubled but their distribution within the economy changed. The most significant change was in the proportion of engineers working in research and design institutes. Taking into account the construction industry, transportation and agriculture as well as manufacturing, where the work of engineers is primarily concerned with operations and production management, 65 per cent of Hungarian engineers are working in this field and 35 per cent are employed in research, development, education and public administration.

This redistribution of the composition of the engineering labour force brought an end to the lack of attention to R & D prior to 1945. At the same time, however, the underdevelopment in the field of industrial production continued. In this period of the formation of an engineering stratum, the work of engineers was concerned mainly with three related tasks: that of design and development; production planning, control and maintenance; and management. While today these functions are still central to the work of engineers, in recent years they have broadened and expanded.

THE MAIN FIELDS OF ENGINEERING WORK WITHIN HUNGARIAN ORGANIZATIONS

The majority of the work of engineers can be considered in terms of two largely comprehensive areas, one concerned with the innovation process and the other with the operations process (Birman 1987). Within the sphere of innovation activities, the following groups can be found: technical/economic planning, analysing and co-ordinating, R & D and experimental testing. The operations activities can be seen as covering technical management, production planning and control, technical information services and training, with an emphasis upon investment and maintenance of plant and facilities.

Although at present in Hungary only a few engineers are employed in sales and marketing, this needs to be noted because of the importance of these activities for both innovation and operations activities.

This provides a general classification of the work of engineers in Hungary, but the areas outlined below derived from empirical work provide a more meaningful picture of the main characteristics of engineering work. In his empirical work, Berkó (1989) identified the groups of engineering activities under design and development, production engineering and sales and marketing activities.

Design and development engineers

The usual task of technical employees engaged in product development activities involves finding technological solutions and implementing them within time and cost constraints. This creative intellectual work requires top-level technical knowledge as well as up-to-date knowledge of market information and the ability to forecast likely user reaction.

However, it has been shown that there is a lack of agreement between the efforts and capabilities of those engaged in product development and the objectives of the enterprise. This is due to the lack of external economic pressure which would force participants to make better use of potential but under-utilized resources. This situation does not arise from the work approach of the highly qualified technical staff engaged in development but from circumstances beyond the control of these engineers. For example, there is a lack of product-oriented management approaches and attitudes and associated supportive systems. In other words, technical development is constrained by the organizational systems and structures.

Hungarian enterprises are now starting to recognize this situation, and many of them have undertaken significant reorganizations in recent years in both the R & D field and the relationship between this and other sections of the enterprise. These changes were made on the one hand to integrate the R & D activity more effectively into the hierarchy of the firm and on the other hand to achieve a better match between technical development and the market. In spite of this, most company managers remain unconvinced of the importance of organizational restructuring for improving the effectiveness of technical development. This is understandable if the restructuring is not accompanied by modifications in the incentive system, i.e. a system which would provide participants with an adequate share in benefits arising from enhanced technical performance.

The rationalization of technical development within the industry would mean the avoidance of duplication of effort. Two types of organizational solution exist, one concerned with creating autonomous work groups where teams of designers and production engineers work together on the development project. An alternative solution is the separation of technical development from the auxiliary activities. Regardless of which solution is adopted, enterprises agree that the reorganized system of technical development activites provides a suitable environment for effective intellectual work.

However, only a few companies have, for instance, introduced computer systems for simplifying data processing. This means that in some companies the modernization of the organization and the development of the technical infrastructure, including the use of computers, has taken place separately. Only a few organizations have realized that the effectiveness of technical development can only be promoted if there is integration between the enhancement of the technical and the organizational systems.

Production engineers

Generally the largest group of technical employees in Hungarian industrial companies are those working in production. The production planning and control activities support the production process. While part of their task is characterized by non-routine activities, their central activities are routine ones, which would be undertaken more flexibly in capitalist countries. This is mainly because of the wider use of local computer systems and instrumentation for monitoring production in western countries.

It is claimed that this failure to introduce modern production planning and control is due to the basically conservative production philosophy, rather than a lack of financial resources. As one financial director of a large Hungarian company put it: 'Production has been carried on essentially without any change for several decades, with only some equipment and products being replaced.' This is the case for other enterprises, as they too have made no significant changes in this respect.

An important group within a company's senior management is the factory managers and chief engineers. However, like their subordinates, they too are concerned with ensuring smooth production output rather than innovation. Most of their intellectual capacity and time are spent on complying with the numerous, and mostly obsolete, formal regulations and instructions. Since their financial incentive system is quantity-oriented, only personal interest in technology would stimulate them to use their qualifications and intellectual capital to pursue new methods. Hence such innovation is not encouraged by financial incentives or other forms of recognition within the organization.

Sales and marketing activities

The number of engineers involved with sales and marketing activities (sales and purchasing, market research, advertising, etc.) is still very low. According to senior managers who were interviewed, the effectiveness of those employed in this area is low in comparison with those in developed countries' industries. This is primarily due to the low level of commercial/marketing knowledge but also to the infrastructural lack of modern information technology (e.g. computing and telecommunications). According to senior managers, because of this situation, marketing/commercial staff could be reduced by 20 to 40 per cent without having any serious impact upon company performance in this area. This would require the remaining staff to work more effectively and to co-ordinate activies better, but also to get more financial recognition. A more dynamic relationship between production and marketing has been achieved by some organizational changes during the last few years in the field of marketing, by the establishment of trade centres, by company shop networks and by acquiring foreign trade rights. However, the potential of these organizational structures and systems are still not fully exploited by engineers in these areas (Fülöp 1989).

MAIN FEATURES OF THE DEVELOPMENT OF HUNGARIAN ORGANIZATIONAL STRUCTURES

The development of organizational structures in Hungary is several decades behind attainments in capitalist countries. It is well known that within the national economy the ratio of large enterprises to smaller more dynamic companies is still too high. It is equally well known that most organizations are out of date in terms of being over-hierarchical, bureaucratic and inflexible. Internal management systems fail to create suitable financial incentives systems, internal accounting and information systems are weak, and there is overstaffing in management.

To understand this situation, Hungarian organizational structures will be examined in terms of the following questions: What kinds of production strategy predominate? As a result, what kinds of organizational structure have been formed? And based on this, what kinds of internal management system have been established? (Marosi 1988; Tari 1988.)

The production strategy of Hungarian socialist industrial companies has been characterized by relatively strong vertical integration. Basically this means production concentration and increasing mass production within specialist units. The managers of the new large industrial enterprises were themselves interested in increasing the vertical integration, since the stronger co-operation between units protected them from decentralization and fragmentation. Also, large industrial enterprises were unwilling to rely on smaller companies as independent suppliers, preferring to incorporate them into their organization through state administrative support.

Increasing vertical integration meant that the structure of production also became more vertical, with increasing complexity and intensity of internal co-operation. As a result, a strongly centralized management system was required to organize the vertical integration, which was similar to developments at an earlier stage of capitalism. The number of staff managers grew not only due to the centralized planning system but also because of the complexities of vertical relationships within organizations.

Between 1948 and 1985 the state dictated not only the production goals but also the organizational framework and the conditions under which production took place. Initially the chief engineer and chief accountant were defined by legal rules as the deputies of the chief executive of the company. The R & D and production departments were responsible to the chief engineer. In the 1960s and 1970s there was a split between R & D and production in order to relieve the chief engineer of responsibility for day-to-day production problems.

From the 1980s onwards, due to the growth of companies, the number of specialized departments has increased (e.g. sales and marketing, human resource management). This trend reflects more specialization at the second level of the hierarchy within companies and in industrial companies more diversification in production. However, most Hungarian industrial companies did not develop a multi-divisional system, or any transitional organizational forms, at that stage. It was only in the last third of the 1980s in Hungary that the objective and subjective conditions made at least partially possible the slow spreading of decentralized divisional systems. The external pressure together with economic incentives, which were so lacking in the earlier stages for the radical restructuring of organizations, now became tangible factors for managers. By this period the external resources necessary to ensure the profitability or even the survival of the companies had become exhausted. Furthermore, the state campaigns for modernizing organizations proved to be mainly ineffective. The question of workshop democracy is also related to decentralization. On the one hand Hungary has managed to ensure that employees participate in company councils, in workshop democratic forums and strategic decision-making. On the other hand, due to the weakness of decentralization and internal accounting systems, it seems that employees within the company are not in a position to enforce their interests properly, even at the level of local issues. The problems of internal administrative systems can be basically attributed to obsolete vertical operational systems.

Beyond doubt, the 'spontaneous' privatization which was initiated by companies in 1988 and 1989 was a further step towards decentralized divisional systems, in which some of the large industrial companies reorganized their production and servicing units to become legally independent economic associations or affiliated companies. Market and budget units were established and they undertake production planning and control and technical development on an independent basis. Although other large industrial enterprises did not grant legal independence to their internal units, they provided an increasing scope for action in their operations in the form of branches and semi-independent units; and as a consequence, a 'sense of ownership' has increased in these units.

Managers of large state-owned industrial companies complain that the small private companies are taking away their employees, because they can offer higher incomes and more interesting work, even though the intensity of work is greater in the smaller companies. In reality, however, the number of highly qualified engineers leaving state companies has remained low. This is because most of them work in the small enterprises at the same time as continuing with their traditional jobs in the state-owned enterprises or co-operatives. This double employment enables them to maintain personal relationships through which they secure contracts for their small enterprise.

During the last few years Hungarian enterprises have also increased their co-operation with foreign firms. In Hungarian and other eastern European firms this takes the following forms: subcontracting, joint ventures, use of western consulting offices, engineering contracts for founding new companies or reorganization of existing firms.

The use of these forms of co-operation can simultaneously serve several different purposes: increasing exports, reduction of imports, obtaining western technologies, elimination of production bottlenecks and imitation of western management techniques, organizational systems and productivity patterns. This co-operation with western companies can serve as a means of retaining employees, especially technical workers, who might otherwise be attracted away to the smaller firms.

HISTORICAL SURVEY OF TRENDS IN HUNGARIAN MANAGEMENT APPROACHES

Here we attempt to describe the development of management approaches and practices in Hungary, by comparing them with those typical in America and Germany during the same period (Balaton and Dobák 1986).

When management and organizational theories developed in the west during the earlier part of this century, through the work of writers like Weber, Taylor and Fayol, at that time Hungary was untouched by these ideas. The development of Anglo-Saxon management theory was influenced by sociological and psychological insights belonging to the 'human relations' school, as well as work on social systems.

The development of theories of management in Hungary included two approaches. Besides being influenced by American methods and solutions like Taylorism, there was also a search for alternatives. At that time the German theory of business economics and organization influenced European, including Hungarian, theories of organization. American approaches which existed before the 1920s were replaced by German doctrines after the First World War. The influence of German business economics and organization touched not only the economy but also the educational sphere. The Anglo-Saxon and French influence only survived in the efforts to rationalize the state administration.

The period between the Second World War and the 1970s is characterized by a concentration on scientific and practical challenges. Between the 1950s and 1960s American management doctrines had influenced practical management and organizational endeavour, as had research in European capitalist countries. Human-oriented and systems approaches brought new colour to business-oriented 'recipe-like' solutions of the managerial sciences. Decision-oriented, mathematical approaches, operational research, cybernetics and systems analysis also spread in Europe due to American influence overseas.

However, in addition to the considerable American influence, attempts were also made to develop a European style of management and organization. This is indicated by the way in which contingency theory based on the relationship between environment, strategy, structure, behaviour and performance is as much European as American, especially British and German. However, by the beginning of the 1990s the eastern European countries had succeeded in replacing these western management and organizational traditions with the Soviet model. The main characteristics of the Soviet model are: priority given to production and work organization, precise production planning, an incentive system based on rewarding quantity rather than quality, internal accounting and a concern with cost reduction. Among the management functions, planning and control were at the forefront.

From the end of the 1950s in some of the eastern European countries certain changes could be observed which were influenced by management and organizational research and a tendency towards reforming economic planning and control in the Soviet Union. Hungary was not excluded from the trends of the 1950s and even those who were influenced by the extreme German mechanistic orientation did not find it too difficult to adjust to the new spirit of the Soviet model. However, things began to change slowly from the 1960s, when management and organizational theory was officially recognized as a science in Hungary.

Developments from the 1970s to the present day

The last twenty years have been characterized by a seeking of new ways and means of managing and by acceleration in the transformation in ways of thinking about these issues. Socio-economic changes and new technologies required further development both in background theory and in prescriptions for practice, to replace older versions.

At that time in the world economy there were qualitative changes associated with modern technology and attempts to follow Japan's lead on productivity and quality assurance. Because of the spectacular results they appeared to achieve, organizations were urged to follow Japanese management methods, like KANBAN, quality circles and 'Theory Z' approaches. During this period, the deterioration in external conditions in most east European countries exposed internal weaknesses within the countries and the urgent need to move to new approaches. This activated more efforts towards reforms in economic management. In contrast to the former standardized solutions of economic management, each country began to develop management systems to suit its conditions and traditions.

These efforts made management and organizational practice in eastern European countries more varied and differentiated. For example, the Soviet Union introduced a programme for restructuring management systems; Yugoslavia established a shopfloor management system; organizational, sociological and praxaeoligical research was carried out in Poland; and there was normative human resources management in East Germany.

In the case of Hungary, greater interest is now shown in the theoretical and practical approach to management in capitalist countries. This is shown by the intensive studying and application of systems theory and cybernetics and the more recent emphasis upon contingency theory and cultural factors. Despite this interest, in some instances only the phraseology has changed and the old outlook persists. Nevertheless the practice of employing western consulting companies shows interest in adapting management approaches from capitalist countries to the Hungarian context.

THE POSITION OF ENGINEERS IN HUNGARIAN MANAGEMENT CULTURES

It has not as yet become general in Hungary to trace back differences of organizational performance to differences in management cultures. Although the concept of management culture appears in the literature on management and organizations, it has not yet received sufficient attention (Susánszky 1985; Branyiczky 1988; Farkasné Déri 1990; Kozma 1990).

Managements now recognize that their approach cannot be constrained by the limitations of a rational planning and control model, however well thought through. Only part of a company's results can be traced back to quantitative aspects, as the rest relates to qualitative cultural elements. Thus the management culture is an important success factor in a company and it is the task of Hungarian managers to understand its internal structure and to develop it. The fundamental question is whether there is a mutually acceptable scale of values which influence the long-term life and behaviour of workers within the company, or whether there is disagreement, or obstruction of the achievements of others, through the methods of applying financial incentives, or the appointment of workers within the hierarachy of the enterprise, which is not based on performance and knowledge but on some other undisclosed basis.

To answer this question the following factors need to be considered:

Values and incentives

The company's value systems are slow and difficult to change. For so long in Hungary companies were used to state intervention and financial subsidies, which influenced the companies strategy. These impacted on the management culture and methods of evaluating worker and company performance. Basic values cannot be changed overnight, even if a new manager means to take a new approach. There may be an opportunity to change the old culture if the environment is supportive and the manager has the authority to intervene in personnel matters. Otherwise failure is inevitable, even if the manager knows what to do.

Hungarian managers have the task of promoting involvement and identification with the company's aims, on the part of engineers as far as possible through creating new values and behaviour patterns and eliminating uncertainty. This is particularly important in companies where workers as a group lack identity with the aims and objectives of the organization. There is a need for a unifying influence to avoid the company fragmenting when faced with new ways of thinking and acting.

A bureaucratic organization will not become an innovative organization simply because there has been a change of management. Employees have to be interested and motivated to change. Managers are unsure how to stimulate the creativity of their technical staff, and in this they require help. There is a need to give engineers the environment in which to become creative, to experiment and develop new ideas in the context of a competitive environment. Alternatively a competitive environment can be created in which they identify as a group and in doing so become more adaptable.

Recognition and hierarchy

Managers trained in a bureaucratic environment had a very limited basis on which to evaluate performance. 'Good engineers' were those who followed all instructions, without question or resistance. Discipline and compliance with company rules were the important requirements. Although companies may have needed talented and well-qualified engineers who were capable of independent thinking, decisiveness, the ability to take initiatives and the willingness to criticize, in practice these requirements were neglected. This was not simply because of the limitations of management but reflected the impact of the economic environment on the organization. This situation resulted in a loss of prestige for the engineering profession and dissatisfaction among engineers themselves.

Studies of the work of engineers indicate that the main cause of dissatisfaction during the 1970s was related to the quality of their working life (Sikora and Tóth 1990). Eighty per cent of engineers were found to be dissatisfied because a considerable amount of their time (10 to 60 per cent) was spent on activities which were below their level of qualifications and did not require a university degree. The problem of adequate utilization of qualified technical staff did not diminish in the 1980s. However, problems concerned with falling standards of living suppressed further their drive for self-actualization. As a consequence of the undervaluing of the work of engineers, their social status and attitudes reached rock bottom. The lack of self-confidence among engineers has been harmful to innovation. This is partly due to the atmosphere in the workplace which influences the role of engineers in the organization and partly reflects the mental attitude of the engineers.

Here the place of engineers in the hierarchical division of labour in socialist enterprises until recently is outlined. According to Marxist ideology the engineer is only a technical expert within a socialist enterprise. Therefore the gist of an engineer's work is dull technical tasks, so that their role in the organization is closer to that of skilled workers than of highly qualified experts. They simply perform the tasks asked of them by management, and if they go beyond these instructions they come up against a strong power system (Harsányi 1961; Huszár 1978; Solymosi and Székelyi 1984).

Thus Hungarian engineers have lived through the last four decades in an environment where entrepreneurial managers were considered to be enemies. The role of capital was not recognized, and egalitarianism was valued over performance. One of the most significant consequences of exaggerated centralization is that hierarchies are dominant, workplace relationships are extremely formal, and managers and subordinates work in isolation from each other (Kozma 1990).

In Hungary half of the engineers employed in industry are working at present in subordinate positions. Their income is determined by their status in the factory's hierarchy, which, contrary to declared aims, does not reflect the extent of their contribution to company performance. This situation has resulted in undesirable consequences. To gain more financial reward the more independent-minded design engineers have either to attempt to mount the hierarchy to senior managerial positions which carry higher incomes, or they have to try to obtain a higher income outside industry. Some engineers, for instance, become associated with small enterprises, where they have the opportunity to engage in teamwork within the organization.

THE DEVELOPMENT OF TRAINING FOR ENGINEERS IN HUNGARY

It is not possible here to survey technical training as a whole, and so the emphasis will be upon basic management education. In many countries of the world it is usual for engineers graduating from universities to gain responsible positions fairly quickly; therefore they need training for such future roles.

General management education

In Hungary demand for preparing engineers for future management positions arose during this century at Budapest Technical University (Ladó 1988). Since then, this issue has reappeared in various forms and with alternative schemes. The situation today has two facets. As far as the past is concerned, considerable progress has been made, especially in the 1970s. Opinions which call for pioneering work to lay the foundations of management are unacceptable, but it is nevertheless undeniable that the progress made so far is unsatisfactory, in the face of the increasing importance of managerial knowledge for engineers.

In graduate education in the field of higher education, the task of the new discipline called business economics is to provide the basic foundation on which managerial decision-making takes place. A second management discipline called basic management and organization, or simply organization, stresses the functions of management. In 1988 the time spent on teaching these subjects at technical universities did not exceed 3 per cent of the total educational time. This is a low proportion compared with other countries. Furthermore, the two above-mentioned subjects cannot offer sufficient management and organizational knowledge to enable engineers to perform even low-level managerial tasks early in their careers. The subject of business economics is complex but does not go into detail concerning such subjects as social psychology, legal systems, finance and information systems which are needed for decision-making. The question is, how can this be achieved?

According to one point of view, the five-year university training of engineers for industry should provide management education for 5 per cent of the total time available. However, recently there has been a reduction in total teaching hours, and representatives of different disciplines inevitably try to stress the importance of their area. Therefore, the above solution could only be achieved by changes in the structure of the whole curriculum, including management education.

A second approach builds on alternative or elective subjects. There are some basic conditions needed for such a scheme, the most important of which is that basic core knowledge has to be compulsory. For example, the engineer who has only studied organizational behaviour would not have acquired the basic knowledge required for the efficient management of an organization. Hence elective subjects can only build on foundation subjects and this is supported by the claim that all engineers should acquire the fundamentals of management. Those who want to know more should be given the opportunity to do so.

Specialization in graduate education

In several industrialized countries there are two kinds of specialization. The first is represented by business schools, originating in the USA. The other form has also developed in the USA but in the field of technical higher education, as branches of industrial engineering. Industrial engineering is only indirect managerial training, but it emphasizes one of the most important aspects of management, that of organizing.

In the 1980s the latter approach was introduced by the government in Hungary. It was introduced as operational management in faculties of mechanical engineering at the technical universities of Budapest and Miskolc and as management at the chemical engineering university at Veszprem. These faculties teach most of the knowledge necessary for future managers.

This teaching does not assume that engineers will necessarily become managers; therefore it does not provide a direct route into management. Thus institutions do not grant diplomas in management but they do prepare people to be able to manage. These faculties are very popular with students and companies, as besides the knowledge of management, information and organization, they also provide core curriculum in mechanical or chemical engineering.

These faculties have a great potential for development, especially if the training of engineer-managers in information technology is introduced. Students specializing in this field would not only become specialists in programming but also have more knowledge of what kinds of information are needed for managerial decision-making and how to develop adequate information systems. A similar specialization in marketing could also be introduced.

A more specific form of management training at the graduate level would also be worthwhile. The basic concept of this would not be to train managers in the traditional sense but to train specialists who would be able to manage innovation processes, be capable of giving assistance to managers initially and later become managers themselves.

The structure of this training would be as follows. The training would be an elective, additional to the full-time training of certified engineers. Students would get an engineering diploma, and the candidate would prepare a thesis on a managerial topic at their company, using the professional experience gained from engineering work during their first year. After defending their thesis, they would get an 'engineer-manager' diploma, the latter being a second diploma recognizing the knowledge necessary for solving complex innovation problems. The realization of such an idea would play an important part in the further development and modernization of Hungarian engineering training and keep pace with ideas from overseas.

NOTE

I wish to acknowledge the contribution of Professor Dr János Susánszky, Doctor of Economics, President of the Committee of Management and Organization Science, Hungarian Academy of Sciences. I also wish to thank Dr Livia Markóczy of the Department of Business Economics, Budapest University of Economics, for her work on the translation of this chapter.

Chapter 7

Symbolizing professional pride: the case of Canadian engineers

Gloria L. Lee

In exploring the relationship between management cultures and the engineer, various contributors to this book have illustrated some of the cultural differences in the formation of engineers and the prestige and place of engineers within that particular society's labour force. Whereas in countries like Germany and Japan differences in cultural traditions as well as language are considerable, for Canada the links with Britain through history and culture are close. Nevertheless, in the case of engineers there are some striking contrasts in the ways in which the engineering profession has developed in the two countries, in the prestige accorded the profession and the popularity of the occupation. Whereas for decades engineering in Britain has had difficulty in attracting young people into the profession, there has been a steady growth in the numbers of professional engineers in Canada over the last forty years (Canadian Engineering Manpower Board 1989). Currently Canadian professional engineers represent 0.9 per cent of the labour force compared with 0.5 per cent for British chartered engineers.

THE GROWTH OF A COUNTRY AND A PROFESSION

The history of the engineering profession in Canada is very closely tied in with the history of the country, as transportation projects in the form of railways and canals provided vital links between disparate pockets of population across the vast territories which by the mid-nineteenth century had come together to form a confederation. With the growth of the railway system, which unlike the canals could operate throughout the year, producer goods industries grew up to serve the railways in the form of foundries, rolling mills and car and locomotive works. These mechanical engineering projects provided the basis for further industrial development, and municipal engineers ensured water and gas supplies, sewers and paved, lit streets in urban areas. While the early engineering works relied heavily upon engineers from Britain or the United States, by 1887 the founding of the Canadian Society of Civil Engineers (CSCE) began the process of signalling the establishment of a distinctly Canadian tradition of engineering and engineers (Millard 1988).

THE EARLY YEARS OF CANADIAN ENGINEERING

Until the mid-nineteenth century, following the British tradition, the education of engineers was primarily through apprenticeships; but by 1887 engineering courses were being offered in five Canadian universities; and by 1921, 87.5 per cent of the membership of the CSCE were university engineering graduates. In their search for power and social prestige, Canadian engineers rejected unionization as a means of occupational closure in favour of professionalization. And by 1922, with the granting of registration laws to Ontario engineers, the Canadian engineering profession had before it a model for gaining substantial monopoly powers through licensing (Millard 1988).

Thus despite dominion status and the many Commonwealth links with Britain, Canadian engineers have carved out a tradition for themselves which has much more in common with American than British experience. Unlike in Britain, where apprenticeship as the basis for technical training dominated for so long, in Canada, with its later industrialization, a graduate basis was much more readily established for entry into the profession.

One association in each province represents the profession and all Canadian professional engineers living and working there. In contrast, in Britain the engineering profession is represented segmentally by nearly fifty different nationally based institutions, covering different branches of engineering, together with the Engineering Council which was created in the last ten years to try to provide a more unified voice for engineering. The interests of individual engineers in Britain are also protected by trade unions, whereas there are only rare and rather isolated examples of unionization among Canadian professional engineers. Although most Canadian engineers do not associate trade union membership with professionalism, in Britain over one-third of chartered engineers belong to a union (Engineering Council 1989b).

Also unlike their British counterparts, Canadian engineers have maintained social distance from other technical workers. Whereas in Britain the Engineering Council and the different engineering institutions have within their membership chartered engineers, incorporated engineers (formerly known as technician engineers) and engineering technicians, in Canada the Canadian Council of Professional Engineers is quite distinct from the Canadian Council of Engineering Technicians and Technologists, and the associations of professional engineers in the different provinces have consistently resisted overtures by associations of other less highly qualified technical workers for amalgamation or any form of recognition.

The status of Canadian engineers is reinforced through licensing, a symbol of occupational control which British engineers, with the exception of very limited aspects of civil engineering, have never achieved. Even though, as in the USA, the necessity to be licensed in Canada is most clearly articulated in the case of consulting work, nevertheless to become licensed is economically rewarding. The licensing system provides an important protection both for professional engineers and for their employers, which is especially significant with the growth of demand-side legislation in North America, which can lead to costly court cases for damages, if for instance negligence can be shown. Demonstration that work has been carried out by or under the supervision of professionally qualified engineers becomes an important element in defending such a case. This is one aspect of the close links between Canadian employers and the professional associations, with the former actively recruiting the professionally qualified and giving every help and encouragement to young engineering graduates entering employment with them to gain their P. Eng.

KEY CHARACTERISTICS OF THE CANADIAN ENGINEERING PROFESSION

The key characteristics of the engineering profession in Canada, then, are that:

1 It is organized from a provincial base.

2 Each provincial association covers all branches of professional engineering.
3 The provincial association is the licensing body.
4 Licensure ensures that only qualified individuals are entitled to offer or provide engineering services *directly* to the public.
5 Entry to the profession is basically a three-stage process whereby the entrant will have completed:
   (i) an accredited engineering programme at a Canadian university;
   (ii) two years of satisfactory engineering work experience, following the conferring of the degree;
   (iii) a professional practice examination.

THE FORMATION OF CANADIAN ENGINEERS

Although the engineering profession is organized provincially in Canada, since 1936 there has been a Canadian Council of Professional Engineers (CCPE), which is a federation of the provincial and territorial authorities that license engineers. In 1965 the CCPE established the Canadian Accreditation Board, which has since become known as the Canadian Engineering Accreditation Board (CEAB). This body, on behalf of the provincial associations, has developed minimum criteria for undergraduate engineering degree programmes and through a process of direct investigation provides engineering schools with a means to have their programmes formally tested against these criteria, to ensure that graduates receive an education which will satisfy the academic requirements for professional engineering registration throughout Canada. Accreditation is far from automatic, as there are some 184 accredited programmes in 31 engineering faculties across Canada, as well as a smaller number of non-accredited engineering programmes.

All Canadian engineering degree programmes involve four years' academic study, and there are also co-operative programmes, the largest of which is at Waterloo University. The latter includes six four-month work terms, as well as the eight academic semesters typical of undergraduate courses at Canadian universities. Many engineering students on four-year programmes also choose to work for companies during their summer vacations, but this is not part of their course, neither does it count towards their requirement for work experience, when applying for professional designation. The vacation employment of engineering students is well established in Canadian companies, who find this a useful method of pre-selecting those they wish subsequently to employ.

Canada has institutionalized a route into the engineering profession which has a number of features in common with that in the USA, where the Accreditation Board for Engineers and Technologists accredits courses from American universities. In the USA, however, there are far more universities than in Canada, and standards between them are generally recognized as much more variable than is the case between accredited schools in Canadian universities. Also in the USA some of the most prestigious engineering schools, like those at Stanford and MIT, have engineering programmes which stand outside the accreditation system.

Canadian engineers are licensed to practise only in the province which has granted them their P. Eng. designation and only in the field of engineering in which they have qualified. If they decide to move to another province, to become professionally recognized there they will have to obtain a new licence and may have to pass the professional practice examination required by the professional association in that province. The PPE is typically a three-hour examination which covers law, ethics, contracts, business practice, etc. The examination is in narrative form and therefore requires the candidate to be competent in English. In the Province of Quebec candidates must show competence in French.

This aspect of the process of professional recognition differs somewhat from the American system, where, instead of the different state licensing boards conducting their own professional practice examinations, a private corporation called the National Council of Examiners for Engineering and Surveying holds the examinations for the state boards. Here each eight-hour-long examination is in two parts, with one written on graduation and another at least four years later, to demonstrate knowledge of business practice.

SYMBOLISM AND THE CANADIAN ENGINEER

In the very early history of Canadian engineering projects, Canadian engineers often found themselves disadvantaged in competition for work with those from the USA and Britain. But over the years considerable pride has grown up in what it means to be a Canadian engineer, and this is symbolically reinforced through traditions which have been institutionalized.

One very clear symbol of professional pride is the wearing of an iron ring by Canadian engineers on the fourth finger of their working hand. In the final engineering year at most Canadian universities a ceremony takes place of the Ritual of the Calling of an Engineer, which entitles the participants to wear an iron ring to remind them of their obligation to maintain the ethics and diligent practice required of the engineering profession. The ceremony was initiated in 1922 by a group of seven prominent engineers, all of whom were past presidents of the Engineering Institute of Canada. They commissioned Rudyard Kipling to write the ceremony to reinforce professional pride and bind members of the Canadian engineering profession more closely together. The ritual is purely symbolic and independently administered by the Corporation of the Seven Wardens, a non-profit organization based in Montreal. It does not imply qualification or licence, but the wearing of the iron ring is nevertheless highly valued by Canadian engineers.

Successful completion of the requirements for the designation P.Eng. is also symbolized by the granting of a personal seal for use on engineering drawings, reports, etc. Improper use of this seal, for instance to seal work outside the area of engineering in which the engineer is qualified, or allowing others to use of the seal, would be contrary to the ethics of the profession and could result in disciplinary action and loss of licence.

PROFESSIONAL STRUCTURES

For professional groups, status, power and authority reside in delineating a body of knowledge and associated practice, in controlling the acquisition of this knowledge and its application. Symbolism provides a powerful mechanism for reinforcing claims to elite status in the eyes of the membership and the wider society. Canadian engineers, then are distinguished from those in Britain in a number of respects which influence their power and authority through mechanisms of occupational control, as well as their professional pride and sense of value and self-worth for the contributions they make to their society.

Essentially for most of this century Canadian engineers have been spared the heart-searching and doubts of their British counterparts about their status and professional standing. The early establishment of a university rather than a craft learning base distinguished them from other technical workers and placed them firmly alongside other traditional professions like medicine and the law. Also, their occupational control and status as professionals are reinforced by licence, and they have created their own ceremonials to symbolize their pride in their undertaking.

One factor contributing to a unity of purpose among Canadian engineers can be attributed to there being one association to cover all branches of engineering. While the profession operates a national body in the form of the Canadian Council of Professional Engineers and its Canadian Engineering Manpower Board, which are based in Ottawa and provide a political lobby at federal level, the professional associations are provincially based, which makes for a strong bond with the local community and its needs.

In contrast, British engineering can be seen historically as having dissipated its voice within the country through the proliferation of different institutions which represent the interests of different branches of engineering (Smith 1984). In recent years some amalgamations have taken place, but rivalry between institutions is still strong, and other attempts at rationalization have been rejected, as in the case of the proposed merger between the Institution of Mechanical Engineers and the Institution of Production Engineers.

The Finniston report (1980) was the latest in a long line of reports which acknowledged the ambiguities surrounding engineering in Britain, whereby in popular perception the work of professional engineers is poorly distinguished from that of other manual and technical workers, and neither industry nor engineering is well regarded in the wider society. The Finniston report based its reform of the profession on a system of registration to be introduced by the newly formed Engineering Council but stopped short of recommending any measure which would add a sanction to registration in the form of licensing. Thus the founding of the Engineering Council became a belated attempt to create a more unified voice for the British engineering profession, which still suffers from an inability to attract sufficient able young people into its ranks.

In the decade since the Finniston report, considerable efforts have been made by the Engineering Council to reform the education and training of British engineers and to make the profession appear more attractive to young people. A university education is now the norm for British professional engineers, with very few non-graduates under the age of 45 years. Overall the proportion of graduates among chartered engineers is now 78 per cent (Engineering Council 1989b). Thus British engineering is attempting to raise its profile and status but still has much to do to emulate the stronger professional image and ethos of Canadian engineering. Although progress is being made in Britain, ambiguities in popular perceptions about what professional engineers actually do persist and this does not help attempts to raise the standing of the profession.

CONCERNS FOR THE FUTURE OF ENGINEERING IN CANADA AND BRITAIN

Britons, then, concerned for the future of engineering in their country, are likely to consider that Canadian engineers are advantaged, particularly as they have achieved some measure of occupational control through licensing. Not only is the way in which professional pride in Canada is reinforced symbolically through their ceremonial traditions impressive, but British engineers may also be struck by the apparent proactivity of Canadian engineers in promoting the image and contribution of their profession at a local as well as a national level, through the work of their provincial associations.

For instance, Wilson (1990) in discussing the distinctiveness of the Canadian engineering tradition, as well as its interdependence with science and technology, pointed to a number of the profession's achievements which were recognized in 1987, during the centennial celebrations of the founding of the first professional association, the Canadian Society of Civil Engineers. Much publicity was given to such monuments to Canadian engineering as the Canadian Pacific Railway, the St Lawrence Seaway, the Transcontinental Microwave Network, the Syncrude Oilsands and Polymer Petrochemical Plants, the Hydro-Québec High Voltage Transmission Line, the 'Alouette' Satellite, the 'Beaver' Bush Aircraft, the CANDU Reactor and the Snowmobile.

However, Wilson saw no room for complacency, as with the presence today of federal agencies, programmes, policies and funding devoted to the development of Canadian science, research and technology, he saw a danger in that the role of engineering in translating all three of these areas into products and processes was not being sufficiently acknowledged. Thus he called on engineers themselves to play a larger part in telling their own story to the general public, young people, politicians, bureaucrats and business decision-makers (Wilson 1990: 17).

In Canada as in Britain, there is also heightened awareness of the need to find more effective mechanisms for balancing the supply of trained engineers with the demands of the economy. This is particularly difficult in the case of Canada, where it is estimated that between 40 and 50 per cent of engineering activity is driven by capital expenditures; and as these are volatile, so are the demands for engineering. This creates a problem in the supply of trained engineers, as enrolments into engineering courses tend to follow the peaks and troughs in demand. As engineering undergraduate courses in Canada are four-year programmes, the number of engineering graduates tends to be out of phase with labour market demand by four to six years. Traditionally Canada has solved its shortages in the supply of engineers through immigration, but concern is being expressed that unless more young people are attracted into the profession, there will be an insufficient supply to meet a growing demand arising from infrastructure renewal, environmental problems, economic growth and advancements in high-technology (Dougall 1990).

In Canada and Britain women are now recognized as a potentially important but largely untapped source of additional entry into engineering today, where they represent only 13 per cent of those on undergraduate engineering courses in both countries. This compares with just under 16 per cent in the USA. However, even this level of representation is very recent in Britain, where for instance in 1984 only 7 per cent of engineering undergraduates were women, compared with 11 per cent in Canada at that time and 16 per cent in the USA.

Since the mid-1980s the engineering profession in Britain has been more proactive in trying to attract women into the profession, and in 1984 the Women in Science and Engineering Programme (WISE) was launched. That there has been an increase in interest in engineering among British women has to be attributed at least in part to the various WISE initiatives in the form of awards, special access courses, schools visits, road-shows, etc., which have raised awareness of engineering as a career for women and provided some limited support to encourage retraining and re-entry into the profession.

While this type of positive action can claim some success, for there to be a more significant swing towards engineering as a career for women the profession itself probably has to become a more attractive proposition generally. It is only then that women are likely to see it as offering the kinds of career opportunity that are apparently perceived within, say, accountancy, which currently attracts into training one-fifth of all British women graduates (Women's Engineering Society 1990). In Canada too, as Baignée has argued, it is not so much a female problem as an engineering problem, as all industrialized nations begin to acknowledge the reality for global competition of a shortage of engineers in their society (Baignée 1990).

While writers like Baignée and others are prepared to acknowledge that engineering as a career in Canada today may appear to lack prestige and other rewards compared with other occupational groups, the profession itself appears to dwell less upon these issues in Canada than in Britain. For instance, status issues are not considered in the Association of Professional Engineers of Ontario's annual *Membership Salary Survey*, which concentrates on salaries, benefits and working conditions. Also, the question of status, power and the perceptions of engineers was not considered in the Canadian Engineering Manpower Board's *Profile of the Engineering Community in Canada*. In contrast, in Britain part of the Engineering Council's biennial Salary Survey devotes a section to career satisfaction, which looks at issues of status and prestige.

For those within the British engineering profession, there are indications of a continued recognition that although they may find their work intrinsically satisfying, other rewards like status and promotion opportunities are less assured. In the 1989 survey 74 per cent of chartered engineers reported that they would recommend engineering as a career for young men and 65 per cent as a career for young women. Their overwhelming reason, however, was in terms of the satisfaction of the work and not of status or pay.

An indication of their perception of the comparative value of their qualifications was also sought. When asked whether the highest position they could reach in their company or organization was higher or lower than or the same as a similarly qualified non-engineer, 22.6 per cent claimed higher, 48.0 per cent the same level and 29.4 per cent lower. In comparison with the survey two years before, there was a very slight increase in those with the most favourable perception of their prospects, but clearly a significant proportion of others felt themselves to be undervalued as engineers, with this view strongest among public-sector employees. Not surprisingly, the average earnings of chartered engineers with the more positive view of their career opportunities were also 17 per cent above those with lesser expectations (Engineering Council 1989b).

Clearly, levels of pay are an important factor in attracting graduates into a profession and keeping them there subsequently. But perceptions of career opportunities and other rewards are also important in convincing people that this is a worthwhile way of pursuing a career.

ENGINEERING AS A CAREER IN CANADA

Whereas in some countries a career in engineering is seen as providing a passport for travelling the world, for Canadians engineering is very much a home-based career. For instance, while 22 per cent of chartered engineers registered with the Engineering Council in Britain are working abroad, the vast majority of Canadian engineers work in their own country, with only 3 per cent located abroad. Two-thirds of those working outside Canada are in the United States, where a number of the larger companies in Canada have their parent organization. Employment opportunities for Canadian engineers occur primarily in Ontario and Quebec, with 39 per cent residing in Ontario and 25 per cent in Quebec (Canadian Engineering Manpower Board 1989). This reflects the concentration of economic activity in these two provinces, which account for 39 per cent and 23 per cent respectively of the gross domestic product (External Affairs Canada 1989).

As in Britain and the USA, the major branches of engineering in Canada are civil, electrical and mechanical engineering, but the balance between the disciplines in the different countries varies, as does the extent to which engineers continue to work in their original field of study. The civil, electrical and mechanical engineering industries employ about 50 per cent of all Canadian engineers; but unlike in Britain or the USA, Canada's economic structure is still heavily dominated by infrastructure and primary industries rather than secondary and tertiary industries. As a consequence, in comparison with the USA, for instance, Canada has almost twice the proportion of engineers working in the field of civil engineering, 32 per cent fewer in electrical engineering and less than 50 per cent of the share in mechanical engineering (Canadian Engineering Manpower Board 1989).

The four major educational disciplines of Canadian engineers are civil engineering (29 per cent), mechanical engineering (23 per cent), electrical engineering (21 per cent) and chemical engineering (8 per cent). While civil and electrical engineers are likely to go on and work in the same area as they originally studied, mechanical engineers are more likely to move into other fields, like petroleum or civil engineering or non-engineering work, which usually means management or administration.

As part of the Finniston report on engineering in Britain various overseas visits were undertaken in order to review the engineering profession in other major industrial countries. Canada was one of the countries visited, and the report comments on the way in which an engineering degree was seen by young people in Canada as a 'ticket into management positions' (Finniston 1980: 200). However, more recent data published by the Canadian Engineering Manpower Board indicate a different picture.

In comparison with the USA and indeed Britain, apparently fewer engineers in Canada are attracted out of engineering and into management as a career. For example, only 17 per cent of Canadian engineers move into management, compared with 30 per cent in the USA (Canadian Engineering Manpower Board 1989: 10). In Britain too, a higher proportion of chartered engineers move into management positions. The Engineering Council's Salary Survey indicates that 6 per cent of chartered engineers are chief executives, 18 per cent are in general management and 11 per cent in technical administration (Engineering Council 1989b: 11).

While fewer Canadian engineers leave their profession in favour of a management career, they are not on the other hand well represented in the most highly technical aspects of engineering work, that of research and development (R & D). In the case of a number of Canadian operations, research and development located outside Canada, and only 7 per cent of Canadian engineers work in R & D compared with 33 per cent of American engineers (Canadian Engineering Manpower Board 1989: 10). In this area of engineering, Canadians more closely resemble their British counterparts. From the national sample of British chartered engineers, only 6 per cent were found to be working in R & D (Engineering Council 1989b: 11). With British companies, however, R & D is not normally located outside the country, and the situation may rather reflect a neglect of this type of investment in Britain.

THE CHALLENGE OF 'GETTING THEM AND KEEPING THEM'

For any profession the initial challenge is that of attracting sufficient numbers of young people to study the discipline at higher educational levels and then subsequently to persuade the majority of these graduates to go on to work in the profession. In Britain, for instance, admission standards for engineering courses have had to fall in the past five years to allow student numbers to rise, according to figures published by the Universities Central Council on Admissions (Ince 1990). Even if access is widened to engineering courses, there are still problems in attracting the most able graduates to carry on and enter the profession on graduation. For instance, a survey by the Institute of Chartered Accountants showed that 7 per cent of their graduate intake in 1988 were engineers; and of particular concern to the engineering profession was that those choosing this alternative to becoming professional engineers were among the most able, with 50 per cent having first- or upper-second-class honours degrees (Training Agency 1989).

In Canada too, some engineering graduates are attracted to non-engineering work, but approximately 70 per cent of those who have studied engineering go on to qualify as professional engineers. The process whereby those who have trained as engineers stay on or move into other areas of work has been studied in Canada, by tracing the early career experiences of a cohort of engineering graduates over a five-year period following graduation. This longitudinal study of Canadian engineers tracked their experiences from graduation in 1982 through their career situations in 1984 and then 1987.

Comparisons have been made between chemical, civil, electrical and mechanical engineers which showed variations in the attachment to the profession itself between the different types of engineer and also to their particular branches of engineering. The reasons for the career decisions were not explored, but in addition to personal preferences, these career moves reflect labour market opportunities over this period.

Changing demands within industries can attract people back

in, even if initial employment was sought and found elsewhere. For instance, among Canadian chemical engineers 62 per cent of graduates were working in engineering by 1984, but the proportion for this cohort had risen to 64 per cent by 1987, representing a small return rate into the profession. However, in the case of civil engineers, whereas 71 per cent were working in engineering in 1984, the proportion fell to 44 per cent by 1987. With the Canadian electrical engineers, 56 per cent were in engineering in 1984 and in 1987, and 43 per cent were still working in their field of study five years after graduation.

Among mechanical engineers, however, movement out of their field of study was greatest. Whereas 59 per cent of mechanical engineers were working in engineering two years after graduation, only 23 per cent were in mechanical engineering, with the rest employed in other types of engineering work. Three years on, a further 20 per cent of those who had started out in mechanical engineering had moved to other fields of engineering, mostly changing to civil engineering, and 10 per cent had gone into administration.

Generally those who had originally trained as mechanical engineers were the most likely among this cohort of Canadian engineering graduates to move into management or administration early in their working lives, with 20 per cent having made this career move five years after graduation, compared with 9 per cent of electrical engineers and 3 per cent of civil engineers (Légaré and Baignée 1990).

Manufacturing industries are major employers of mechanical and electrical engineers, and in these organizations until fairly recently the supervisory/management route has often been seen as a faster source of promotion than technical work. There are, however, some indications that Canadian companies are rethinking their career structures for engineers, as indicated in recent fieldwork by the author in Canada.

In March and April 1990 the recruitment and career development schemes of twelve major companies employing engineers and finance and accounting people were examined through interviews with twenty-six key personnel, mainly in senior positions responsible for human resource development in these organizations. Further insights into links between education and professional employment were gained from an additional twenty-four interviews with representatives of the professions, academics and university careers officers.[1]

The companies studied were in a range of Canadian industries employing engineers including telecommunications, automotives, electrical, computing, adhesives, chemicals and food processing. With the exception of those in food processing, all offered some form of dual career structure for engineers, so that they could remain in technical work for a significant proportion of their working life without having to move into managerial work in order to progress their career. In the larger companies, it was possible to remain in essentially a technical function to a very senior level, although such posts did not represent the typical career progression for most engineers.

For the companies with technologically complex products it was particularly important to sustain a regular intake of well-qualified engineers, and they worked to maintain links with particular universities where they were most keen to recruit their graduate engineers. The same prestigious universities were targeted by most of the employers covered in the study, but links with more local institutions were also recognized as important by the companies. Offering regular vacation work to students was seen as one way of sizing up potential recruits, well before the company attended career fairs and began the selection process in earnest. There is also a growing interest in the products of cooperative education, and this system was viewed very positively by a number of respondents, especially where they are already offering placements to co-op students.

The companies essentially fell into three categories: those that wanted to attract able engineers to work in specific technical areas; those that saw bright engineers as an important human resource to be deployed widely within the company in both technical and other functional areas; and those that recruited engineers primarily at plant level to work within production facilities. The first two groups of organizations, in particular, circulated elaborate recruitment literature to university careers centres, which in addition to describing the company usually set out details of the range of career openings for engineers and the types of career progression which were available to them.

These companies were well aware of the importance of starting salaries in attracting young people to them, but found it better to share knowledge with other companies recruiting from the same potential pool of applicants. Hence the major players circulate salary level details between themselves on a semi-confidential basis. In practice the interviews confirmed that they were all offering very similar basic levels of starting salary for those with undergraduate or postgraduate levels of qualification, together with the same sorts of package of benefits. Starting salaries would then be adjusted primarily according to any prior work experience which the applicant might have.

It appears, then, that salary levels are not a closely guarded secret among Canadian employers, who not only want to ensure that they are meeting the market rate but are also prepared for this information to be available in various forms to prospective applicants. For instance, companies in Ontario participate in the Association of Professional Engineers of Ontario's *Report on Engineers' Salaries - Survey of Employers*, which is produced annually as well as the *Membership Salary Survey*.

The University of Toronto Career Centre also, for instance, prepares an *On-Campus Recruitment Programme Salary Survey* based on the salaries offered by employers who participated in the On-Campus Recruitment Programme during each academic year. This survey gives a salary breakdown by discipline and by sector. The surveys covering 1988, 1989 and 1990 show that employers are prepared to pay higher average salaries to engineering than either business, arts or science graduates. While there are few differences between salary levels for students in the different areas of engineering, there are differences by sector of employment. For instance, in 1990 for engineers with bachelors' degrees, manufacturing employers were offering an average salary above that for all the sectors, with the percentage gain over 1989 salaries higher for manufacturing than the other sectors where representative returns were shown (University of Toronto Career Centre 1990).

Essentially, then, employers are not so much competing between each other for the best engineering graduates on the basis of salary, as competing on the ways their companies present themselves to graduates. This involves employing designated specialist human resources staff who are knowledgeable about the discipline, their sector and the ways in which they can convince those that they wish to employ that their company offers the most attractive career opportunities. While these specialist staff manage the recruitment of particular types of graduate, such as engineers, finance or marketing specialists, the selection of candidates is not left to those in the human resources function, as line managers are also involved, either at the preliminary interview stage or at the second stage when applicants are invited to come into the company for further interviews. Line managers are given training to participate in the selection process, and decisions are typically reached immediately following the final interview stage and communicated swiftly to those candidates whom the company wishes to recruit.

Psychometric tests are not normally used, as these are seen as off-putting to applicants at this level and time is rather spent when applicants are visiting the company to convey to the applicant the dynamic nature of the organization, often with the stress on teamworking. This means that successful applicants have to be particularly good at demonstrating social as well as technical skills in order to impress prospective employers. Companies appear to have a very clear perception of the kinds of young person who would 'fit in' and become 'part of the team'.

A very important part of selling the company to the candidate on the other hand hinges upon the opportunities which can be shown to open up to those who join it. Potential career paths are spelled out in some detail, together with explanations of the career development programmes offered by the company. The stress is very much on enabling the candidate to get to know the company and to understand its ethos, as on joining they would be expected to be ready to fit into the culture of the company and perform effectively straight away.

Once companies have successfully recruited those they feel capable of meeting these expectations, efforts then turn to ensuring that they do perform effectively. Initial career development programmes often extend over at least a two-year period. Regular performance appraisal is the norm, with frequent salary reviews for those in the early years of their career with the company.

Some organizations have a well-publicized internal promotion policy whereby they reckon to hire only at entry level and to 'grow their own' people from then on. With the move towards flatter structures in many Canadian companies, it is recognized that ways have to be found to give people a sense of career progress in the absence of hierarchies of authority through which people can see themselves progressing. Salaries are therefore increasingly related to personal performance, rather than particular positions within the organization. Ongoing career planning is encouraged, with large companies in particular working to ensure good communications concerning opportunities within the wider organization. For example, one company put on regular monthly 'career forwarding' presentations to encourage people to look inwards rather than outwards when they wanted a career change or were simply seeking wider experience.

Through the careful nurturing of a person's development and career paths, people joining the company are given powerful signals about their importance to the organization, which it is hoped will persuade those who continue to perform well to remain with the company. For the system to work, the companies not only need committed human resource specialists but also have to invest in training their managers to ensure that they participate effectively in the appraisal and counselling process. The overall impression, then, is that a great deal of time, thought and effort goes into the recruitment of graduates in the more dynamic Canadian companies and that this is particularly the case with those needing a regular intake of young engineers.

CONCLUSIONS

For young Canadians today, then, becoming an engineer appears to mean entering a seller's market for their services, where they can anticipate good career prospects within their chosen profession. Notwithstanding the vicissitudes of world markets, advancements in technologies, economic growth, infrastructure renewal and increased consciousness about environmental issues are likely in the long term to increase demand for their services well into the future. While some will decide to move into management in the course of their career, others more wedded to technical work are likely to find increasing opportunities, accompanied by good incentives, for continuing along the technical path in the flatter organizations of the day.

These young engineers enjoy good levels of starting salary in comparison with many studying alongside them in other disciplines. Successful students can expect to be offered attractive packages to join a company which promises challenging opportunities and clear indications of a range of career openings before them. The extent to which these promises are met can to some extent be judged by turnover rates, which some companies acknowledge as around 10 per cent per annum among engineers.

Also, although certain companies work hard at maintaining an internal promotion policy, others acknowledge that in practice they often have to look outside too, to maintain the engineering workforce which they require. While turnover may be a matter for concern to the company, it does indicate a buoyancy in demand for the services of engineers, which, notwithstanding certain downturns, as in the early 1980s, has generally been good in Canada for most of this century.

Essentially, then, young engineers in Canada today join a profession which has managed to combine the symbolic with the practical. The traditions and ceremonies of the profession give a sense of pride in belonging to a profession which maintains much of its exclusivity in the face of a changing world and where the material rewards are generally satisfactory if not spectacular.

They are also likely to derive some satisfaction from knowing that they are entering an occupation where the links between the profession and employing organizations are strong. Engineering in Canada today still appears to be a well-respected profession within industry as well as the wider society. Most companies employing young engineers encourage them to go ahead and seek their professional designation, often paying the subscription for them.

Although the numbers of those entering the profession have risen over the years, demands for their services are clearly distinguished from those with other less prestigious technical qualifications. Professional engineers continue to enjoy a measure of exclusiveness associated with licensing of the profession, even though the designation is not necessarily essential in all areas of engineering work, outside the field of consultancy. Employers recognize the distinction between professional engineers and other types of technologist, and the vast majority of professional engineers do not find themselves doing work which would be seen as more appropriate for those less highly qualified.

The engineering profession and employers in Canada have developed a series of linkages which serve to benefit both those who join the profession, the industries in which they work and in some respects society as a whole. Since the products of engineering touch everyday life at every turn, the standards of proficiency of practitioners are clearly important. There is some comfort to the public too in the knowledge that professional bodies exist at provincial level, to act as guardians of ethical standards within the profession. Also, the profession, informed by its membership, provides a lobby to government at national and provincial levels, on behalf of the engineering industry, which provides an important source of employment in the country.

The role of the professional bodies as qualifying associations is significant to employers as well as members. As immigration is a feature of Canadian society, employers could be faced by applicants for jobs with a plethora of overseas qualifications, the standards of which are difficult to assess. In practice, employers rely upon the professional associations to provide a filtering mechanism for overseas qualifications. Hence if the association is prepared to recognize the qualification, this gives an assurance to the employer that the applicant may be worth consideration.

Also, with the growth of demand-side legislation in North America, questions of professional competence become particularly important, as this can be a key element in the defence, if an organization facing claims is able to cite the widely respected professional qualifications of its employees.

These are powerful considerations which link companies with the profession, but other regular services are also valued, like the annual salary surveys carried out by the associations. These provide one of the mechanisms used by employers to ensure that their rates of remuneration remain competitive, as well as keeping members informed about their professional market-place.

Perhaps of greatest significance, however, is the way in which employers and the profession work together to monitor the programmes through which young engineers receive their university education. Provincial associations, in supporting the work of the Canadian Engineering Accreditation Board, provide through their membership participants for the volunteer accreditation teams, who monitor the form and standards of university engineering education. In this way senior engineers from industry have an ongoing input into the content and style of education to be offered to engineers of the future, thus providing an important link between producers and consumers of a skilled engineering labour force in Canada.

NOTE

1 This fieldwork was funded through a Canadian High Commission Faculty Research Program award. Also see Lee (1991c).

Chapter 8

Engineers and trade unions: the American and British cases compared

Peter Meiksins and Chris Smith

INTRODUCTION

Most writing on engineers, including the majority of chapters in this book, assume that engineers are part of management or the natural allies of management and therefore unlikely to be associated with labour unions. This is, in fact, only partially true. Engineers as salaried employees share with other employees many of the uncertainties of waged labour, and in many countries have sought economic protection through labour unions, rather than professional associations or individual deals with their employers. This side of engineers' employment experience makes them different from other professional groups, such as accountants, and makes their relationship with management more contested and problematical. This chapter examines the link between engineers and labour unions through a comparative perspective. It takes two countries, Britain and America, with many similar characteristics in terms of managerial cultures and ideologies, but with quite marked differences with regard to the unionization of engineers.

UNIONISM AND PROFESSIONALISM

Traditional explanations of low rates of unionization among professionals have tended to focus on the nature of professionalism itself. Professional ideology and professional forms of organization are seen as antithetical to unionism; those occupations which define themselves as 'professional' eschew unionism as incompatible with their ethical principles, social status and employment conditions.
    The simple version of this argument can no longer be defended.

Even a cursory glance at the case of engineers shows that professionalism and unionism are not inherently irreconcilable. Thus, in the American case, considerable social science research on engineers' attitudes has shown that professional ideology is not the primary barrier to unionism (Kleingartner 1969; Zussman 1985). Professionalism may colour the unions professionals create – giving them a distinctive preoccupation with issues such as salary differentials, merit pay and career structures (Goldstein 1959; Sturmthal 1967; Zussman 1985). But professionalism is not the opposite of unionism in principle. Moreover, if one considers the British case, it is noteworthy that the period of greatest expansion of engineering unionism (the 1960s) was also the period when American-style models of engineering professionalism began to displace the older craft tradition. It was in the 1960s that a new emphasis on university training, in particular, as the privileged route to engineering practice emerged; yet, despite this more 'professional' mode of occupational recruitment, engineering unionism took off.

All in all, it is abundantly clear that unionism and professionalism can be and have been reconciled in specific cases. But does this mean that an analysis of professionalism is *irrelevant* to understanding the different histories of engineering unionism in the United States and Great Britain? We contend that it is highly relevant. However, in order to understand its impact, a number of over-simplifications implicit in the argument criticized above need to be avoided. First, we need to recognize that professionalism is not monolithic. Different occupations, because of their different situations, give rise to a diversity of forms of professional organization, which are not equally powerful as alternatives to union organization. Second, even within a single occupation, several different professional ideologies may take root; since not all of these are equally hostile to unionism, students of engineers' unions need to consider the pattern of conflict among different professional ideologies. Finally, and perhaps most important, the impact of professionalism on unions does not occur in a vacuum. On the contrary, as our comparison of the United States and Great Britain shows, a variety of 'contingent' historical and cultural factors condition the interaction between professionalism and unionism in very important ways.

ORGANIZATIONAL PROFESSIONALS

Let us begin with the question of the character of engineering professionalism. As Larson (1977) has argued, the 'professional' project takes on quite a different meaning for different occupations, depending upon their historical and social context. Some occupations, such as medicine and the law, emerged outside the context of organizational employment. For them, the professional project has meant *both* the defence of autonomy and the pursuit of status and privilege. By contrast, other occupations emerged primarily within organizations – corporations and the state. Lacking the ability to assert their economic autonomy from these relatively powerful, unified employers (Johnson 1971), the professional project for such occupations was primarily ideological and limited to the pursuit of status and privilege.

There is no doubt that engineering is an example of the latter situation, which Larson calls the 'new' professions. In both the United States and Great Britain, engineers experienced organizational employment at early stages in the development of the profession; as a result, one finds relatively little emphasis on self-employment and professional independence within engineering.

This is reflected in the form and ideology of both British and American engineering associations. In neither case does one find engineers endorsing the 'medical model' of professionalism, with its emphasis on self-employment and professional independence. On the contrary, American engineers have traditionally rejected the idea of mandatory licensing for engineers as a method of creating professional control over engineering work. Indeed, representatives of the major professional associations have openly attacked this idea and have actively opposed legislation which would have required engineering licensing (SPEE 1930; Layton 1986; Meiksins 1989). Similarly, although the 'school culture' triumphed quite early in American engineering, so that the normal route into the profession is through formal engineering education (Calvert 1967; Noble 1977), there has been real reluctance to make this into a hard-and-fast principle. It remains the case, even now, that a minority of engineers lack formal engineering credentials (Zussman 1985).

This is even more true for the British case. As Smith (1987) has argued, one of the more notable features of British engineering has been its strong links to a craft tradition. Until fairly recently, formal credentials played a relatively weak role in the British engineering profession. Indeed, a very common route into engineering was from the shop-floor. Skilled workers could aspire to technical occupations, which were not 'closed' to those who lack university training. Moreover, even in recent years, when the emphasis on university training as a prerequisite for engineering has increased, traditional recruitment patterns have not entirely disappeared. Although there has been an important trend towards strong professional credentialism in upper technical occupations, which has weakened the craft tradition there, it remains the case that engineering is not defined by engineers or their associations as a closed caste.

The engineering associations in Britain and the United States, thus, have not been mechanisms for occupational control. In both Britain and the United States, engineering professional associations have been relatively weak, and their impact on engineering has been markedly less than was the impact of the American Medical Association (AMA) on medicine. In both countries, engineering associations are fragmented, with different engineering specialisms having their own professional societies. The bewildering alphabet-soup of professional associations that this produces, and the lack of an overall, unified engineering organization, has been held partly responsible in both countries for the profession's lack of influence over social policy and over employers (see Gerstl and Hutton 1966 and Watson 1975 for the British case; for the USA see Perrucci and Gerstl 1969).

The leadership of the professional societies in both countries is dominated by engineers with strong ties to the major private-sector employers of engineers. These strong ties with business help to explain the typical conservatism on economic questions of professional engineering bodies. Reflecting this relative conservatism, both British and American engineering societies define themselves primarily as 'learned societies'. They see their role as involving the promulgation of professional knowledge and, when necessary, representing engineering opinion in public and private debates over technical issues. Neither British nor American engineering societies have exhibited much willingness to become active political advocates on major social issues or to represent engineers in disputes over material issues with government or private-sector employers of engineers. Rates of participation by rank-and-file engineers in engineering societies are generally low in both countries, although it is probably true that rates of membership in the societies are somewhat higher in the United States. In the United States, surveys of engineers have found that there is relatively little emphasis on publication and participation in professional associations as measures of professional status or success (LeBold and Howland 1966). Perrucci (1971) estimates that as many as one-third of American engineers belong to no professional associations at all (including local or regional ones). For the British case, Whalley's (1986: 156) case studies found that 'many of the younger engineers in particular regarded the institutions as antiquated organizations, with little to offer the practising engineer. They seemed irrelevant.' Membership was generally viewed by the older engineers as 'an instrumental device to get a job'. Active participation in the institutes was non-existent. All in all, professional engineering organizations in both the United States and Great Britain are relatively weak and do not correspond to the 'medical model' of the professional project.

Thus, if engineering is a profession, it is a 'new' profession, in Larson's terms. One important implication of this argument is that engineering professionalism is less powerful as an alternative to unionism than is medical professionalism. Doctors could argue that unionism was inappropriate to their circumstances, since they were able to use mechanisms of professional closure and control to win autonomy and a strong market position. Engineers were not in this position; professionalizing engineers could not respond to the challenge of unionism by pointing to effective alternative mechanisms of self-defence and occupational control. It is thus hardly surprising that there has been a much more spirited debate about unionism within engineering than there has been in professions such as medicine and law.

CONSTRUCTING THE TECHNICAL DIVISION OF LABOUR

The fact that engineering is, in Larson's terms, a 'new' profession also helps us to understand one of the more distinctive features of the history of professional engineering unionism. Larson suggests that occupations such as engineering pursue a professional project focused largely on status questions. As we shall see, this has been the case for both British and American engineers. In both cases, engineering unionism has been powerfully shaped by engineers' preoccupation with status issues. The manner in which these status questions were resolved is one of the key elements distinguishing the history of British and American engineering unionism. Perhaps the most important manifestation of engineers' concern with status has been their preoccupation with their relationship with non-professional technical workers. The question of professional boundaries has, in fact, been central to the history of engineering unionism in both the United States and Great Britain. However, the 'boundary question' is not the crucial one for explaining the failure of engineering unionism in the USA and its success in Great Britain. Engineers in both countries have shown similar concerns with professional boundaries; but in the British case this concern was expressed *within* a union context, while in the United States it helped to undermine the emergence of unionism.

Historians have identified the question of engineers' relationship to non-professional technicians as a central theme in the history of American engineering unionism. It has been suggested that this was the Achilles' heel of engineering unionism in the United States (Walton 1961; Kuhn 1971). When professional engineers began to experiment with union organization, they were confronted with the question of whether or not to include technical workers in their unions. Fearing the loss of professional status for engineers that the inclusion of technicians implied, many engineers argued for their exclusion. This produced significant levels of conflict within engineers' unions, and led, ultimately, to their collapse.

This account of the demise of American engineering unionism is true enough at one level. An analysis of the rise and fall of engineers' unions in the period between 1935 and 1950 shows clearly the importance of the 'boundary question'. Thus, right at the start, the initial impetus to the formation of the engineers' unions was, to some extent, the fear of inclusion in industrial unions of non-professional workers. As Walton (1961) has shown, the passage of the National Labor Relations Act encouraged industrial unions such as the United Auto Workers to mount major organizing drives in many American industries. These organizing drives often sought to include a wide variety of employees, including engineers, as part of the new bargaining unit. Since engineers would constitute a distinct minority within any industrial union, and since there was concern that involvement with blue-collar unions would produce a decline in the engineer's status, engineers began, with the encouragement of their professional societies, to form separate engineers' unions as a way of preventing their subsumption into the industrial labour movement.

This concern proved rather unnecessary. The National Labor Relations Board (NLRB) generally refused to include engineers in production workers' bargaining units (Northrup 1946); and, in any case, the Taft–Hartley Act (1947) included provisions, promoted by the engineering societies, which prevented the forced inclusion of professionals in non-professional unions (Kassalow 1967). Nevertheless, engineers' unions survived for at least another decade, indicating that American engineers could accept certain kinds of unionism and had found that this type of organization met some of their needs. Most observers concluded that engineers wanted a form of collective organization that would defend them materially but which was not linked to the larger labour movement (Walton 1961; Kleingartner 1969; Kuhn 1971).

Yet the 'boundary question' continued to dog the union movement and was crucial to its eventual decline. Thus, many of the engineering and technical unions which survived in the 1950s became embroiled in bitter disputes over the inclusion of technicians. Some argued for their inclusion, on the grounds that greater numbers led to greater strength and that it made sense to include all technical workers in a single bargaining unit. On the other hand, many engineers did not wish to be associated with technicians, fearing that they would be treated as technicians by employers and the general public. Many unions eventually split over this kind of issue. Most notably, the Engineers and Scientists of America (ESA), founded in an attempt to provide a national federation for professional engineers and scientists, fell apart over such status questions.

In short, there is no doubt that the 'boundary question' was at the heart of the decline of American engineers' unions. Comparisons with the British case indicates that British engineers have developed similar concerns about the boundary between them and non-professional workers. Clegg (1976) has noted that, in the confused pattern of trade union structure in Britain, white-collar workers' preference to join white-collar organizations is one of the only safe facts. While even this structural given began to erode in the 1980s, up until that time it was true that the first experience of unionism for technical workers and white-collar labour in general was through their own exclusive organizations.

Craft exclusiveness was the dominant form of unionism for technical workers in Britain until well into the 1960s, the technical unions such as the Draughtsmen's and Allied Technicians' Association (DATA), having increased membership on a lateral basis, decided to expand into higher grades of designers and engineers. In the 1960s British engineers started to be produced through the universities, not through part-time courses in technical colleges and 'premium' apprenticeships, and a 'graduate barrier' began to emerge within the broad technical engineering labour process. This was a new phenomenon in Britain. Engineers were being 'professionalized' and not socialized through the craft traditions where acquiring a union card and experience had been part of the general apprenticeship. 'Professionalization' opened new opportunities and challenges for collective organization, and there have been several drives to generate organizational forms adapted to new patterns of occupational closure. These have not, however, taken place within a political or historical vacuum, and competition for newly professionalized engineers has been divided between an evolving but entrenched union movement and new exclusivist professional bodies.

Established unions, like DATA, launched membership drives in the late 1960s aimed at the professional engineer. Initially, engineers were incorporated as a standard category of membership with no sectional autonomy. This was only partially successful, and the union policy towards accommodating engineers has been through several changes, until by the late 1970s granting limited autonomy within the union was decided to be the best method of recruiting these groups. The union followed the pattern of sectionalism developed by another technical union, Association of Scientific, Technical and Management Staff (ASTMS) (initially formed by a merger of foremen and scientists' craft unions), and consciously adapted the union structure and character to the status consciousness and exclusivity of engineers (Smith 1986). DATA, later Technical, Administrative and Supervisory Staff (TASS), modified its strategy through competition with other unions who emerged to recruit the newly 'professionalized' engineers.

From the late 1960s 'professionalization', however partial, offered other organizations an opportunity of moving into the area via exclusive engineers' unions based on educational segmentation. It was the professional engineering institutes and the Engineers' Guild which made the running for these new 'qualified engineers'. In 1969 the Engineers' Guild, with a scattered membership of 6,000, established the United-Kingdom Association of Professional Engineers (UKAPE) as an exclusive 'professional engineers' union'. Other 'professional' unions appeared at the same time in an attempt to recruit engineering, science and technology graduates in industry in opposition to established white-collar unions (Dickens 1972; Gill, Morris and Eaton 1977; Snape and Bamber 1989). This first professional union strategy failed partly because of employers' opposition to the further proliferation of unions within an already overcrowded multi-union environment (Dickens 1972). But equally important was the determined opposition to the unwelcome newcomers from established technical unions such as TASS and ASTMS. Significantly, the old unions could claim efficacy in collective bargaining, while calling on the political power of the Trades Union Congress and wider union movement to block any encroachment into their job territories by professional and anti-TUC, right-wing rivals (Smith 1986).

A second wave of professional engineering unionism occurred in the late 1970s, when a single-industry engineers' union, the Electrical Power Engineers Association (EPEA), formed the Engineers' and Managers' Association (EMA) to recruit outside the power engineering industry. The union capitalized on the failure of UKAPE to make any inroads into recruiting engineers from scratch. The EMA was sponsored by the collective voice of the engineering institutes, the Council of Engineering Institutes, to challenge the growth of TASS and ASTMS (Glover and Kelly 1987: 202–3). Unlike UKAPE, the EPEA had well-established trade union roots, dating back to 1913, and represented a more serious challenge to established technical unions.

The challenge was seen by some commentators, such as Roslender (1983), as inaugurating a 'new model unionism', combining an established trade union effectiveness with a strong orientation towards professionalism which would act like a magnet for graduate engineers, and a strategic model for other organizational professions such as accountants, personnel managers, systems analysts and marketing staff (Snape and Bamber 1989). However, such a scenario has failed to materialize. The EMA was blocked from establishing a wider recruitment base due to established union opposition, a general decline in union growth from the late 1970s and the non-viability of small unions within an increasingly concentrated British union environment. Employers were reluctant to grant recognition to another union when a strategy of reducing the number of bargaining units had been their aim for a number of years. The EMA continued to experience organic decline and only picked up four 'transfers of engagement' of engineers' and managers' staff associations between 1977 and 1987. Less than 20 per cent of its 41,000 paper membership were outside its original base in electricity supply (Snape and Bamber 1989: 98). It remains a small, exclusive right-wing union within the TUC, and will only survive through merger, which is most likely to be with the equally right-wing Electrical, Electronic, Telecommunications and Plumbing Union (EETPU).

The established home of engineers' and managers' staff associations outside technical unions is the right-wing EETPU; this marks a new development in the British trade union environment. The union has the largest number of engineers in a separate section called the Electrical and Engineering Staff Association (EESA). The EETPU-EESA absorbed five engineers', managers' and foremen's staff associations between 1976 and 1987, and four 'professional unions' which appeared in the late 1960s, including Association of Supervisory and Executive Engineers (ASEE), the Steel Industry Staff Association (SIMA), UKAPE and Association of Managers and Professional Staff (AMPS). All of these organizations were launched on the basis of 'professional exclusiveness', hostile to white-collar-unions, let alone manual ones. That these supposedly professional unions should have ended up within a manual union underlines the fact that their concern with occupational exclusiveness existed alongside a right-wing political practice, and the latter is probably a more significant determinant of union form and character in Britain.

TASS became a technical white-collar union with a sizeable craft manual union base by absorbing craft unions in the 1980s. It changed again in 1988, when it merged with ASTMS, to form Manufacturing, Science and Finance (MSF), the biggest white-collar union in Europe, with a paper membership of 600,000 and a reach across the staff/manual and industrial divides between manufacturing and service. The two unions combine different traditions, but represent the single largest concentration of technical labour in Britain today. This is a 'new-wave unionism', conglomerate and big, within an increasingly concentrated union environment.

Engineers in Britain today, in so far as they have a choice of unions to join, are faced with the two political poles of the MSF and EEPTU, and the occupational exclusivity and right-wing character of the EMA. The project of occupational exclusivity as a basis for collective organizatior looks increasingly untenable, and it will be union size and politics, not occupation or class, that determine the pattern of union structure in the future. This is not new; but the balance between the two determinants of union form seems to have tilted decisively in favour of the political in recent times.

Unionism among engineers in the British case represents a complex interaction between exclusivity and efficacy. Craft exclusiveness defined the effective pattern of technical unionism until the late 1960s, when there was a marked decline in craft apprenticeships for engineers and a move towards more 'American' concern with professional exclusivity. British engineers, like their American counterparts, began to place an educational boundary between themselves and non-professional co-workers. However, in the British case, established technical unions were adept at accommodating these concerns by granting separate bargaining facilities, defending wage differentials, and the like, while at the same time blocking professional-only unions from either entering or expanding into their domain. In other words, British technical unions have found a variety of means of meeting the changing aspirations of engineers while keeping them in membership of the wider union movement. In short, while the kinds of professional status concern characteristic of a 'new' profession *have* shaped the union movement in both cases, the British case indicated that the presence of such concerns alone is not inconsistent with unionism. If we are to explain the failure of American engineering unionism, therefore, the influence of professionalism must be examined in conjunction with the role played by other factors.

BUSINESS PROFESSIONALISM: ENGINEERS AND MANAGEMENT

Before turning to a consideration of these other factors, one final point must be made regarding the character of engineering professionalism. If engineering is a 'new' profession, with a distinctive concern for status, and not autonomy, it is also a 'business' profession. As has been noted by virtually all observers of the engineering profession, the category of engineer is enormously heterogeneous, containing practitioners in significantly different social, indeed *class*, positions. Thus, 'engineer' can mean a relatively low-level technical worker performing largely routine work in testing. Or it can mean the chief executive officer of a multinational corporation whose career began in engineering. It is the presence of engineer-managers within the professional community which is of particular importance to the history of engineering professionalism and engineers' unionism, because they have been very influential within the national engineering associations of both the United States and Great Britain (which has helped fuel the argument that these associations are, in some ways, extensions of business rather than independent professional associations). To a great extent, it has been their brand of professionalism which has been the official ideology of the organized engineering profession. And, not surprisingly, their professionalism has often been particularly hostile to unions.

We have already noted the reluctance of engineering associations in both the United States and Great Britain to advocate and implement traditional mechanisms of professional closure such as licensing and formal educational requirements for entering engineering practice. Whalley (1986: 183) suggests that, in the British case, 'engineers . . . lack the power and will to support a credential-based exclusionary strategy'. But this is not due, as Whalley and others (P. J. Armstrong 1987b) maintain, to the 'inherently practical' nature of engineering, where 'only so much can be learned in the classroom' (Whalley 1986: 57). Law and medicine are equally practical, combining theoretical and craft elements. What sets engineering apart is the enormous influence of engineer-employers over the profession and its institutions. Strict rules limiting membership of the profession to those with formal educational credentials would have the effect of excluding some of these employers, a fact which has been a very important impediment to the development of such rules in the American case (Layton 1986; Meiksins 1988). Moreover, engineer employers have often used their dominant position within engineering associations to discourage the formation of inflexible restrictions, in the form of credentials, which would limit their flexibility in the use of technical labour (Meiksins 1988). It should not surprise us that engineer employers have not favoured the development of a strong, independent profession analogous to the medical profession, capable of restricting the supply of technical labour and of achieving significant control over its own labour.

In short, the influence of engineer employers has been one factor underlying the engineering profession's lack of emphasis on closure and professional autonomy. Moreover, the professional ideology which has emerged within engineering, coloured in various ways by these elites, has had a distinctively anti-union cast. It is possible to argue, in other words, that engineering *employers* have attempted to present professionalism as an *alternative* to unionism, as inconsistent with union organization, as a means of trying to impede, or at least control, the emergence of engineers' unions.

Thus, as we have seen, it has been the employer-influenced professional associations which have been active proponents of the view that professionalism and conventional unionism are incompatible. In the British case, this is evident in the efforts by the engineering institutes to encourage the development of 'separate' quasi-unions such as UKAPE which would not be linked to (and presumably strengthened by) other union organizations. In the United States, the national engineering associations have consistently opposed unionism. In the 1920s they helped to undermine the emergence of a quasi-engineers' union in the form of the American Association of Engineers (AAE), arguing that it was not professional (Meiksins 1986). And in the 1940s they initially opposed the formation of engineers' unions outright. Once it became apparent that it would not be possible to avoid the inclusion of engineers in conventional unions, the engineering associations, most notably the American Society of Civil Engineers (ASCE), moved to advocating the development of separate bargaining units for professionals (Walton 1961). Goldner and Ritti (1967) have argued that employers often encourage, or even impose, professional ideology among their engineering employees, because it serves as a form of social control. The history of the relationship between employer-influenced professionalism and engineers' unions seems consistent with this view.

This is not to suggest, however, that employers alone create the conflict between professionalism and unionism. There can be no doubt that many practising engineers are sceptical about unionism, in part because, as professionals, they see themselves as 'above' the kind of activities and social groups conventionally involved in unions. Nevertheless, the existence of a conscious effort to counterpose professionalism and unionism by engineering employers *has* served to make their reconciliation more difficult and more complex.

To sum up, the 'new', 'business' professionalism that has emerged within engineering does present real obstacles to the development of unionism. The overwhelming emphasis on status associated with the new professionalism has made the question of boundaries between professional engineers and other technical workers a sore point in engineering organization. And the rhetoric of professionalism has been used quite deliberately to try to impede and/or channel union development. Yet, although this has been true in both the United States and Great Britain, the outcomes have been very different in the two cases. In order to understand how and why professionalism has shaped engineers' unionism in the two cases, we need to consider *when* professionalism and unionism developed in the two cases as well as the role played by a variety of social factors outside the engineering profession itself.

THE TIMING OF PROFESSIONALISM

One weakness of 'sociological' discussions of professionalism and unionism has been their neglect of the 'timing' of the emergence of the various ideas in question. One major difference between the British and American cases lies precisely in this timing. In the British case, unionism among engineers emerged relatively early and established itself well before the solidification of a strong, graduate-based professional identity. By contrast, American engineers developed their professional identity relatively early, turning to unionism only after this identity had stabilized.

In part because of this timing, American engineers have been much more likely than their British counterparts to look to their professional associations for assistance in periods of material crisis. Lacking an acceptable, viable union outlet for their concerns, and encouraged by their professional rhetoric to do so, American engineers tended to see the professional associations as their first resort in solving their material problems.

In the American case, like the British one, engineering associations have not defined themselves as defenders of engineers' material interests. On the contrary, they have resolutely resisted being drawn into this role, as we have seen. However, in periods of economic hardship among engineers, members of the profession have tended to look first to the professional associations in the history of American engineering in the twentieth century. Thus, in the period after the First World War, when engineering employment slipped and engineering salaries were losing ground to those of manual workers, many engineers turned to their professional societies for assistance with their material problems. The societies were reluctant to become involved in such activities, which led to a significant amount of internal conflict and helped fuel what Edwin Layton has called 'the revolt of the engineers' (Layton 1986). However, fearing the development of engineers' unionism, most of the professional associations responded with some concessions to dissidents within the societies and with a variety of half-measures such as employment services and talks and publications on finding a job (Meiksins 1986, 1988).

A similar pattern emerged in the Great Depression. Like most Americans, engineers were hard hit by the Depression. A federal government study of the engineering profession (Fraser 1941) estimated that 34 per cent of American engineers had experienced unemployment between 1929 and 1934 and reported a 33 per cent decline in median earnings during the same period. This stimulated calls for action on behalf of engineers; and, while there was some interest in unionization, most engineers looked first to their professional associations for help. While the associations shied away from anything that resembled collective bargaining, they did recognize the need to do something and responded, as in the earlier period, with employment services, employment advice, and the like. Once again, engineers turned to their professional associations as their first resort in a period of crisis. And once again, the associations responded with half-measures which seemed designed to discourage the development of more assertive forms of engineering organization.

Finally, in the late 1960s when cuts in the space programme and the winding down of the Vietnam War led to a decline in engineering employment, engineers again turned to the professional associations for assistance. As in the previous crises, pressure was placed on the societies to do something about the plight of unemployed engineers; typically, the societies responded with employment advice and similar programmes. And, as in earlier periods, the dissatisfaction with these relatively weak measures produced heated debate *within* the professional societies. The debate focused on such questions as whether engineering societies could serve their members' professional interests if they were closely tied to employers and whether it was appropriate for such societies to confine their activities to what was possible within the confines of a self-defined 'learned society' (Sinclair 1980; McMahon 1984; Meiksins 1989).

In sum, American professional engineers have consistently

turned to their professional associations when a material crisis developed within the professions. This is in marked contrast to the British case, where, by and large, the societies have been seen as irrelevant to material issues. At the heart of this tactical difference lies the question of history. In Britain, professionalism emerged as a significant force only after technical unionism had taken root.

By the lateness of the professionalization of British engineers, we mean the relatively slow development of exclusive, university-based entry systems into the occupation, and the persistence of diverse, apprenticeship-based access routes. This reflects traditional training patterns in Britain, and employers' hostility to purely academic training and their resistance to empowering engineers with exclusive credentials. Graduate entrants into engineering accounted for 35 per cent of total engineers in 1945, but we see a progressive increase in the proportion in the post-war period, rising to 50 per cent in the mid-1960s, and over 90 per cent in the 1980s (McCormick 1988b:589). By contrast to American engineers, graduate status as a boundary badge of professional identity is a relatively recent phenomenon in Britain.

This difference meant barriers between professional associations and trade unions could not be built on an educational divide, and the apprenticeship system persistently exposed engineers to unionization. British engineering institutes have, as a consequence of this, and the altogether more legitimate place of trade unions within the society, had to adopt a more flexible and strategic posture towards technical unions.

British engineering institutions, like their American counterparts, see material issues as inappropriate concerns for professional organizations; indeed, many are restricted by charter from engaging in activities to better the material conditions of engineers. For example, the charter of the Institute of Mechanical Engineers states: 'the Institution shall not carry on any trade or business or engage in any transaction with a view to the pecuniary gain or profit of the members thereof' (Gerstl and Hutton 1966: 10). They have therefore been vulnerable to competition from trade unions claiming to do just that, especially where employers are unwilling to accept as given established wage differentials, and therefore treat engineers as skilled labour, rather than a class apart. One response to the restrictive economic function of the institutions was the establishment of the Engineers' Guild in 1937 to promote the material interests of all engineers in corporate membership of the institutions. The Guild, in addition to promoting the public image and professional standing of engineers, advised individuals on terms of employment, pensions, salaries and status questions. It is significant that the Guild appeared at a time when unionization of technical labour was increasing. The Guild, however, was no answer to workplace union organization provided by the technical unions, and central to the post-war British industrial relations environment, and it struggled along with a scattered membership of around 5,000 to 6,000 until dissolving its membership into the UKAPE, a quasi-union set up by the institutes in the late 1960s when technical trade unionism was again booming. Indicative of the failure of this strategy, apart from the low membership of the Guild, has been the support for particular trade unions by the engineering institutions to block challenges by less welcome trade unions.

An early instance of this appeared when the Electricians' Trade Union (ETU) began to bring within its membership engineers of all ranks in the power-stations in 1917. The Institution of Electrical Engineers (IEE) attempted to form its own 'exclusive' association to block this drive. However, this failed, as a moderate 'exclusive' union was already in competition with the ETU: the Electrical Power Engineers' Association (EPEA). The IEE sided with the EPEA, recommending power-station engineers to join this union to block the threat from the manual craft union (Slinn 1989: 43). Another example is the setting-up of UKAPE by the Engineers' Guild in 1969 to compete with established technical unions that were actively recruiting graduate engineers. And in 1975 the Council of Engineering Institutes (CEI), an organization formed to promote the public interest of all engineering institutes, openly but reluctantly supported, for the first time, engineers joining trade unions. This was a strategic decision aimed at promoting a new right-wing union, the Engineers' and Managers' Association, formed out of the EPEA to recruit engineers outside of the power industry (Smith 1986). The CEI recommended members join the EMA and three non-affiliated 'professional unions' – UKAPE, the Association of Professional Scientists and Technologists (APST), the Association of Supervisory and Executive Engineers (ASEE). The large technical unions, where the majority of engineers are organized, TASS and ASTMS, were not recommended, as 'they were considered insufficiently professionally orientated and did not incorporate in their rules provision for a ballot before taking industrial action' (May 1979: 112). The voice of the professional associations, as expressed through the CEI or the Engineering Council established in 1982, has continued to promote the EMA and what became the home of the failed professional unions in the 1980s, the Electrical, Electronic, Telecommunications and Plumbing Union–Electrical and Engineering Staff Associations (EETPU–EESA) against the larger technical unions (Engineering Council 1986). The British case therefore exhibits an opportunistic attitude of engineering institutes towards trade unions, and a keen political strategy of promoting right-wing organizations against what are perceived as large, left-wing unions. In comparison with the American case, however, what is striking is the complete failure of the institutions themselves to form the organizational arena within which engineers' material grievances are satisfied. This has always taken place within a trade union form.

Thus, the late emergence of engineering professionalism in Great Britain helped facilitate the emergence of engineers' unions. By contrast, American engineers' unions had to contend with a well-established, deeply entrenched professionalism. The different results of engineering professionalism in the two cases were, in other words, heavily influenced by the historical sequence of events.

Yet this leaves open one important question regarding the relationship between unionism and professionalism. Does the failure of engineers' unions in the United States indicate that it is impossible for unionism to emerge if it is *preceded* by developed professional ideology and organization? If so, we are left with a modified version of the traditional argument that professionalism as such is incompatible with unionism.

The key to answering this question lies in remembering that professionalism is not monolithic. Although it is true that the professionalism of American engineering leaders, the official professionalism of the engineering associations, was irreconcilably opposed to unionism, there have been other strains of professional ideology within the American engineering community which have been more open to unions or union-like organization.

Thus, students of the rise and fall of engineers' unions in the 1940s and 1950s found that rank-and-file engineers' professionalism was, in many ways, rhetorical and not incompatible with the principle of unionism as such. Research on American engineers' attitudes (as well as those of other organizational professionals) has shown that professional ideology is not an inherent barrier to unionism (e.g. Kleingartner 1969). The case of the American Association of Engineers (AAE) illustrates well the relationship between engineering professionalism and union organization and the diversity of opinion within the engineering community (Rothstein 1968; Meiksins 1986). Professionalism may colour the unions professionals create – giving them a distinctive preoccupation with issues such as salary differentials, merit pay and career structures (Goldstein 1959; Sturmthal 1967; Zussman 1985). But the professionalism of the rank-and-file engineer is not the opposite of unionism.

THE COMPARATIVE STATUS OF THE ENGINEER

While there are many significant differences between British and American society, several are of particular importance to understanding the history of engineering organization. We have emphasized three in our analysis here: the relative status of the engineer in British and American society; the manner in which the labour movement has approached engineers in each society; and the overall conditions for labour organizing in general.

One of the major differences between engineers in Great Britain and engineers in the United States is the status accorded them by society as a whole and management in particular. It has been well documented in a variety of contexts (ranging from social scientific research to government inquiries such as the Finniston report) that the status of engineers in Great Britain is lower than their counterparts in other societies, including the United States (Ahlström 1982). Where British engineers routinely complain of being treated like workers, American engineers, except in periods of salary compression and unemployment, seem relatively secure in their 'middle-class' status and are seen by both the public and managers as relatively high-status professionals (although not as high-status as doctors or lawyers).

These differences in status reflect larger social attitudes towards technology and industry in Britain and the United States (Chandler 1989; Elbaum and Lazonick 1986). American culture has long exhibited extremely positive attitudes towards technology and those individuals and groups who work with it. This positive evaluation of technical men and women is apparent in the widespread idealization of mythical figures such as Benjamin Franklin or Thomas Edison, whose virtues consist in their having been 'practical men' who invented valuable new technologies or discovered important scientific principles. Similarly, American culture is also characterized by a deep respect for the activities of the business man and woman (Bendix 1956). Although there are complexities here (e.g. the strong antipathy to 'bigness' in business), figures such as the early captains of industry (Carnegie, Rockefeller, etc.) or more recent examples of corporate 'excellence' (Iacocca, Watson, etc.) are routinely lionized in the popular media.

American engineers have benefited from these positive evaluations of business and technology. Most obviously, since Americans tend to value technology, and since engineers are clearly linked to technology, there is a generally positive view of engineers in American society as valuable, useful employees. They also have gained a degree of status from their association with business. Early on, engineering was linked to entrepreneurial modes of business. Sons of prominent figures (including Frederick Taylor, the father of scientific management) saw engineering as a dignified occupation because, although it might mean getting one's hands dirty, it involved the prospects of a career culminating in the proprietorship of a small machine-shop (Calvert 1967). While the days of the entrepreneurial engineer did not survive long in the context of corporate capitalism, the fact that respected middle-class families sent their sons into engineering lent the occupation a degree of status which carried over into the organizational age. More recently, engineers have been associated with many of the positive technical accomplishments of American business. Corporate slogans emphasizing 'better living through better technology' routinely present Americans with an image of the engineer as the fusion of the positive sides of both technology and business. While there have also been criticisms of engineering activities, criticisms which have grown louder since the 1960s as a result of the growing doubt about the virtues of scientific 'progress', engineers have occupied a relatively privileged place in the American view of things.

One of the more important consequences of this positive cultural stereotype of the engineer has been that American managers have tended to see engineers as an important type of employee. Since technology is seen as important to business success, and since engineers have long been regarded as 'middle-class' professionals, major employers have taken engineers seriously as prospective managers. While the United States is not the country with the greatest tendency to recruit top management from the engineering profession (Germany probably is; see Lawrence, chapter 5 in this volume), it is certainly true that American engineers are seen as prospective managers. Moreover, as David Noble (1977) has shown, American managers, because they regarded engineers as important to business success and because they were aware of the need to recruit engineers into managerial roles, took an active part in shaping the curriculum of American engineering schools. By encouraging business courses and certain kinds of practical training in engineering programmes, managers ensured that the schools would produce trustworthy engineering personnel who were socialized to the needs of the corporation and who would constitute a pool of potential managers.

For all of these reasons, engineers in the United States have had a relatively high status and relatively close ties to the managers who employ and supervise them. There can be no doubt that this has accentuated their tendency to question the relevance of unionism to their situation. By contrast, British engineers, handicapped by the stigma associated with working with one's hands in an elitist managerial culture, have occupied a rather lower status. This difference is one of the factors helping to explain their greater willingness to adopt union forms of organization. We can examine the nature of the status of British engineers through the formation of the profession, their place in the structure of managerial hierarchies and the failure of various attempts to enhance engineers' status in society.

British engineers have historically entered the engineering profession through premium apprenticeships and pupillage to particular employers who exercised a massive influence on the structuring of the engineering profession. Not only did such systems emphasize the importance of engineering as a 'practical craft' and not a theoretical discipline, but the supply of engineers qualified through such routes was never sufficient to undermine the reliance on manual crafts. When technical education appeared in the nineteenth century to supplement craft practices, it was 'defined so narrowly that the classes it sponsored for workers in fields such as engineering offered little competition to long established methods of craft oriented training' (Wrigley 1986: 168). While in the late nineteenth century American capital restructured engineering through the universities, in Britain engineering courses were restricted to a few institutions, and did not in any way disrupt the apprenticeship system. Moreover, teaching business, economics and management on engineering degrees did not develop until the 1960s, and then only in a marginal way. Engineering education was overwhelmingly technical in content.

Part-time study and apprenticeships remained the dominant method of training engineers until the 1960s. This served to ensure that entry channels were not monopolized by the middle class, but open to workers. Indeed, engineering did not figure as an appropriate profession for the middle class, who preferred pure science and the arts to the applied disciplines (Weiner 1981). Recent studies of engineers in Britain, such as Smith (1987) and Whalley (1986), confirm the continued importance of the craft tradition for socializing engineers into a practical orientation where theory, credentialism and a strict separation between intellectual and manual labour are rejected in favour of fluidity between learning and doing. This is not inherent in engineering, but rather its peculiarly British structure.

If we look at the growth of managerial hierarchies in Britain and the place of engineers in them, what is striking is that engineers fail to make top management positions. Being a manager in Britain is all about general decision-making. Moreover, as Lazonick (1985) has noted in comparing the growth of British and American managerial hierarchies, in Britain top managers were initially recruited from the elite public schools and universities as 'surrogate family members'; having a technical skill was not only unnecessary for selection, but probably a disadvantage. Having the right background, not the right qualifications, remained the most important factor in recruiting in senior management until the emergence of business education in the 1960s.

Obvious similarities in the decline in status of the engineer in the two societies exist, even if the timing of this is different. In Britain the entrepreneur-engineer was a folk hero of nineteenth century industrial progress, although the salaried engineer inside twentieth century corporate capital has been a marginalized figure within management. By contrast, the Taylorite corporate engineers in American companies were dominant figures within managerial hierarchies until well into this century, although, as Armstrong (Chapter 3 in this volume) points out, this productivist ideology has now given way to views of management drawn from finance and marketing. In both societies there has been an absolute decline in manufacturing, and strong financial and commercial factions dominate corporate capital and management elites, especially when compared with the centrality of engineers and the manufacturing ethic in Japan and Germany – the two major economies of the late twentieth century (see McCormick and Lawrence, Chapter 4 and 5 in this volume).

CONCLUSION

Our comparison demonstrates that patterns of union formation among professional engineers are strongly influenced by a variety of historical contingencies and cultural differences. There is, first, the question of timing – does engineers' unionism begin to take root before or after the emergence of strong professional patterns of recruitment and organization. While the latter do not prevent unionization entirely, their existence clearly makes it somewhat more difficult. As the British case suggests, the timing of the emergence of professional forms depends, in part, on managerial (and cultural) attitudes towards engineering. In Britain, where engineering has not traditionally been highly valued, and where professional engineers have not been defined as apprentice managers, the development of formal university training for engineers emerged relatively late. In general, the strength of managerial efforts to define engineers as professionals and part of management is an important factor shaping the history of engineers' unionism. The approach of the union movement towards engineers is also important. Where, as in the British case, unions developed a strong commitment to organizing white-collar constituencies, and where unions were flexible enough to accommodate the peculiar needs of professional employees, unions developed more easily. In the American case, the relative lack of organizing activities directed at professionals and other white-collar groups and the scepticism regarding their appropriateness as union members helped to impede the development of engineers' unions. The politics of the labour movement also played a role; the fact that it was the more militant, egalitarian Congress of Industrial Organizations (CIO) that approached American engineers had a distinct chilling effect on attempts to organize these relatively conservative employees. Finally, and perhaps the most important, the overall climate for union organization has had profound effects on the fate of union organization. In the United States, where there are a strongly anti-union culture, militantly anti-union managers and a restrictive legal framework for union organization, the labour movement has been placed on the defensive. The failure to organize engineers in the United States is, in part, a symptom of the weakness and lack of organizing activities by American labour. By contrast, British unions, while hardly popular with employers, have faced less resolute opposition and have not had to contend with complex statutory restrictions. They have, as a result, been seen as more legitimate and effective, and have had much greater success in extending union organization beyond the ranks of manual labour.

These conclusions regarding the importance of historical and national peculiarities for the emergence of engineers' unionism are broadly consistent with Bain's classic (1970) analysis of the development of white-collar trade unions. Bain argues that it is precisely historical factors, and in particular the attitude of government and employers towards unionizing activities, that determine whether white-collar unions will succeed in developing and growing.

While we agree, up to a point, with Bain's analysis, we reject the view that engineers' unionism is purely a matter of historical contingency. On the contrary, we share Carter's (1985) critique of Bain – there are important structural factors that also condition the emergence of engineers' unionism. Two, in particular, are worthy of emphasis here. First, our analysis suggests that there is an underlying reality in the conditions of engineering employment creating tendencies towards unionization. Professional engineers are employees and, as such, share the kinds of experiences that promote unionism – conflicts over wages, bureaucratic conditions of employment, job insecurity, and the like. These conditions do not automatically produce unionization but they do place unionism on the agenda. There is a persistent question built into the engineers' situation – shall we unionize? – which does not go away even when, as in the United States, historical and national conditions are not conducive to union formation. Second, Carter is right to stress that the emergence of what he calls 'middle-class' unionism depends on the structural realities of class conflict. Where class conflict becomes more intense, and the lines of conflict are more sharply drawn, the pressure on employees to unionize grows more pronounced. If we think back over the various periods in which engineers have attempted to organize, and/or have succeeded in doing so, it has tended to be periods in which levels of class conflict in society as a whole were relatively high. Moreover, as Carter (1985) points out, the historical factors emphasized by Bain depend, to some extent, on levels of class conflict. Why does the state become more favourable to union organization in certain periods? Clearly, it is related to the pressures put on the government by employees and their organizations to create more favourable conditions. The failure of engineers' unionism in the post-war United States and its concomitant success in Britain are clearly related to the strong position of British labour and the weakness of its American counterpart.

It is our contention that the emergence of unionism depends on the interaction between the structural forces that promote engineers' unionism and specific national and historical factors that either assist or impede it. In short, despite the American case, engineers' unions are not an oxymoron. The forces which have impeded such unions in the United States have been largely historical, not structural, and there exist real structural pressures towards the unionization of professional employees in all industrial capitalist societies. It is true that professional engineers are not 'just like' manual workers; like many skilled employees, they do desire separate organizations and their professional ideologies do foster powerful status concerns which make unionization problematic. These do not, however, represent insuperable class differences any more than do the concerns of skilled craft workers. As the labour force in industrial capitalist societies shifts further towards professional and service employees, the fate of the labour movement may depend on its ability to make the most of the opportunities for organizing these new constituencies.

NOTE

A version of this chapter appeared in the journal *Theory and Society*, 1992.

Chapter 9

Irish engineers: education for emigration?

James Wickham

INTRODUCTION

'Ireland – Powered by People' reads an advertisement which greets visitors arriving in Dublin airport. Placed by the state's Industrial Development Authority (IDA), the poster shows a group of young, bright, keen Irish men and women shining with entrepreneurial zeal and technological competence, ready to work for the next foreign-owned company to open up in the country.

In Ireland's continuing drive to modernize and industrialize, its young and educated labour force has now become one of its major selling points. This chapter looks at the reality behind that image by focusing on one key group of such young technically qualified professionals – Irish electronics engineers. By examining their education, work and career it shows the contradictions created for engineers by the attempt to create an industrial base in a peripheral European country.

ENGINEERING EDUCATION AND INDUSTRIALIZATION POLICY

For the last thirty years Irish industrial strategy has been largely one of 'industrialization by invitation'. Industrial success has been seen to be dependent on attracting to Ireland subsidiaries of foreign corporations which produce for the export (i.e. European Community) market. Today such firms employ a third of all the workforce in Irish manufacturing industry and account for more than two-thirds of all manufacturing exports (O'Malley 1989: 155f).

This process was already well established by the late 1970s, when

US electronics firms began to expand production abroad. In the heyday of Silicon Valley fever, such firms were wooed by European development agencies, each one of which seemed to believe that all its problems would be solved if it could persuade enough 'high-tech' firms to open plants in its bailiwick. As one of the first countries to attempt to attract foreign investment systematically, Ireland had a head start in the competition: government policy had no ambiguities; the institutional mechanisms were already in place.

In this situation employment in electronics firms reached 12,000 by 1981. This was hardly significant in international terms, but 5 per cent of the total Irish manufacturing labour force (Wickham 1988). However, compared to existing industry, electronics seemed to make a rather novel demand on the host country: it needed qualified electronics technicians, and above all, it needed electronics engineers.

This perceived need pushed engineering as a whole into a new status within higher educational policy. Nation-building in Ireland, as elsewhere, had involved engineering. In the late 1920s the newly independent state embarked an ambitious electrification programme: the Shannon Scheme harnessed the country's longest river for hydroelectric power and created a national electricity distribution system. In the subsequent decades the Rural Electrification Programme ensured that the national grid reached even the remotest parts of rural Ireland (Manning and McDowell 1984). The nationalized Electricity Supply Board (ESB) wired the nation together – and was the largest employer of engineers in the country. Especially for electrical engineers, employment prospects within Ireland meant the ESB.

By the end of the 1970s, however, various pressure groups were demanding a rapid expansion in the output of electronics engineers. Existing firms were complaining of a growing shortage of engineering graduates, and the IDA believed that this would hamper its attempts to bring in new firms.

In this context the government attempted for the first time to link the content of education with economic growth. From the mid-1950s enrolments in third level had been growing by about 30 per cent every five years (Clancy 1988: 9). This expansion had been justified in general human capital terms, but there had been no attempt to fine-tune the educational system to produce clearly specified skills. Now the government created a

Manpower Consultative Committee whose brief was to do just that. Its major achievement was to sanction a rapid expansion of engineering between 1979 and 1983, so that the number of electronics engineers graduating annually rose from 163 in 1980 to 385 in 1986 (National Economic and Social Council [NESC] 1985: 176, 324; Higher Education Authority [HEA] 1987: 93).

These new electronics engineers were very different from their predecessors in the older engineering disciplines: their employment was in foreign, not indigenous industry, in the private not the state sector and in an area where technical change was much more rapid.

These changes enhanced the already relatively high prestige of engineering within Irish education. Critics of Irish culture and education (J. Lee 1990) have bemoaned the historical tendency of the Irish middle class to seek the comfortable blanket of a conventional 'professional' career in law or medicine rather than to venture out into business. None the less, an engineering education and an engineering career have never had the low status that – notoriously – they have had in England.

In one of the first studies to compare British and German engineers, Hutton and Lawrence (1981) argued that German engineers' higher prestige was shown by the fact that in Germany, unlike in Britain, students from better-off backgrounds were disproportionately likely to study engineering. Furthermore, German students with good results at the *Abitur* (the German school-leaving examination) were more likely to study engineering than were equivalent students in Britain. On both counts Ireland appears closer to the German than the British case. The Irish data on students' origins (derived from students' application forms for third-level places) shows that engineering is certainly no low-status occupation: the social background of students is roughly 'normal' for university students as a whole (Table 9.1). In addition, competition for university engineering places is intense, so that entry standards in engineering are higher than for all subjects apart from the professional degrees (veterinary medicine, medicine, law, dentistry and architecture) (Clancy 1988: 41).

However, the attractiveness of engineering appears to be part of a wider process of change within the Irish middle class. Engineering, like other obviously 'applied' university courses, seems to be particularly attractive to well-qualified students from rather less privileged backgrounds. In general, such students seem to be more adventurous in their subject choice than students from more established professional middle-class homes, being more likely to apply for new courses which are directly linked to specific job areas. In other words, as the middle class comes to include more professional jobs which involve technical expertise, so this is the area where its new recruits (in terms of social origins) are clustered. Thus, some of the courses with the highest entry level are those at the new technological university of Limerick, which has a less privileged student social profile than the older Dublin universities.

Such was the education that was expanded at the beginning of the 1980s, but the decision to do so was based on a very naive understanding of the demand and supply of qualified labour.

First the demand for engineers was based on the projections of employment in the Irish electronics industry made by the Industrial Development Authority. In retrospect these have turned out to be astonishingly optimistic. They predicted that by 1985 there would be approximately 30,000 employees in electronics, of whom 2,500 would be engineers (Killeen 1979: 15).

The reality has been rather different. Certainly, skill levels in the industry have been rising; 'professionals' (including engineers) comprised 5.5 per cent of the workforce in 1981, but 10.2 per cent in 1985; by 1985 engineers themselves amounted to 5.6 per cent of the workforce (Wickham 1988). None the less, this meant that the *total* number of engineers in the industry was only 900, less than half the number originally predicted. Such figures could only

Table 9.1 Social origins of engineering students, 1986

Socio-economic groups	Engineering students (%)	All students (%)
Farmers, etc.	19.7	18.6
Professional	29.3	28.2
Employers and managers	15.2	17.4
Salaried employees	7.7	8.1
Non-manual employees	15.8	16.4
Manual workers	12.4	11.4
Total	100.1	100.1

Source: Calculated from Clancy (1988)

have been produced by assuming that (1) aggregate employment in electronics would rise at a similar rate to that already experienced in the USA; and (2) the skill structure of the workforce would be similar to that of the US industry. In other words, it was assumed that the Irish industry, although based on the 'branch plants' of multinational corporations (MNCs), would resemble the electronics industry in Silicon Valley!

Second, the projections blithely treated the Irish labour market as existing in splendid isolation from the rest of the world. This might seem a bizarre achievement, given the importance of emigration in Irish experience, although the excuse can be made that during the 1970s the country had the novelty of net immigration. However, more recent research has shown how even during the 1970s substantial numbers of people were leaving the country (National Economic and Social Council [NESC] 1991) Equally, there has always been a substantial middle-class element of emigration from Ireland: emigration has been a career option for Irish graduates in a way that would be unthinkable in England (Lynn 1968; Hanlon 1991).

Through most of the 1980s the Irish economy stagnated: unemployment reached 20 per cent of the labour force, while those in employment saw virtually no increase in their disposable income, not least because of high levels of personal taxation. Meanwhile in Britain, still Ireland's major emigration destination, real incomes were increasing, in particular above-average ones. Thus, according to the NESC, between 1980 and 1988 the differential in net real wages between Britain and Ireland rose from 11 per cent in 1980 to 41 per cent in 1988 for those on average earnings, and from 16 per cent to fully 86 per cent for those with earnings one and half times above the average (NESC 1991). For graduates with an internationally marketable qualification, emigration therefore became increasingly attractive. As Table 9.2 shows, electronics engineers were a classic example: of all the electronics engineering students who graduated in 1987, nine months later nearly half had left the country.

In this respect, Ireland's first attempt at 'manpower planning' in engineering appears to have been a complete disaster. Indeed, turning from the mere numbers of engineers produced to the work that they actually did reveals a further deficiency in the planning. There seems to have been no attempt made to find out what engineers were needed to do, or more precisely, how the engineers' education and engineers' work would be related. Thus, the closest two conferences held on the theme of 'Engineering Manpower and Economic Development' came to defining the work of graduate engineers in industry was to cite a UNESCO definition of the professional engineer (O'Donnell 1980).

The rest of this chapter therefore changes focus and examines the work of Irish electronics engineers in manufacturing industry.

ELECTRONICS ENGINEERS AT WORK

By the beginning of the 1980s decisions about Irish engineering education had been made which would ensure a substantial growth in the number of graduate electronics engineers. But what work awaited such young engineers in industry? This section of the chapter looks at the structure of the Irish electronics industry as it developed in the 1980s and how this shaped the sort of work carried out by electronics engineers.

The data used in this and the subsequent section derive mainly from two surveys carried out by the author in 1985–6 as part of the Irish National Board for Science and Technology's study of the manpower needs of the industry (for summary see Eolas 1989). For the 'industry survey', all 186 firms operating in the industry in 1985 were asked to complete a questionnaire, 144 firms replied, and these firms were estimated to employ 81 per cent of the industry's labour force. This survey provided data on firms' use of engineers from two angles. First, it looked at engineering as an occupation by asking firms to break down their workforce into occupational

Table 9.2 Graduate emigration rates, 1984–9

Percentage in employment abroad nine months after graduation

Year	All graduates	Electronics engineering
1984	11	27
1985	13	40
1986	17	36
1987	23	43
1988	23	32
1989	21	43

Source: HEA, *First Destination* . . . (relevant years)

categories, one of which was 'engineer'. Second, it looked at engineering as a qualification by asking firms to report the main functional area occupied by each individual with an engineering degree.

In a second stage of the research a stratified sample of twenty firms was selected for the 'engineers survey'. In each of these firms semi-structured interviews were held with senior management and questionnaire-based interviews with a sample of technicians and engineers. The latter also completed a 'task sheet' in which they described in their own words the main features of their job (for details of the research methodology see Wickham 1989).

In 1985 the Irish electronics industry consisted overwhelmingly of subsidiaries of international (largely US) companies. In total about a third of the industry's workforce was in the computer sector, which was dominated by the assembly plants of US minicomputer manufacturers DEC in Galway and Wang in Limerick. As Table 9.3 shows, MNC plants accounted for 93 per cent of total employment in the computer sector.

Irish-owned companies were (and are) much smaller in average employment, and include many specialist firms in niche markets, in particular in the instruments sector. In addition, there are a growing number of Irish-owned firms carrying out sub-supply for the large MNCs.

Although the MNC firms started as assembly plants, they cannot be stereotyped as 'screwdriver plants' carrying out only semi-skilled operations. Through the 1980s firms bolted on other functions such as product documentation, customer service, marketing and warehousing to their existing assembly operation, so that a facility

Table 9.3 Irish electronics industry employment by sector and ownership, 1985

Sector	Irish	Foreign	Total
Computers and related	363	5,074	5,437
Components	419	4,422	4,841
Consumer products	315	1,335	1,650
Instruments, etc.	255	1,787	2,042
Telecommunications	270	1,853	2,123
Total	1,622	14,471	16,093

Source: Eolas (1989), based on industry survey

devoted purely to manufacturing is now a rarity. The IDA believed that such qualitative expansion was desirable because it 'deepened' the company's involvement in the Irish economy, making closure less likely, while also ensuring that more skilled jobs were created. Research and development (R & D) were seen as particularly important for both these reasons.

All such additional activities tend to require engineers, but as we shall now see, the main work of engineers in the industry is in the production process itself. Even a plant carrying out only the simplest assembly operation requires extensive testing and quality control; as the production process becomes more automated (for example, the move to surface-mount technology), so production engineering becomes more important. Finally, the Irish electronics industry in general and the computer sector in particular involve mainly batch production processes, which tend to require relatively more engineers than does mass production.

The industry survey shows how the proportion of engineers in the factory workforces varies between firms. As would be expected, engineers are particularly important where the firm is carrying out product innovation. Table 9.4 reports engineers as a percentage of the workforce of different groups of firms. Thus in firms carrying out no product innovation, engineers are only 4.8 per cent of the workforce, compared to 7.1 per cent of the workforce of all firms with product innovation.

Table 9.4 Engineers and innovation: engineers as percentage of total employment, by industry sector and product innovation

Sector	Product innovation No (%)	Yes (%)	Total (%)	(N of engineers)
Computers	7.2	11.4	8.3	(358)
Components	2.3	5.4	3.3	(131)
Consumer	2.7	3.1	2.9	(45)
Instruments	6.9	9.9	8.2	(31)
Telecommunications	2.4	5.6	4.0	(70)
ALL	4.8	7.1	5.6	(635)

Source: Industry survey

Note: Cells give the number of engineers employed in the relevant group of firms expressed as a percentage of total employment in the same firms.

The importance of the industry's production process as a determinant of the relative number of engineers is suggested by the clear differences between the sectors for firms that do not carry out any product innovation. Engineers comprise 7.2 per cent of the workforce of such firms in the computer sector, but only 2.3 per cent for equivalent firms in the component sector. This can be explained by the fact that computers involve batch production, while components are more a mass-production sector. Consequently engineering work is disproportionately important in the computer sector. Here engineers make up 8.3 per cent of the total workforce, while at the other extreme in the consumer products sector engineers only comprise 2.9 per cent of all employees. In fact, in 1985 the computer sector employed 32.8 per cent of the industry's workforce, but fully 48.7 per cent of its engineers.

The actual work of these engineers can also be examined by looking at where qualified engineers work. In the industry survey firms reported the task areas of the 842 qualified engineers they employed (this number naturally differs from the 735 individuals carrying out an engineering occupation). Table 9.5 aggregates these into five main functions. It shows how of all qualified engineers, by far the largest number (44.3 per cent of the total) worked in manufacturing, whereas 'information support' (which includes R & D activities) occupies only 25.1 per cent.

However, the clearest evidence of the importance of manufacturing comes from the engineers survey. Here 'engineer' is defined by occupation rather than qualification. Table 9.6 shows that of the

Table 9.5 Qualified engineers' function

	(%)
Management	19.1
Administration	6.1
Manufacturing	44.3
Information support	25.1
Customer support	3.5
N/a	1.9
Total	100.0
(N)	*(842)*

Source: Industry survey

total sample of 116 engineers, 53 per cent defined themselves as working in production, as against only 24 per cent in R & D. The engineers' own descriptions of their work reveal the wide range of activities covered by the rubric 'production'. This variety can by understood in terms of two dimensions: the time horizon of the tasks and the extent to which they involve contact with people outside the firm.

At one extreme on both dimensions lies the work of test engineers, testing the assembled printed circuit boards and the whole computer system as they are manufactured. In one plant assembling mainframe computers, almost all the engineers were 'test engineers' and their work was similar to that of test technicians in other plants. One young engineer gave this description of his main work:

> I perform diagnostic testing on our company's computer products. This means that I have to 'run' a program in the computer and ensure that it has worked OK. If not, I have to find out why . . . have to find and replace the faulty part, if any, or find out why a test program would fail.

However, such cases were very much an extreme. Even in this case, the engineer spent some of his time on less routine work: 'I have to perform a number of other duties broadly termed "projects". This involves ensuring that test equipment is correctly maintained, the test floor is tidy, etc.'

In the component sector, where production is essentially process production, engineers' main work involves monitoring the

Table 9.6 Engineers' location

	(%)
Production	52.6
Marketing	2.6
Management services	11.2
R & D	24.1
Other	9.5
Total	100.0
(N)	*(116)*

Source: Engineers survey

reliability of the equipment. Thus an engineer in one high-volume component plant reported his main work as 'monitoring the results obtained from process check, i.e. recording operating parameters of machines to ensure that they are functioning within spec.'. In this case too, process innovation was involved. The engineer described one of his tasks as 'computer programming – developing software to automate monitoring of results'.

This engineer defined his functional area not as 'production' but as 'management services'. In this he was not unusual: those engineers whose work involved maintaining, monitoring and improving the production process allocated themselves randomly to 'production' or 'management services'. Since the task sheets of virtually all those defining themselves as in 'management services' show them to be closely involved in the manufacturing process, the differentiation between management services and production is an artifact of the questionnaire: of the engineers in the sample, at least 60 per cent should therefore be considered as working in production.

In other computer assembly plants it was the majority of technicians who worked in the test area. Engineers by contrast were involved in a wide range of production-related functions. Nearly all were involved in some medium-term planning – preparing changes in the existing production process and preparing for the production of new products. Furthermore, such engineers were likely to have quite extensive contacts outside the plant, whether with suppliers, customers or colleagues in other plants of the same MNC. Thus one described one of his tasks as 'resolution of current production problems with the suppliers', while another gave his main task as 'co-ordinate activities of, "working group" of CAD/CAM engineers from all [Firm X] plants in Europe'.

The task sheets for those who defined themselves as working in R & D do show them as doing rather different work. Unlike other engineers, these describe their work – usually their main task – as involving 'design'. For example: 'At this stage in the project I am involved in, most of my time is spent in simulating the chip I designed.' Engineers' work in R & D appears rather less likely to involve contact outside the plant than does that of their colleagues in production. More importantly, the extent to which this work involves product design suggests how far the Irish electronics industry has moved from simply a collection of assembly plants. However, such R & D is in no sense basic research and its extent cannot detract from the single basic fact: most engineers work in production and production-related areas. The next section of the chapter shows how this effects engineers' careers and the use they make of their education.

THE USES OF PRACTICAL EDUCATION

Engineering education has been expanded in Ireland because it was believed to be 'useful' education, needed for the growth of the electronics industry. Yet such terms are rather vague. This section of the chapter therefore examines how young graduate engineers evaluated their qualification in the workplace.

First it is necessary to consider the different ways in which an educational qualification can be 'useful'. Sociologists have long made the distinction between the use of a qualification as an entry ticket *to* a job and the actual use that is made of a qualification *in* a job. This distinction is at the basis of arguments of 'qualification inflation' (Dore 1976). However, studies of labour market segmentation also stress that some groups of jobs form relatively distinct markets with few entry ports. In other words, some jobs are only open to occupants from a determinate range of other jobs. From this perspective, an educational qualification can also be useful in that it allows its holder initial access into a labour market: once through the entry port, the holder then may use other 'qualifications' to acquire subsequent jobs.

These arguments clearly apply to engineering work in the Irish electronics industry. The distinction made earlier between engineer as occupation and engineer as qualification already suggested that not all engineers have an engineering qualification. This turns out to be the case: of the total 116 engineers in the engineers survey sample, about a fifth had no degree qualification at all (Table 9.7). These engineers tended to be older than the engineering graduates (mean age of 28.9 as against 27.1), to have worked in a larger number of companies and to have worked as a technician before reaching an engineer's post. As Table 9.7 also shows, such engineers work almost entirely in the production area. In their case a formal engineering qualification was clearly not necessary to do their work.

An educational qualification can also be useful in another way unrelated to the actual content of the job. The friends and contacts a student makes at college may well turn out to be useful in their subsequent career. Quite apart from all the intangibles of national culture, the small size of the Irish labour market makes 'who you know' important in any specialist area – and electronics is no exception.

During the 1980s college departments were encouraged to build closer links with the industry. This makes personal contacts more important for young engineers' careers. As undergraduate and postgraduate students share their department's industry contacts during their studies (through vacation jobs, work experience schemes, student projects), so these increasingly shape an individual's career possibilities. Such 'networking' gives the 'old boy network' (the use of the male gender is deliberate) a new lease of life.

Even when we turn to the technical core of the work itself, a qualification can be used in three different ways. It can provide a detailed knowledge which is applied directly (knowledge of particular products, components, etc.); it can provide a general knowledge which is a background resource (more theoretical knowledge of the fundamental principles involved); it can provide a problem-solving methodology. Clearly, in different jobs (and even at different times within the same job) one or other of these dimensions will predominate.

Table 9.7 Engineers and qualification by functional area (percentages by row)

Most recent qualification	Production (%)	R & D (%)	Other (%)	Total (N)
B.Sc. Engineering (electrical/electronics)	54.2	25.0	20.8	(48)
Other B.Sc. (engineering/science)	70.6	17.6	11.8	(17)
Postgraduate M.Sc./Ph.D. (electronics/computing)	18.2	72.7	9.1	(11)
Postgraduate diploma (engineering/management)	76.9	15.4	7.7	(13)
No primary degree (technician qualification)	96.0	4.0	0	(25)
No information	0	100.0	0	(2)
Total	63.8	24.1	12.1	(116)

Source: Engineers survey

Researching the usefulness of qualifications involved operationalizing these considerations. In the interviews the engineers were asked to evaluate their qualifications on six different dimensions. Two dimensions are concerned with the qualification as entry qualification – to the first job and to the current job; three are the different ways in which the qualification can contribute to the technical work task; one concerns the qualification as a career resource. For each dimension respondents were asked whether they considered their qualification 'very important', 'important', 'desirable', 'not important' or 'irrelevant'. The responses are reported either as the percentage ranking a particular aspect 'very important' or as the mean score for that dimension when the responses are scored from 5 (very important) to 1 (irrelevant).

Table 9.8 focuses on those engineers who both were under 30 and had a degree in electrical/electronic engineering, i.e. those for whom their qualification should have been most directly relevant to their current work. It shows that such engineers do indeed see their degree to have been more important as an entry ticket to a particular labour market than for actually carrying out their work. When asked about their degree 'as a qualification for applying for my first post in the electronics industry', 70 per cent rated it 'very important' (mean 4.6). As a qualification for applying for their current post the proportion fell to 58 per cent (mean 4.4). In terms of its relevance to the actual work, the proportion fell further still: to 16 per cent for detailed knowledge (mean 3.6), to 33 per cent for background knowledge (mean 4.0) and to 21 per cent (mean 3.6) for general approach. Finally, while only one individual went so far as to consider his degree 'very important' as a route to useful social contacts, the mean score of 2.6 shows that this dimension had some reality for most of the sample.

For these engineers, therefore, their education is *primarily* an entrance qualification to their work. While very few considered it actually irrelevant in the task itself, nearly all felt it was of less importance here. Clearly, the relevance of the degree to the job's task content is related to the functional area in which the engineer works. A conventional degree appears least directly relevant in production. In the computer sector many engineers are working as test engineers, and this tends to require knowledge very specific to the particular product. By contrast, where production is more mass production, engineers tend to be working as production engineers, and this requires a mix of highly 'practical' skills. In the words of one manager:

> The people involved in line jobs of its [sic] very nature tend to be more practical on a day to day thing and have to integrate with a hell of a lot of people on a minute-to-minute basis. You know, production operators, production supervisors, finance, anywhere, so they have to be very adaptable, whereas the design people can be much more product focused, specialist focused.

Thus Table 9.8 also shows that R & D, presumably the most technical area, is where an engineering qualification is more directly used in work itself. While only one of the graduates working in production found his qualification 'very important' for providing detailed knowledge in the work (mean 3.3), this was the case for 50 per cent of those working in R & D (mean 4.2).

The extent to which the qualification can be irrelevant is confirmed when we look at how this group of graduate engineers evaluated their degree as a whole. Asked 'In general are you able to use most of what you have learnt [in your degree] in your current job?' only 14 per cent felt able to answer positively. Once again, perceived usefulness was concentrated among those working in the R & D area; yet even here the majority felt that their qualification was not of general use. Certainly, most engineering graduates

Table 9.8 The relevance of degree qualification by functional location (engineers with B.Sc. Electronics Engineering only)

	Functional location			
	Production	R & D	Other	All
Percentage considering qualification 'very important' for:				
Entry to industry	72	80	80	70
Entry to current post	52	90	38	58
Detailed knowledge	4	50	13	16
Background knowledge	16	70	38	33
General approach	20	30	13	21
Personal contacts	0	0	13	2
Total (N)	(25)	(10)	(8)	(43)

Source: Engineers survey

claimed that they had not expected to use their education in work. However, it is noticeable that, of those who had expected to do so, the majority were disappointed.

All young engineering graduates felt that lack of 'practical experience' was the main deficiency of their education. Thus there was little demand for formal business skills, with the exception of personnel issues, but they felt strongly that they lacked an awareness of the demands of business for engineering, and, in the technical area, that they lacked practical experience of using equipment. Correspondingly, these were the areas where engineers felt they had gained knowledge and experience on the job. In particular, those working in production tended to feel that their most important gain had been in personnel and supervisory skills. Once again, young engineers in R & D had a rather different perspective, being more likely to suggest that their education was deficient in specific areas of technical knowledge.

In taking this attitude the engineers were very much concurring with the views of their managers. In the management interviews managers showed little interest in particular weaknesses of education. For them, the overall academic quality of Irish engineering education was if anything too high, since it tended to orient students towards research issues rather than production. As one said:

> It's less true now than it used to be, but engineers tend to want to become research and development people. And technicians likewise. They all have this idea that design and development is the perfect job and actual production involvement is not their first choice.

Indeed, 'technical' deficiencies tended to be seen in terms of over-specialization: a few managers felt students needed to study analogue as well as digital electronics, others that more mechanical as well as electronic engineering would have been desirable; still others bemoaned engineers' lack of software skills. What unites these disparate comments is that managers felt engineering graduates lacked much of the knowledge required to work in the production area of an electronics factory.

Such criticisms were relatively reticent. By contrast, managers vociferously criticized Irish engineering education as 'impractical'. Like the engineers themselves, they saw this as involving two aspects. First, students were seen to lack *practical* engineering skills, a view epitomized by the manager who found university students weak because 'they have never held a soldering-iron'. Second, students were felt to lack 'business sense'. Managers did not expect engineering students to have a knowledge of accountancy, but they did frequently criticize students for lacking any sense of the time and cost constraints of a commercial environment. Interestingly, unlike the engineers themselves, managers commented rarely on the lack of personnel and supervisory skills transmitted by education. For them such skills could be acquired by experience and were not particularly important. By contrast, the engineers, with their daily involvement in this area, were less likely to see such skills as the prerogative of management proper.

Engineering education has been developed in Ireland in order to service the needs of manufacturing industry. Graduate engineers have been most likely to gain jobs in the production area, yet to them their education appears particularly 'impractical'. Engineering education turns out not to be self-evidently useful at all.

CAREERS IN ELECTRONICS: UP AND OUT?

Engineers' work and careers are shaped by the organizational context of the firm and the wider labour market. This section of the chapter shows how the career opportunities for engineers are limited by the truncated labour market of the Irish electronics industry – and how individual engineers respond to this situation.

Overwhelmingly Irish electronics engineers work in foreign-owned companies. In virtually all such companies all senior posts are, as a matter of policy, filled by Irish nationals, so foreign ownership does not of itself place any limit on internal promotion. Furthermore, foreign (effectively US) ownership provides some limited scope for movement to the company's operations in other countries, and contacts with the company's US operations are one way that Irish engineers gain information on openings abroad.

The few Japanese firms in Ireland are rather different. These companies have a small layer of senior management which is entirely Japanese, so that there is a clear limit on the internal promotion that their Irish engineers can expect. Although Irish employees visit Japan, permanent jobs in Japan remain completely closed to them.

Far more important than the nationality of job holders is in fact the structure of employment within the firm. The Irish plant is a small part of an international organization, and as such even its senior management rank relatively low within the corporate hierarchy. Furthermore, the plant is *primarily* a production plant: the existence of the additional functions mentioned earlier cannot detract from the fact that most jobs for engineers are in production, with few high-level technical positions. Electronics engineers are compelled to take on managerial roles very early, since promotion within the Irish plant will very quickly be promotion out of engineering. Since virtually all Irish plants are managed by engineers, the Irish electronics industry does offer a career *for engineers*, while at the same time it provides few opportunities for a career *in engineering*.

For the engineer working for an Irish-owned company the situation is equally restrictive. A growing number of Irish-owned companies exist in the industry. Such companies cannot or do not match the salary offered by the MNCs: in 1986 in the sample the mean engineers' salary was IR £11,700 in Irish-owned companies, as against IR £15,700 in MNCs; this differential held within all age and qualification categories. The only effective 'promotion' route within the company is the hope that the company will grow, and with it the rewards of its engineers. However, the experience of the 1980s has punctured the heady dreams of the beginning of the decade: a 'successful' firm employs at most a few hundred employees. And that provides very few extra jobs for engineers.

Most engineers enter this structure as engineers. The 'usual' engineer is young, male and has recently finished full-time third-level education: 74 per cent of the sample had ended their full-time education with a B.Sc. or postgraduate qualification; just over 90 per cent were men. These are the engineers as understood by the manpower planners: entering industry immediately after they have been 'produced' in third-level institutions with their relevant qualification.

To a much greater extent therefore than in many other countries, in Ireland engineering as an occupation is entered immediately on completion of full-time education at university. There is, however, another route. With a high profile as 'good modern employers', firms in the electronics industry attempt to provide internal promotion as a reward for loyalty and commitment. Accordingly, the remaining quarter of the sample had been promoted into an engineering job by their current or by their previous employer. Many of these 'promoted' engineers had started work as technicians and most had worked as a technician at some stage in their career. Usually too they had gained a further qualification, in some cases a degree, by part-time study. Such individuals are more likely to come from manual working-class backgrounds and, less obviously perhaps, include virtually no women (only one of the eleven women engineers in the sample was 'promoted' in this way). Earlier research on women in the Irish electronics industry (Wickham and Murray 1987) has shown that such internal promotion has been strongly sex-tracked, with women who do come forward for promotion being channelled away from the technical area.

Given this context and these routes, what makes for a successful career in engineering within the industry? One answer is to take the fifty-four engineers aged between 25 and 30 in the sample and isolate the top 25 per cent in terms of salary. It turns out that this upper quartile of 'achievers' do differ from those engineers of the same age with lower salaries: almost all have degrees and all work for multinational companies; they are less likely to work in the production area, are more likely to report themselves as having management than technical positions and are more likely to define themselves as managers rather than engineers. Even by age 30 therefore, success is being defined as taking on managerial (and to some extent *non*-technical) roles. Interestingly, women are disproportionately likely to be included in this top quartile of earners, though there is a suggestion in the data that this has involved choices which their male colleagues have not had to make: *none* of the women engineers in the sample had children, unlike 25 per cent of their male colleagues of the same age group.

Many engineers feel frustrated by the limited technical demands of their work. The survey asked respondents to rate six different dimensions of their current job on a five-point scale (from 'very bad' to 'very good'). As Table 9.9 shows, only a minority were prepared to rate their current job as 'very good' in terms of being technically challenging. At the same time, when asked what they would consider to be the most important of these dimensions when choosing a future job, 'technically demanding work' was by far the most popular choice. Most engineers want technically demanding work, and feel they are not getting it. There are two exceptions. On the one hand those currently working in R & D are more likely to feel their current work is technically satisfying, and on the other hand the achievers are less interested in technical work: for them 'high responsibility' comes far ahead of technical challenge as a criterion for choosing a future job. Most engineers, however, remain committed to the technical side of their work. While a quarter of the sample expected to be promoted to a management position within the next three years, fully 20 per cent claimed they would reject promotion if it led them away from technical work. For many engineers their work involves little technical challenge, and they resent the fact that promotion will take them away from what little technical work there is. In the words of one of them:

> Looking at the guys on the floor out there, who've had the opportunity to move into supervision, they haven't chosen that, because they would rather stay technical. The problem with a lot of companies here is that you can't go much further. Once you get [to be] in charge of a few engineers, there is nowhere else to go technically.

Interestingly, such attitudes of commitment to engineering itself are particularly pronounced among young engineers with an engineering degree.

In such circumstances a small minority (7 per cent) of engineers envisaged setting up their own business within the next few years, and a much larger minority (44 per cent) were considering emigrating. Overall a quarter of the sample reported already having taken practical steps towards emigrating (e.g. inquiring

Table 9.9 Engineers' evaluation of current job

	R & D	Functional location Production	Other	All
Percentage considering currentjob 'very good' for:				
Technical challenge	42.9	24.6	18.5	27.6
Secure employment	32.1	24.6	33.3	28.4
Promotion prospects	7.1	6.6	11.1	7.8
Salary	7.1	16.4	29.6	17.2
Fellow workers	39.3	36.1	25.9	34.5
Responsibility	10.7	15.0	22.2	15.7
Total (*N*)	(28)	(61)	(27)	(116)

Source: Engineers survey

about jobs and visas), and this was the case for fully 32 per cent of those under 25. Perhaps surprisingly, emigration plans are not directly linked to the level of frustration with the current job. At its simplest, those considering emigration were likely to be better paid than those who were not, even when age is held constant. Within the production area, fully 56 per cent of engineers under 30 were considering emigration, as against 37 per cent of those in R & D. However, within R & D those who were more satisfied with the work tended to be more likely to be considering emigration, whereas in the production area the relationship was, if anything, the other way round.

Technically demanding work is crucial for young engineers' careers because to have worked in a technically advanced firm at the leading edge of technology is itself a passport to the international labour market. On the international labour market, it is the experience of technically demanding work which provides the young engineer with access to other interesting – and well-paid – jobs. Hence in R & D those who felt their current job was technically demanding clearly felt in a strong position on the international labour market – and were ready to take advantage of it. By contrast, in the production area, those who were dissatisfied with the technical level of their work wanted to get out – before it was too late. In the words of one of them: 'I'm not going to stay. I'll stay for a while, but my ultimate aim would be someplace like California. There are more opportunities there. I think anyone that's driven technically enough, that should be their ultimate goal.'

CONCLUSION

During the 1980s it became commonplace for Irish engineering graduates to be recruited by firms in Europe or even before graduation: the much heralded Euro-graduate, educated for a European labour professional labour market, is already a reality in Ireland. Such 'milk-round' recruitment is, however, only part of the story. This chapter has shown how the relationship between engineering education and the structure of the labour market has built emigration into the very culture of high-technology industry in Ireland.

Paradoxically, the over-production of over-educated engineers suits almost all the stakeholders involved. Educational institutions benefit, gaining government funds for expansion for apparently 'relevant' education, while the focus on research ensures that academic careers can be oriented to the prestigious centres of knowledge abroad. Firms benefit, because the ready supply of young recruits ensures that salaries can be kept relatively low, and, even more important, those who leave because they are frustrated by the limited opportunities can easily be replaced. The government benefits, since the over-supply of engineers becomes one factor attracting further mobile investment into the country.

Indeed, the wheel has now turned full circle. Originally more engineering graduates were produced because existing firms needed more technically qualified labour; now a policy objective has become to create jobs for these same graduates. Thus, when the US electronics giant Intel announces it is setting up a plant in Ireland, this is celebrated because it will provide jobs . . . for the engineers who have emigrated. Equally, colleges are lauded for setting up research-oriented campus companies to keep engineers at home who would otherwise emigrate, since, in the words of one entrepreneur professor, 'Manufacturing usually only offers a couple of exciting jobs, and the rest are fairly mundane' (Industrial Development Authority 1991:6). Given such attitudes, it is hardly surprising that engineering education has become education for emigration.

Chapter 10

British engineers in context

Gloria L. Lee and Chris Smith

This book has set out to review some of the available evidence on the position of engineers in Britain in the decade after the Finniston report and to draw comparisons with the situation of the profession in other parts of the world.

The 1980s have been a period of rapid change for British industry. The recession which began in the late 1970s resulted in a decline in the size of the manufacturing base of the country, and a period of economic recovery has been followed by further recession by the end of the decade.

Commenting on the period between 1979 and last quarter of 1988, Coutts and Godley examine a series of key indicators of economic performance. They conclude that Britain's economic growth has been similar to that of the main European countries, but that in that time the country's balance of payments has deteriorated rapidly. Also, although there have been improvements in productivity in the UK during this period, these were mainly confined to manufacturing, where there was no associated improvement in performance, whether measured by output growth or by ability to compete in world markets, including Britain's own domestic market (Coutts and Godley 1989: 150). Further, business growth in the 1980s has still left Britain with productivity levels below those of the more advanced countries in Europe (Bannock 1990). All this has taken place in the context of a government committed to a market ideology and deregulation, which have had particular implications for various professions (Lee 1991a).

This period of change has been accompanied by growth in the application of information technology and a growing recognition of the need for organizational restructuring to regain competitive advantage and to facilitate the potential benefits from investments in IT.

There have been other changes which influence management generally and engineering in particular. These include movements to reform management education and development and to create a more unified voice for the engineering profession through the establishment of the Engineering Council. These changes in Britain have occurred against a backdrop of external environmental changes, including increasing globalization of economic activities, major political changes in eastern Europe and moves towards the completion of a Single Market in Europe in 1992.

This chapter will start by overviewing some of the debates raised in this book and elsewhere concerning the role of engineers in the context of manufacturing and the relationship with management thinking and practice during the 1980s. Inferences will then be drawn from the accounts of engineering in different countries, which provide a context in which to discuss possible ways forward for engineering in Britain.

THE CASE OF ENGINEERS AND MANUFACTURING

The Finniston report started from the premise that the future of both the engineering profession and manufacturing industry are closely intertwined. While acknowledging that improvements in manufacturing performance would not be achieved solely through changes regarding engineers and engineering, nevertheless it was claimed that 'There are few – if any – areas of manufacturing where the competitiveness of a company's products and processes does not depend upon its corporate engineering capabilities' (Finniston 1980: 21).

The report mounted a case for the importance of manufacturing to Britain's prosperity and hence to the welfare and living standards of its people. The point was made that by the late 1970s 30 per cent of gross domestic product and 32 per cent of employment were in manufacturing. Also, manufacturing contributed 66 per cent of the export of goods and services at that time (Finniston 1980: 7–8).

A decade later manufacturing was accounting for less than a quarter of GDP and was employing little more than a fifth of the workforce, although, due to the fall in the value of oil exports, manufacturing accounted for 80 per cent of exports in Britain (Wood 1991a). Therefore, in the global context, the comparative importance of manufacturing and hence engineers has increased in Britain.

Against such a background, this book takes forward the case for the continuing importance of both engineers and manufacturing. In Chapter 2, Glover reinterprets the arguments for engineering and manufacturing, by mounting a powerful critique of the post-industrial society thesis and 1980s thinking about organizational culture and its focus upon human resource management.

He challenges the view of work in manufacturing as more dehumanizing than that in the service sector and the association of an information society with that of post-industrialism. He argues that, in English-speaking countries like Britain and America, people have been educated to 'avoid rather than to prioritize and run manufacturing and related activities'. This leads to the higher status accorded financial capitalism over industrial capitalism. Yet in many ways the barriers between 'manufacture' and 'services' are increasingly artificial, as computer technology penetrates both spheres.

This has interesting implications because the growth of information technology provides a particular paradox for engineers, in that their work has been central to both the radical product innovations and the subsequent development of both hardware and software. Thus engineers have had a pivotal role in the process of technological change as developers of systems, as well as end-users. More senior engineers are particularly well placed to make explicit the choices to be made when implementing such technologies. IT provides opportunities for skills enhancement and improvements in autonomy and the quality of working life or for deskilling and further routinization of work (Lee 1988).

Nevertheless various studies of the implementation of CAD/CAM systems, for instance, suggest that there is little empirical evidence to support earlier assumptions about the deskilling potential of such technologies (McLoughlin 1989; Lee 1991b). However, whether this suggests that engineers with influence within management hierarchies have successfully argued in favour of upskilling as a management strategy, rather than exploiting the potential of the technology for increased management control, is debatable. It may be that command over the knowledge base of this far-reaching technological innovation has given engineers a greater sense of their own authority to argue for a more human-centred approach to implementation. Alternatively or concomitantly, it could be that managers have recognized the cost of some of the earlier attempts to push through such changes in ways contrary to the wishes and needs of their workforce (Lee 1989). Job losses during the early 1980s and reductions in union membership and the power of organized labour have been part of the changing manufacturing scene during which increased implementation of IT has taken place. Attempts by trade unions to introduce technology agreements have only rarely been successful (McLoughlin 1989). However, the very existence of such campaigns can help to ameliorate management actions in favour of greater consideration towards the perspectives of end-users. The perceived need by management for organizational restructuring to improve competitiveness can predispose management to avoid confrontation over issues such as IT, in order to foster a co-operative climate for organizational change. There is also a growing recognition that new forms of work organization are in any case required to facilitate the potential benefits from investments in IT.

What is clear is that, where IT has been implemented in process technologies, this has often been at the behest of engineers, who have successfully argued for such investments. Where radical innovations are being introduced, it is not always possible to meet the requirements for returns on investment which their accountancy colleagues would have wished to see. In discussing some of the findings from a nine-country study of the implementation of information technology in service sectors (Child and Loveridge 1990), Loveridge comments that normal accountancy bench-marks of cost/performance ratio and risk assessment were found to be relatively useless, other than as a means of convincing sponsors of such investments (Loveridge 1990: 342).

Notwithstanding the often expressed view of British engineers that their companies are controlled by accountants, it has been noted that post-audits on the results of these investments have not been the norm. For instance, in a study of British companies implementing CAD/CAM, Winch noted that only one company had attempted to measure the performance of their system against the criteria laid down in the initial financial justification (Winch 1989). In a study of the implementation of these technologies in British and Canadian companies it was also found that methods of evaluating the outcome of such investments were generally underdeveloped and not regularly or systematically undertaken in either country (Lee 1991b).

This all suggests that British engineers may indeed be finding that IT offers them new opportunities to assert their voice of authority and impose their rationality over those of their traditional rivals within manufacturing, the accountants.

THE INFLUENCE OF MANAGEMENT EDUCATION

In challenging a simplistic view of culture which has influenced much management thinking and writing during the 1980s, Glover in Chapter 2 argues that the notion of human resource management is the culmination of a liberal crusade against authoritarian management. While he commends the latter approach, he points to the need to recognize that organizations are cultures; i.e. culture is not something to be handed down by top management to the rest of the organization.

He sees the absorption in the problems of 'cultural' change in organizations as all too often involving 'quick fix' solutions instead of careful analysis of the technical and social division of labour which is an integral part of the institutional context of organizations. He blames much of the inadequacies which flow from this approach within management upon the case, which has been argued widely elsewhere, that the British educational system has prioritized the pursuit of knowledge for its own sake and that this has led to an arm's-length approach to manufacturing and top-heavy management structures.

Armstrong, in Chapter 3, takes a more detailed and specific look at the British management education movement (MEM) which emerged during the 1980s in the form of a lobby for major changes in the formation of managers. His main premise is that the importance of the 'engineering dimension', as spelled out in the Finniston report, has simply not been accepted by the MEM in Britain.

He sees the growth of the MEM as having major implications for engineers for two main reasons. First, as more business and management graduates appear on the labour market, they will provide engineers with additional competition for senior positions in management. Second, people with management education backgrounds will have inculcated the peculiarly British concept of *management* being distinct from *technical* expertise.

He cites the ways in which various writers on management separate out all technical activities, even though they may be performed by managers, in order to focus on a common core of activities which are presented as the *essential* elements of management, whatever the setting. In this way he argues that not only students of management but also providers of management education and management consultancy offer essentially the same package of abilities, which fail to take account of the actual processes which are to be managed. Thus the importance of operational expertise is ignored, as attention is given to the centrality of interpersonal roles within management activity.

Armstrong concludes by offering the other side of the coin to the arguments which, as he points out, he has himself made in the past, concerning the need for more management education to be incorporated into the engineering undergraduate curricula. Here he puts the case for inserting the missing 'engineering dimension' into current management education.

The Handy report (1987) and that by Constable and McCormick (1987), together with a number of earlier studies, all pointed to the neglect of management education and development in Britain compared with its industrial competitors. This has resulted in what was initially and in the main an industry-led and industry-funded movement to bring together employers, government and educators to reform management education and development to enhance the effectiveness of managers (G.L. Lee 1990).

While the university sector in particular among management educators has been somewhat reluctant to engage actively in this movement's approach to reforming and greatly extending the scope of management education, other providers have been more ready to work with what is now known as the Management Charter Initiative (MCI). Their *Guidelines* for certificate- and for diploma-level qualifications stress the importance of competence-based, rather than the more traditional knowledge-based, forms of education; and one of the four key areas of activity is singled out as 'operations'.

'Managing operations' emphasizes improving services, products and systems with a special regard for quality and monitoring functions. The other areas distinguished in the *Guidelines* are 'managing finance' and 'managing information', but an even greater emphasis is apparently placed upon the fourth function, 'managing people', judging from the number of units devoted to this area of activity (MCI 1990).

With its insistence upon open access and output assessment,

together with the development of personal competences, if the adoption of the MCI approach does become widespread among providers of management education and development, then it would change the character of much current provision. However, there is nothing to suggest that the 'engineering dimension' would be any better integrated into management education and development than in the past.

What continues to be clear is that Britain still has a long way to go before the education and development of those entrusted with the tasks of management are in any way comparable with those in other industrialized societies. A recent study by Wood of the educational backgrounds of the main boards of directors of fifty-five of the UK's largest manufacturing companies confirmed the low level of educational qualifications in management, already detailed in the Handy report. Among directors in this study, 46 per cent had no degree or professional qualification. Of those with a degree or professional qualification, 15 per cent were accountants and 12 per cent engineers, which, as the author notes, is interesting, since all the companies were engaged in manufacturing. In the case of the chief executive officers (CEOs) of these companies, however, the balance between qualifications changed, as 16 per cent were qualified engineers, compared with 13 per cent qualified accountants and 7 per cent MBAs. Although no *causal* relationship should be attributed, in comparing the performance of companies, in terms of their profitability and the qualifications of their CEO, the researcher noted a statistically significant difference, in favour of those companies with CEOs who had qualifications. There was, however, no significant difference in performance between companies where the CEO was a qualified engineer and any of the other categories of qualification (Wood 1991b: 442-4).

With only small numbers involved in this study, it is not possible to draw any conclusions about trends in the abilities of engineers to rise through management hierarchies to the very top of industry. Yet it could be seen as portraying a slightly more hopeful scenario for the central role of engineers within top management than most previous writings on the topic, including the Handy report.

Scientific management principles and mass-production techniques have kept engineers very closely involved in day-to-day operational matters, and this did not provide engineers with a fast track into top management. However, the growth in the use of IT and the structural changes which have been taking place within manufacturing could be seen as pointers to a situation where engineers have new opportunities opening up to them.

Although Britain's manufacturing base may have become smaller relative to other forms of economic activity, it is still a major source of employment and a particularly important contributor towards export efforts. A number of manufacturing companies have made significant moves towards simplifying and streamlining their organizational structures. For instance, a study by the Fellowship of Engineering showed how in leading British manufacturing companies traditional interfaces between departments have been dismantled and the use of multi-disciplinary teams has been encouraged. In moving towards a more market-led approach, they are finding new ways to use highly qualified technical personnel in technical marketing and selling, as well as customer services. Most companies were now spending substantial sums on research and development programmes and between 1 and 3 per cent of turnover on education and training on a continuing basis (Fellowship of Engineering 1991). Companies of this sort clearly offer wider employment opportunities for engineers in more innovative settings, for traditional as well as newer spheres of activity. Whether there will be an adequate supply of appropriately educated and trained engineers to meet the demands of such organizations, however, remains an open question.

THE ENGINEERING COUNCIL AND THE PROFESSION

One of the other major events for engineering in the 1980s was the establishment of the Engineering Council, which received its Royal Charter in 1982, as a response to some of the recommendations of the Finniston report. The Finniston committee had recognized that the institutions' joint body, called the Council of Engineering Institutions, had failed to establish 'one voice and one ear' for a unified engineering profession and it lacked authority with industry. The report proposed the creation of a new body intended to reform the engineering profession and with it the engineering industry, in order to strengthen the manufacturing base of the economy.

The Finniston committee envisaged a statutory body, but after lengthy discussions between the Department of Industry, the engineering institutions, the employers and the universities to decide upon its composition and powers, instead a new chartered body was created. Commentators at the time noted the determination of the engineering institutions to try to prevent this body from taking over control of the registration of engineers and the accreditation of engineering courses (*Engineering Today* 1981).

The Engineering Council was created with a chairman and up to twenty-four members, two-thirds of whom have to be chartered engineers. However, it was specified from the outset that the sixteen chartered engineers did not hold their seats as representatives of their particular institutions but rather as individuals with a concern for engineering as a whole. The Engineering Council holds a listing of nominees from the engineering institutions, employers and educational organizations, from which the sixteen are drawn. The other eight seats are held by people with an interest in engineering but who are not chartered engineers. The latter group are drawn from nominations by a wide range of bodies, including trade unions, the Women's Engineering Society and the Fellowship of Engineering.

Its Royal Charter requires the Engineering Council to set standards for the engineering profession, to create awareness of engineering and technology, to secure the supply of the next generation of engineers and technicians and through these activities to encourage competitiveness in British industry. The Engineering Council describes itself as speaking for the engineering profession as a whole and has industry affiliates with which it meets regularly at various locations across the United Kingdom, to exchange views and factual information. This system is intended to help the Engineering Council to speak authoritatively to government, as well as providing a balance between the three key players in the demand for and the supply of qualified engineers, namely engineering interests in industry, the professional institutions and academia (Engineering Council 1989a).

One of the limitations of the influence of the Engineering Council is that it was set up as a chartered rather than a statutory body. Although this means that it can act independently of government, since the latter does not provide its funding, the price of such independence is a lack of real power to bring about change. The Engineering Council has to rely upon its ability to persuade and this is often difficult, even within the profession, which is fragmented into forty-seven different institutes. The inevitable rivalries between them have long bedevilled British engineering, leaving it much weaker than its counterparts in other countries.

In recent years there has been some attempt to tackle fragmentation, by a coming together of some institutes, but this is often the outcome of long and hard-fought battles, and not all negotiations have been successful. For instance, attempts to achieve a merger between the Institution of Mechanical Engineers and the Institution of Production Engineers fell through after lengthy discussions. More recently the Production Engineers changed their name to the Institution of Manufacturing Engineers and they have since merged with the Institution of Electrical Engineers. At the time of writing the proposed merger between the Electricals and the Mechanicals has been on the agenda, but there are serious reservations on both sides and negotiations are now withdrawn.

The inability of these two large institutions to find common cause suggests that a more radical approach is needed. One solution would be for registration and accreditation to become the sole responsibility of one body, instead of the current situation where it is in effect contracted out by the Engineering Council to the individual institutions. This would create a body with more authority to speak for engineering as a whole; but for the institutes to be ready to see such a transfer of power, and to concentrate upon their role as learned societies, would require new thinking and a very clear break with the traditions of the past.

Attempts to try to tackle the fragmentation of British engineering have been a long time in coming about. The contrast between such time-consuming and energy-diverting moves and the situation for instance in Canada is very marked. As discussed in Chapter 7, the strength of the Canadian system is that there is one professional association representing all types of engineers which operates federally, and through its provincial associations, to provide a powerful source of influence in society, industry and academia.

THE WORK OF THE ENGINEERING COUNCIL

Notwithstanding the difficulties facing the Engineering Council in its current form, it has worked steadily to influence the future of engineering in a number of ways, despite an often contrary tide of events. Most of its efforts are directed towards the wider task of improving the education and training of engineers, towards capturing the interests of schoolchildren, young people and adults in engineering as an exciting and rewarding activity, and towards helping to ensure that qualified engineers and technicians keep up to date throughout their working life through continuing education and training.

Unlike the engineering profession in many other countries, the Engineering Council has avoided distancing a professional elite from all other types of technical worker. Rather, it has built upon the British tradition of drawing together the varying interests of those engaged in engineering work, by representing within one organization those with different backgrounds and levels of qualification. It has established a register of qualified engineers and technicians, with the titles and designatory letters of chartered engineer (C.Eng.), incorporated engineer (I.Eng.) and engineering technician (Eng.Tech.). Each of these qualifications is obtained in three stages which represent the required academic, training and experience standards, and the titles may only be used at the third stage. This hierarchy is seen as providing the range of qualified personnel required by employers, but the latter have often been slow to distinguish clearly their needs in terms of these designations.

In many respects the 1980s have been far from a propitious decade in which to undertake the work of securing the supply of the next generation of engineers. The vicissitudes of the economy have made manufacturing industry less attractive as an employment environment; and, partly as a consequence, engineering and technology have declined significantly in popularity with those going into higher education, with a fall from 13 per cent of applicants to higher education choosing engineering or technology in 1982 down to 8 per cent of applicants by 1990 (Universities Central Council on Admissions 1983, 1991).

Even some of the changes in the content of undergraduate engineering education, brought about as a result of the Finniston report, have proved to be something of a mixed blessing. The aim, admirable in itself, was to strengthen the 'engineering applications' elements in courses, in order to produce engineers with a more appropriate background and preparation for going into industry. As a result of implementing these changes, however, engineering courses became very crowded in content, which had the unfortunate and totally unintended effect of reinforcing their lack of attractiveness to students.

Concern over declining applications for engineering higher education and unfilled places have led to calls for changes in the structure and content of engineering education in Britain to improve its popularity. A need is seen to broaden undergraduate engineering into a more general engineering approach to start with, to be followed by later specialization. There is also recognition of the need to find new ways to tap a wider pool of applicants to the profession (Engineering Council 1990).

BROADENING ENGINEERING EDUCATION AND THE EUROPEAN DIMENSION

In the 1990s various events have been taking place which have important implications for the future of British engineering. The completion of the Single Market in Europe and the opening up of eastern Europe to a market economy call for a broadening of engineering education in Britain which has to be considered in relation to engineering formation here and in mainland Europe.

The Single Market programme, to reach fruition in 1993, is widely recognized as bringing fundamental changes in the economic environment. As part of this programme, action has been taken on professional qualifications, as a free market is seen as inhibited if member states insist on qualifications gained within their own state. In 1985 the European Commission announced a new approach through a general directive on the mutual recognition of professional qualifications throughout the Community. The main features are that it is a general directive applying to any regulated profession involving at least three years of higher education. It is based on mutual recognition of qualifications leading to membership of the profession in the receiving state. The consequence is to sweep away many of the remaining barriers to the free movement of professionals (Adler 1989).

Although this directive still has various implications for the engineering profession, in practice the movement to get recognition of European engineering titles across Europe dates back to 1951, with the founding of the Fédération Européene d'Associations Nationales d'Ingénieurs (FEANI). FEANI produced its first register of engineers in 1970 and this was replaced in 1987 by one which included the European Engineer title (Eur.Ing.).

Until the mid-1980s member states with longer-duration degree courses were very reluctant to accept the British pattern of three-year degrees followed by professional experience as a basis for professional recognition. However, very active participation in negotiations by the UK representative body, the British National Committee for International Engineering Affairs (BNCIEA), which is a consortium of representatives from British engineering institutions, the Fellowship of Engineering and the Engineering Council, led to acceptance by FEANI's twenty member countries of a seven-year formation package.

Under the FEANI agreement a professional qualification in engineering needs a planned and monitored package with elements of training and experience in addition to education. British chartered engineers are eligible to apply to the FEANI register and thus be able to use the Eur.Ing. title before their names.

One more step along the way towards greater integration within Europe arises from the European Commission directive on a general system of recognition for higher education diplomas. There has been concern throughout the member countries that this general directive would represent a standard lower than that demanded for Eur.Ing. or indeed in the case of Britain the chartered engineer title. The European Commission has requested FEANI to produce a draft of a special directive for engineers, but largely because of strongly held views on the significance of varying lengths of degree course in different countries, at the time of writing, this issue is still under discussion.

Although Britain has achieved a large measure of acceptance in mainland Europe of the standards which can be achieved from a three-year degree course, discussions are now taking place over the possibility of rethinking the traditional British pattern. There has already been a growth in the establishment of four-year M.Eng. courses in a number of British universities. There is also interest in a movement towards a 2 + 2 pattern of higher education in engineering. This can be seen as more commensurate with the changes in patterns of education and qualifications taking place within the schools system and to resemble more closely the continental practice of two years of science to be followed by two years of specialized engineering education. A similar pattern is also operated in North America, so this would be seen to bring the educational background of British engineers much more into line with the extent of education seen as necessary for the profession in other parts of the world and distance it from its technical college heritage.

A number of the changes which are forcing Britain to become less insular have implications for the engineering profession and those who might be attracted to it. As the qualifications of British engineers are increasingly seen as standing alongside those of professional engineers in mainland Europe, it may be that some of the higher esteem with which the profession is held in Europe and other parts of the world may influence attitudes in the British context. At a practical level too, as the Single Market in Europe takes effect, British industry will increasingly have to pay salaries to engineers which are competitive with rates in mainland Europe.

As illustrated earlier in the case of Canadian engineers, symbolism can be a powerful element in the pride people take in their profession and the prestige accorded them by others. For instance, by conforming to the continental practice of prefixing titles, this gives British engineers an opportunity to symbolize more overtly their pride as an engineer. Today there is heightened awareness among young people, through media coverage and work undertaken within the schools, of the European dimension to life. If the practice of using the prefix Eur.Ing. is widely adopted by British engineers, this could be one factor which raises the visibility of engineering among young people and helps to improve the attractiveness of the profession.

OTHER ATTEMPTS TO MAKE ENGINEERING A MORE ATTRACTIVE PROFESSION

Other moves to try to make engineering more attractive to applicants have taken the form of more general engineering degrees which combine the discipline with others. Ten years ago what have become known as the Dainton courses were established in eight universities. These courses, which took four years in England and five in Scotland, were restricted to the educationally most able students and offered a significant element of management, accountancy and in some cases foreign language study. Some concern has recently been expressed, however, over the way students from these courses are then spurning a career in engineering. The point is made that attracting able students and giving them a stimulating course will not retain them within engineering while poor image and low pay are offered to graduates in the manufacturing sector (Patel 1991).

Industrial sponsorship has traditionally been offered by a number of companies to try to maintain a high profile with universities and their engineering students. Recently, however, the Association of

Graduate Recruiters has indicated that a number of engineering and manufacturing companies are now doubting the value of these schemes, as they are finding that so many of the students they sponsor through university end up working for someone else. Thus new approaches are being tried out. For instance, the Rover Cars Commercial Division is now giving students an opportunity to get some experience of the company at the end of their second year of undergraduate studies, before the company decides which ones to sponsor through the final stages of the programme (Dunn 1991). If the opportunities for sponsorship through university decrease, this could further reduce the attraction of engineering courses, as hitherto the possibility of such sponsorship has been a very positive factor in attracting people into this area of study. The situation is a matter of some concern within engineering circles, as conversely sponsorship is rising among retail and service organizations, which could further attract young people away from engineering.

TAPPING A WIDER POOL OF APPLICANTS

Two major ways of widening the pool of applicants for engineering are to attract into the profession groups who have previously not considered engineering as a possible career and/or to open up access routes into higher education to accommodate those who do not have conventional entry qualifications.

In a general attempt to attract more applicants, the Engineering Council has supported various initiatives to raise the profile of engineering among schoolchildren. For instance, there is the Neighbourhood Engineers Scheme which was started by the Institution of Electrical Engineers and the Institution of Mechanical Engineers and is now being co-ordinated by the Engineering Council. This involves three or four engineers in a neighbourhood adopting local schools. The engineer goes into a school to provide a link with the profession – for instance, helping with project work, providing introductions to industry and sometimes assisting with placements. Under this scheme the one-thousandth school was recently adopted, out of some 5,000 schools in the country.

Through the Women into Science and Engineering Programme initiated by the Engineering Council and the Equal Opportunities Commission, efforts to attract more young women into engineering have had some success. Over the decade, applications by women for engineering courses in higher education have risen from 2 per cent in 1982 to 12 per cent in 1990. This increase has to be seen in the context of an overall decline in applications, indicating that in contrast, engineering has clearly become less popular among male applicants.

While the WISE Programme can claim some success in raising the profile of engineering and science among female schoolleavers, it is generally recognized that national awareness campaigns also have to take more account of the larger adult population who could be attracted to the profession, which includes in particular women returners (Engineering Council 1990). This last report called for different arrangements to accommodate students with a wider range of academic and practical experience, involving more flexible arrangements for entry, transfer and qualification at a number of points. Carter and Kirkup (1990) show how rewarding and challenging women working in engineering find the profession but that they also find enormous obstacles in their way.

Historically the process of feminization of an occupation has not necessarily raised its prestige. The case of accountancy provides a good example of the way in which a profession can be very successful in attracting people generally and women in particular into its ranks. For instance, until the mid-1960s under 1 per cent of the membership of the Institute of Chartered Accountant in England and Wales were women; but by 1987, 39 per cent of young members were women (Crompton and Sanderson 1990: 88). Patrick Holme, dean of engineering at Imperial College, is attributed with the comment that not only does engineering not pay as well as management consultancy or accountancy but also it does not have the same highly structured training and career programme. He cites in particular the way in which accountancy firms will give graduates two months out of work to revise before exams and he compares favourably the well-organized, well-presented image of accountancy, which makes it attractive to graduates, with some contrasting images of British industry (Goodwin 1991).

EXPERIENCES IN OTHER COUNTRIES

This book has included chapters on engineers and engineering in seven different countries, to provide a context in which to evaluate where engineering in Britain stands today and where it might be going in the future.

The essential message from reading these chapters is that the place of engineering as a profession and as a powerful force within manufacturing varies considerably with the cultural context of particular countries. Even when in a technical sense engineers in different countries are performing largely similar tasks, they are likely to be doing them in very different organizational settings; their status and the regard with which their role in society is accorded will vary widely, and the relationship of engineers to management will also differ between countries. This has been illustrated in the case of Japan, Germany and Hungary, where cultural traditions are demonstrably very different, but also in the case of Canada, the USA and Ireland, where British traditions have left a mark but outcomes are very different.

One of the most striking contrasts is between the relationship in Japan and Germany, where engineering is highly regarded and closely integrated with management, and in Britain, where the status of engineering is low and many engineers, at least until very recently, have been confined to largely technical specialist or support roles, at the expense of their participating fully in management decision-making arenas.

McCormick (Chapter 4) reminds us that in the 1870s the Japanese government sent missions studying engineers and engineering to this country, as Britain was then the most advanced industrial nation. Today Britain has been looking to Japan to find ways to improve economic performance, and it is widely believed that the Japanese way of educating and training engineers and managing engineering within manufacturing has much to do with the success of that country's economy.

In Germany too, Lawrence (Chapter 5) has shown how the German understanding of management and the structuring of organizations have made companies much more 'hospitable' to engineers. They have also caused the wider society to value the technical competences of engineers more highly than in Britain.

Earlier in this chapter the issue of a fall-out from engineering by graduates was touched upon, and it is worth noting the point made on this topic by Lawrence. Not only is engineering recognized in Germany as a route to the top in manufacturing organizations, but young people's commitment towards this type of career is made before going to university and is subsequently very unlikely to change. In other words, in Germany the commitment to engineering is established at a fairly early stage. Also, manufacturing industry is so structured that engineers do not have to give up their technical activities to take on a management role. Equally, having taken this career route, there are good prospects for career progression within companies, which will include gaining top 'management' jobs.

While the situation in Germany portrayed by Lawrence suggests a very positive working experience for those who train as engineers, the contributions by Fülöp on Hungary (Chapter 6) and Wickham on Ireland (Chapter 9) show how other cultural contexts can create very different environments and opportunities for engineers. In the case of both Hungarian engineers and those in Ireland, the point is made that they feel frustrated by the limited technical demands of their work. Some Hungarian engineers resolve their frustrations by becoming involved with small enterprises. This solution has taken them beyond the narrow confines of their technical work in the state socialist enterprise, giving them more opportunities for teamwork within the organization. While some Irish engineers consider setting up their own business, emigration is more likely to be seen as the alternative to the limited opportunities open to them in their own country.

While both Hungarian and Irish engineers report frustrations with their working experiences, the underlying factors behind this situation are very different. Although there are clear differences in the economic structures of Hungary and Britain, Hungarian engineers have sentiments about their profession which have much in common with those of many British engineers, in that both feel that there is an undervaluing of their work by the wider society.

In the case of Ireland, however, it is argued that their case is closer to that of Germany, in that engineering is not a low-status occupation. Engineering in Ireland enjoys high prestige and attracts bright students. However, as Wickham sees it, the relationship between engineering education and the structure of the labour market in Ireland has built emigration into the very culture of high-technology industry in Ireland.

These experiences point to the importance of both time and place when trying to understand why what is essentially the same occupational group, carrying out very much the same types of technical task in organizations, can nevertheless attract very different responses from the wider society in terms of status, prestige and rewards. Indeed, engineers themselves respond in varying ways. The importance of historical timing has been emphasized by Meiksins and Smith in their analysis of the relationships between professionalism and unionism in America and Britain (Chapter 8).

They point to the historical roots of engineering in Britain as a practical craft, rather than a theoretical discipline, and the associated late entry of engineering into university education. In the discussion of Canadian engineers by Lee (Chapter 7), the contrast is also made between the early establishment there of engineering as a university-based discipline and the British experience. The craft heritage of engineering in Britain has made it a more fertile ground for establishing trade union representation. In contrast, in both Canada and the USA professionalism rather than trade unionism has been the major source of identity for engineers in these countries.

CONCLUDING THOUGHTS

The historical perspective highlights the way in which Britain has suffered from being the first country to industrialize and from a lack of shocks to its social fabric to cause it to change rapidly (Bannock 1990). The power of inertia has been very strong in Britain, where institutions change both slowly and painfully. However, the pressures against remaining isolated and inward looking have been growing, with events in Europe, the effect of market forces and attacks by government on professions generally, through deregulation, all creating a new environment for the 1990s (Lee 1991a).

Engineers in Britain have never achieved the autonomy and control enjoyed by their counterparts in many other countries or indeed by other professions in Britain. But, as discussed earlier, they have been outward looking in relation to the changes affecting professional recognition in Europe. As a country, Britain has always exported engineers across the world and played an important role in educating and training engineers from overseas. As the effects of the Single Market are increasingly felt, the demand for British engineers in Europe is likely to rise. One scenario would be that Britain could go down the Irish road of exporting many of its engineers, especially if salaries, job opportunities and the image of engineering in Britain remain poor. Alternatively further shortages of engineers in Britain, because of competition for their services from overseas, could push British employers towards offering engineers here the kinds of salary level enjoyed by their counterparts in, say, Germany and France. Closer associations with mainland Europe could also help to raise the profile of engineers within management hierarchies, as it is seen how other countries value the authority of their specialist knowledge.

The accounts of the place of engineers in other cultures have made it clear that there are no simple recipes or 'quick fixes' which can be applied to the British situation to raise the profile of engineers and engineering in this country. There is a strong case, however, for the continuing integration of the profession through the work of the Engineering Council and for the maintenance of a clear presence in Europe at the level of the company, the profession and academia.

Changes in the environments in which engineers work open up new horizons of opportunity for employment. They also provide a prospect for British engineers to put behind them their concerns with lack of status and prestige in the domestic economy and to grasp new opportunities for association with engineers in other parts of the world, where the profession is held in much higher esteem.

The Engineering Council could provide a central political reference point from which British engineering institutes and unions could start to press for change with employers and government. It remains to be seen whether they will seize this opportunity.

References

Abernathy, W. J., Clark, K. B. and Kantrow, A. M. (1983) *Industrial Renaissance: Producing a Competitive Future for America*, New York: Basic Books.

Adler, G. (1989) 'An engineer's perspective', in *Single Market, Europe Open for Professions*, conference transcript (London, October), London: Department of Trade and Industry.

Ahlström, G. (1982) *Engineers and Industrial Growth*, London: Croom Helm.

Aldington, Lord (1986) 'Britain's manufacturing industry', *Royal Bank of Scotland Review* 151, 3–13.

Alford, B.W.E. (1988) *British Economic Performance, 1945–1975*, London: Macmillan.

Allaire, Y. and Firsirotu, M.E. (1984) 'Theories of organizational culture', *Organizational Studies* 5 (3), 193–226.

Amsden, A. (1990) 'South Korean capitalism', *New Left Review* 182, July/August, 5–32.

Aoki, M. (1988) 'A new paradigm of work organizations: the Japanese experience', WIDER Working Paper No. 36, Helsinki: World Institute for Economic Development Economics Research, United Nations University.

Armstrong, M. (1987) 'Human research management: a case of the emperor's new clothes?', *Personnel Management*, August, 30–5.

Armstrong, P.J. (1984) 'Competition between the organizational professions and the evolution of management control strategies'; in K. Thompson (ed.) *Work, Employment and Unemployment: Perspectives on Work and Society*, Milton Keynes: Open University Press.

——(1987a) 'The abandonment of productive intervention in management teaching syllabi: an historical analysis', Warwick Papers in Industrial Relations No. 15, Coventry: Industrial Relations Research Unit, University of Warwick.

——(1987b) 'Engineers, managers and trust', *Work, Employment and Society* 1 (4), December, 421–40, 4.

Armstrong, P.J., Carter, B., Smith, C. and Nichols T. (1988) *White Collar Workers, Trade Unions and Class*, Croom Helm: London.

References

Ascher, K. (1984) *Masters of Business: The MBA and British Business*, London: Harbridge House.
Association of Professional Engineers of Ontario (1989) *1989 Report on Engineers' Salaries – Survey of Employers*, Toronto: APEO
——(1990) *APEO Membership Salary Survey 1989*, Toronto: APEO.
Baignee, A. (1990) 'Women in engineering then and now', *Indicator* 2 (4), 13–15.
Bain, G. S. (1970) *The Growth of White-Collar Unionism*, Oxford: Clarendon Press.
Bain, G. S., Coates, D. and Ellis V. (1973) *Social Stratification and Trade Unionism*, London: Heinemann Educational Books.
Balaton, K. and Dobák, M. (1986) 'A mérnöki szemlélettöl a társadalmi megközelïtésiz ['From the engineer's attitude up to the social approach'], *Közğazdasági Szemle* 5.
Bamber, G. (1986) *Militant Managers*, Aldershot: Gower.
Bannock, G. (1990) 'Britain makes up some lost ground: the 1980s story', *Quarterly Enterprise Digest*, November, 8–13.
Barnard, C. (1938) *Functions of the Executive*, Cambridge, Mass.: Harvard University Press.
Barnett, C. (1972) *The Collapse of British Power*, London: Eyre Methuen.
——(1986) *The Audit of War*, London: Macmillan.
Barsoux, J.-L. and Lawrence, P. A. (1990) *Management in France*, London: Cassell.
Bayer, H. and Lawrence, P. (1977) 'Engineering education and the status of industry', *European Journal of Engineering Education* 2.
Bell, D. (1973) *The Coming of Post-Industrial Society: A Venture in Social Forecasting*, New York: Basic Books.
Bendix, R. (1956) *Work and Authority in Industry*. Berkeley: University of California Press.
Berkó, I. (1989) 'A müszaki fejlesztök teljesitményét meghatározó tényezök az iparban' ['Factors determining the performance of technical developers in the industry'], *Ipargazdasági Szemle* 2.
Berthoud, R. and Smith, D. J. (1980) *The Education, Training and Careers of Professional Engineers*, London: Department of Industry/HMSO.
Bessant, J. and Grunt, M. (1985) *Management and Manufacturing Innovation in the United Kingdom and West Germany*, Aldershot: Gower.
Bhasavanich, D. (1985) 'An American in Tokyo: jumping to the Japanese beat', *IEEE Spectrum*, September, 2–81.
Birman, E. (1987) *Innováció* ['Innovation'], Budapest: Müszaki Könyvkiadó.
Blackburn, P. Coombs, R. and Green, K. (1985) *Technology, Economic Growth and the Labour Process*, London: Macmillan.
Boisot, M. H. (1986) 'Markets and hierarchies in a cultural perspective', *Organization Studies* 7 (2), 135–58.
Boltanski, L. (1987) *The Making of a Class: Cadres in French Society*, Cambridge: Cambridge University Press.
Boltho, A. and Hardie C. J. M. (1985) 'The Japanese economy', in D. Morris (ed.) *The Economic System in the UK*, Oxford: Oxford University Press, 3rd edn.

Booz, Allen and Hamilton (1973) Report, English translation, 'German management', *International Studies of Management and Organization*, Arts & Science Press Inc., spring/summer 1973, 223–28.
Branyiczky, I. (1988) 'A szervezeti kultúra és a vezetés' ['Organizational culture and management'], *Vezetéstudomány* 12.
Brinkmann, G. (1967) *Die Ausbildung von Führungskräften für die Wirtschaft*, Cologne: Universitätsverlag Michael Wienand.
Bryant, C. G. A. (1970) 'In defence of sociology: a reply to some contemporary philosophical criticisms', *British Journal of Sociology* 2 (1), 95–107.
Budde, A., Child, J., Francis, A. and Kieser, A. (1982) 'Corporate goals, managerial objectives, and organizational structure in British and West German companies', *Organization Studies* 3, 1–32.
Calvert, M. (1967) *The Mechanical Engineer in America, 1830–1910*, Baltimore: Johns Hopkins University Press.
Canadian Engineering Manpower Board (1989) *A Profile of the Engineering Community in Canada*, Ottawa: CEMB, November.
Capital (1964) 'Jeder Dritter Manager hat nicht Studiert', 4.
Carter, R. (1978) 'Class militancy and union character: a study of the Association of Scientific, Technical and Managerial Staffs', *Sociological Review* 27, 297–316.
——(1985) *Capitalism, Class Conflict and the New Middle Class*, London: Routledge.
Carter, R. and Kirkup, G. (1990) *Women in Engineering*, Basingstoke: Macmillan.
Chandler, A. C. Jr (1980) 'The growth of the transnational industrial firm in the United States and the United Kingdom: a comparative analysis', *Economic History Review* 23, 396–410.
Chandler, A. D. (1984) 'The emergence of managerial capitalism', *History Review* 58 (4), winter, 473–503.
Child, J. (1981) 'Culture, contingency and capitalism in the cross-national study of organizations', in B. M. Staw and L. L. Cumings (eds) *Research in Organizational Behaviour* 3, 303–56.
Child, J. and Loveridge, R. (1990) *Information Technology in European Services: Towards a Microelectronic Future*, Oxford: Blackwell.
Child, J., Fores, M., Glover, I. and Lawrence, P. (1983) 'A price to pay? Professionalism and work organization in Britain and West Germany', *Sociology* 17 (1), 63–78.
Chokki, T. (1977) comment, in K. Nakagawa (ed.) *Strategy and Structure of Big Business*, Tokyo: University of Tokyo Press.
Clancy, P. (1988) *Who Goes to College? A Second National Survey of Participation in Higher Education*, Dublin: Higher Education Authority.
Clark, R. (1984) *Aspects of Japanese Commercial Innovation*, London: Technical Change Centre.
Clegg, H. (1976) *Trade Unionism under Collective Bargaining*, Oxford: Blackwell.
Cohen, S. S. and Zysman, J. (1987) *Manufacturing Matters: The Myth of the Post-Industrial Economy*, New York: Basic Books.

References

Constable, J. and McCormick, R. (1987) *The Making of British Managers*, London: British Institute of Management/Confederation of British Industry.

Cool, K. O. and Lengnick-Hall C. A. (1985) 'Second thoughts on the transferability of Japanese management styles', *Organization Studies* 6 (1), 1–22.

Coutts, K. and Godley, W. (1989) 'The British economy under Mrs Thatcher', *Political Quarterly*, April–June, 137–51.

Crawford, S. (1989) *Technical Workers in an Advanced Society: The Work, Careers and Politics of French Engineers*, Cambridge: Cambridge University Press.

Crompton, R. and Sanderson, K. (1990) *Gendered Jobs and Social Change*, London: Unwin Hyman.

Csath, M. (1990) *Stratégiai vezetés – vállalkozás* ['Strategic management – venture'], Budapest: Közgazdasagi és Jogi Könyvkiadó.

Czabán, J. and Nováky, E. (1990) *Vállalati prognosztik I* ['Company prognostication I'], Budapest: Tankönyvkiadó.

Dalton, M. (1959) *Men Who Manage*, New York: Wiley.

Dickens, L. (1972) 'UKAPE: a study of a professional union', *Industrial Relations Journal* 3, 2–16.

Dobson, S. and Stewart, R. (1990) 'What is happening to middle management?', *British Journal of Management* 1 (1), 3–16.

Dore, R. (1976) *The Diploma Disease: Education, Qualification and Development*, London: Allen & Unwin.

——(1985) 'Japan', *ESRC Newsletter 54*, London: Economic and Social Research Council, March, 9–11.

——(1986) 'Where will the Nobel Prizes come from?', *Public Policy* 13, vi.

Dougall, J. R. (1990) 'Canadian engineering into the future', *Indicator*, 2 (4), February, 3–12.

Drucker, P. L. (1955) *The Practice of Management*, London: Heinemann.

Dunn, J. (1991) 'Rethinking the price of loyalty', *The Engineer*, 31 January, 35.

Elbaum, B. and Lazonick, W. (1986) *The Decline of the British Economy*, Oxford: Clarendon Press.

Engineering Council (1986) *Guidance Statement on the Engineering Council Registrants and Trade Union Membership*, London: Engineering Council, July.

——(1989a) *Shaping Britain's Future*, London: Engineering Council.

——(1989b) *Survey of Chartered Engineers, Incorporated Engineers and Engineering Technicians*, London: Engineering Council.

——(1990) *Engineering Futures*, London: Engineering Council.

Engineering Today (1981) 'Government gambles desperately with the new Engineering Council', 3 August, 10–11.

Eolas (Irish National Board for Science and Technology) (1989) *Electronics Manpower Study: Trends in the Irish Electronics Manufacturing Industry up to 1995*, Dublin: Eolas.

Ettlie, J. I. (1988) *Taking Charge of Manufacturing: How Companies Are Combining Technological and Organizational Innovations to Compete Successfully*, San Francisco: Jossey-Bass.

Eustace, P. (1985) 'Training Graduates for Greatness', *The Engineer*, 5 December, 43–54.
Evans, F. (1986) 'History versus the rivet counters', *The Times Higher Education Supplement*, 14 February, 11.
External Affairs Canada (1989) *1989 Canada Facts*, Ottawa: Prospectus Investment & Trade Partners.
Farkasné Déri, K. (1990) 'A vállalati kultúra és helye a paradigmák változásában ['The company culture and its place in the change of paradigms'] *Ipar-Gazdaság 10*.
Fayol, H. (1949) *General and Industrial Management*, London: Pitman.
Fellowship of Engineering (1991) *The Management of Technology in United Kingdom Manufacturing Companies*, London: Fellowship of Engineering.
Fielden, G. B. R. (Chairman) (1963) *Engineering Design*, London: Department of Scientific and Industrial Research HMSO.
Fincham, R, (1987) 'From "post-industrialism" to "information society": comment on Lyon', *Sociology* 21 (3) 463–6.
Finniston, Sir Montague (1980) *Engineering our Future*, Report of the Committee of Inquiry into the Engineering Profession (Sir Montague Finniston, Chairman), London: HMSO.
Fores, M. (1972) 'Engineering and the British economic problem', *Quest* 22, autumn.
——(1979) 'The myth of technology and industrial science', Discussion Paper 79-49, Berlin: International Institute of Management.
——(1981) 'The myth of a British industrial revolution', *History*, June, 181–98.
Fores, M. Glover, I. and Lawrence, P. (1991) 'Professionalism and rationality: a study in misapprehension', *Sociology* 25 (1), 79–100.
Fores, M. and Sorge, A. (1978) 'The rational fallacy', Discussion Paper 78-84, Berlin: International Institute of Management.
——and——(1981) 'The decline of the management ethic', *Journal of General Management* 6 (3) 36–50.
Forrester, P. G. (1986) *The British MBA*, Cranfield: Cranfield Press.
Frankel, B. (1987) *The Post-Industrial Utopians*, Cambridge: Polity Press.
Franks, Lord (1963) *British Business Schools*, London: British Institute of Management.
Fraser, A. (1941) *Employment and Earnings in the Engineering Profession, 1929–34*, US Department of Labor, Bureau of Labor Statistics Bulletin No.682, Washington, DC: US Government Printing Office.
Freeman C. (1987) *Technology Policy and Economic Performance: Lessons from Japan*, London: Frances Pinter.
Friedman, A. (1987) 'Specialist labour in Japan: computing staff and the subcontracting system', *British Journal of Industrial Relations* xxv (3), 353–69.
Fukuda, K. J. (1986) 'What can we really learn from Japanese management?' *Journal of General Management* 11 (3), 16–26.
Fülöp, Gy. (1989) *A észak-magyarországi iparvállalatok műszaki fejlesztési szinvonalának vizgálata* ['Scientific investigation of the technical developing level of the industrial enterprises in north Hungary'], Borsodi Müszaki-Gazdasági Elet, Miskolc: (1), 4–9.

——(1990) 'A robottechnika bevezetésének vállalati stratégiái' ['Company strategies of the introduction of robot technique'], *Vezetestudomány* 10.
Gallagher, C. C. (1980) 'The history of batch production and functional factory layout', *The Chartered Mechanical Engineer* 27 (4) 73–6.
Gallie, D. (1978) *In Search of the New Working Class*, Cambridge: Cambridge University Press.
——(1983) *Social Inequality and Class Radicalism in France and Britain*, Cambridge: Cambridge University Press.
Gershuny, J. I. (1978) *After Industrial Society?* London: Macmillan.
——(1983) *Social Innovation and the Division of Labour*, London: Oxford University Press.
Gershuny, J. I. and Miles, I. D. (1983) *The New Service Economy*, London: Frances Pinter.
Gerstl J. E. and Hutton, S. P. (1966) *Engineers: The Anatomy of a Profession*, London: Tavistock Publications.
Giddens, A. (1973) *The Class Structure of the Advanced Societies*, London: Hutchinson.
Gill, C., Morris, R. S. and Eaton, J. (1977) 'APST: the rise of a professional union', *Industrial Relations Journal* 8, 50–61.
Gispen, K. (1990) *New Profession, Old Order: Engineers and German Society, 1815–1914*, Cambridge: Cambridge University Press.
Glover, I. A. (1978) 'Executive career patterns: Britain, France, Germany and Sweden', in M. Fores and I. Glover (eds) *Manufacturing and Management*, London: HMSO.
——(1980) 'Social science, engineering and society', *Higher Education Review* 12, 327–42.
——(1985) 'How the west was lost?: decline of engineering and manufacturing in Britain and the United States', *Higher Education Review* 17 (3) 3–34.
——(1987) 'Functionalism, reification and managerialism in the notion of science and technology', paper presented to the Annual Conference of the British Sociological Association, University of Leeds, March, and to the Conference on the History of Technology, University of Surrey, August.
Glover, I. A. and Kelly, M. P. (1987) *Engineers in Britain: A Sociological Study of the Engineering Dimension*, London: Allen and Unwin.
——and——(1991) 'Engineering better management: sociology and the Finniston report', in G. Payne and M. Cross (eds) *Sociology in Action*, Basingstoke: Macmillan.
Godley, W. (1986) 'A doomed economy?', *New Society*, 17 January, 106–7.
Goldner, F. and Ritti, R.R. (1967) 'Professionalization as career immobility', *American Journal of Sociology* 72, 489–502.
Goldsmith, W. and Clutterbuck, D. (1984) *The Winning Streak*, London: Weidenfeld & Nicolson.
Goldstein, B. (1959) 'The perspective of unionized professionals', *Social Forces*, 37, 323–7.
Golzen, G. (1987) 'Company culture shock', *Sunday Times*, 21 June, 85.

Goodwin, B. (1991) 'The less attractive option?', *The Engineer*, 31 January, 32-3.
Gouldner, A. W. (1957-8) 'Cosmopolitans and locals: towards an analysis of latent social roles', *Administrative Science Quarterly*, December–March, 281-306, 444-80.
Graham, I. (1988) 'Japanization as mythology', *Industrial Relations Journal*, 19 (1), 69-75.
Griffiths, B. and Murray, H. (1985) *Whose Business?*, London: Institute for Economic Affairs.
Guardian, The (1989) 'Graduates in engineering shun profession', 8 December.
Gunz, H. and Whitley, R. (1985) 'Managerial cultures and industrial strategies in British firms', *Organization Studies* 6 (3), 247-73.
Halberstam, D. (1987) *The Reckoning*, New York: Avon Books.
Handy, C., Gow, I., Gordon, C., Randlesome, C. and Moloney, M. (1987) *The Making of Managers: A Report on Management Education, Training and Development in the USA, West Germany, France, Japan and the UK*, London: National Economic Development Office.
Handy, C., Gordon, C., Gow, I. and Randlesome, C. (1988) *Making Managers*, London: Pitman.
Hanlon, G. (1991) '*Graduate emigration – a continuation or a break with the past?*', Department of Sociology mimeo, Trinity College, Dublin.
Harsányi, I. (1961) *A mérnökök-technikusok munkájáról, társadalmi – anyagi helyzetéröl* 'About the work of engineers and technicians and their socio-material position', Budapest: Közgadasági és Jogi Könyvkiadó.
Hartmann, H. (1956) 'Der zahlenmässige Beitrag der deutschen Hochschulen zur Gruppe der industriellen Fuhrungskräfte', *Zeitschrift fur die gesamte Staatswissenschaft* 112.
Hartmann, H. and Wienold, H. (1967) *Universität und Unternehmer*, Gutersloh: Bertelsmann.
Harvey-Jones, Sir J. (1986) 'Bright future for British industry?', *Reader's Digest*, November, 85-8.
Hayes, R. H. and Abernathy, W. J. (1980) 'Managing our way to economic decline', *Harvard Business Review*, July–August, 67-77.
Heidenreich, M. (1991) 'White-collar culture and computer policies', paper to Tenth EGOS Colloquium **'Societal Change between Market and Organisation'**, Vienna, 15-17 July.
Hickson, D. and McMillan, C. (eds) (1981) *Organization and Nation – The Aston Programme, vol. IV*, Aldershot: Gower.
Higher Education Authority (1987) *First Destination of Award Recipients in Higher Education (1986): A Compromise Report*, Dublin: HEA.
Hirschorn, L. (1984) *Beyond Mechanization: Work and Technology in a Post-Industrial Age*, Cambridge, Mass: MIT Press.
Horovitz, J. (1980) *Top Management Control in Europe*, London: Macmillan.
Huntford, R. (1983) *The Last Place on Earth*, London: Pan.
Hurst, D. K. (1986) 'Why strategic management is bankrupt', *Organizational Dynamics*, autumn, 4-27.

References 211

Huszár, T. (1978) *Értelmiségiek, diplomások, szellemi munkások* [Intellectuals, graduates, white-collar workers'], Budapest: Kossuth Könyvkiadó.
Hutton, S. P. and Lawrence, P. A. (1981) *German Engineers: The Anatomy of a Profession*, Oxford: Oxford University Press.
Hutton, S.P., Lawrence, P.A. and Smith, J.H.(1975) *The Engineer in Germany: a Review of the Literature*, London: Department of Industry.
——(1977) *The Recruitment, Deployment, and Status of the Mechanical Engineer in the German Federal Republic*, 2 vols, London: Department of Industry.
Ince, M. (1990) 'Engineering lowers the odds to successful entry', *The Times Higher Education Supplement*, 31 August, 2.
Industrial Development Authority (1991) *Academics – Journal for Campus Entrepreneurs*, Dublin: June.
Iwata, R. (1977) 'Marketing strategy and marketing structure in three nations: the United States, the United Kingdom and Japan', in K. Nakagawa (ed.) *Strategy and Structure of Big Business*, Tokyo: University of Tokyo.
Jaeger, A.M. (1984) 'The appropriateness of organization development outside North America', *International Studies of Management and Organization* XIV (1) 23–35.
Japan Productivity Centre (1985) *Kenkyu kaihatsu gijitsusha no shogu ni kansuru chosa hokoku* 'Survey report on the treatment of research and development engineers', Tokyo: JPC.
——(1987) *Gijutsu kei jinzai no ryudoka jittai to jinji kamri chosa* ['Survey on the mobility and personnel management of technical manpower'], Tokyo: JPC.
Johnson, T. (1971) *Professions and Power*, London: Macmillan Press.
Kaplan, R. S. (1984) 'The evolution of management accounting', *Accounting Review* 59 (3) 390–418.
Kassalow, E.M. (1967) 'White collar unionism in the United States' in A. Sturmthal (ed.) *White Collar Trade Unions*, Urbana: University of Illinois Press.
Kempner, T. (1984) Review of *In Search of Excellence – lessons from America's Best Run Companies* by T. J. Peters and R. H. Waterman, Harper & Row, 1982, *Journal of General Management* 9 (3), 95–6.
Kennedy, P. (1987) *The Rise and Fall of the Great Powers*, New York: Random House.
Killeen, M. (1979) 'The electronics revolution: its Impact on Ireland', mimeo, Dublin: Industrial Development Authority.
Kleingartner, A. (1969) 'Professionalism and engineering unionism', *Industrial Relations* 8, 224–35.
Kocka, K. (1980) *White Collar Workers in America, 1890–1940*, London: Sage Publications.
Kogon, E. (1976) *Die Stunde der Ingenieure*, Duesseldorf: VDI Verlag.
Koike, K. (1988) *Understanding Industrial relations in Japan*, Basingstoke: Macmillan.

Koontz, H. and O'Donnell, C. (1968) *Principles of Management: An Analysis of Managerial Functions*, New York: McGraw-Hill, 4th edn.
Kotter, J. P. (1982) *The General Managers*, New York: Free Press.
Kornai, J. (1980): *A gazdasági vezetés túlzott központositása*, ['Extreme centralization of economic management'], Budapest: Közgazdasagi és Jogi Könyvkiadó.
Kozma, F (1990) 'Helytállás a világgazdaságban és vezetési kultúra' ['Self-maintenance in the world economy and management culture'], *Ipar-Gazdaság* 6.
Kravetz, D. J. (1988) *The Human Resources Revolution: Implementing Progressive Management Practices for Bottom-Line Success*, San Francisco: Jossey-Bass.
Kruk, M. (1967) *Die Oberen 30,000*, Wiesbaden: Betriebswirtschaftlicher Verlag Gabler.
——(1972) *Die Grossen Unternehmer*, Frankfurt: Betriebswirtsche Ftlicher Verlay Gable.
Kuhn, J. (1971) 'Engineers and their unions' in A. A. Blum *et al.* (eds) *White-Collar Workers*, New York: Random House.
Kumar, K. (1978) *Prophecy and Progress: The Sociology of Industrial and Post-Industrial Society*, Harmondsworth: Penguin.
Ladó, L (1988) 'A vezetést szolgáló alapozó ismeretek oktatásának egyes variánsai a müszaki felsöktatasban'. ['Some Variants of the teaching of basic knowledge serving management in technical higher education'], paper presented to the National Conference on Management Science, Balatonföldvar, April.
Lane, C. (1987) 'Capitalism or culture? A comparative analysis of the position in the labour process and labour market of lower white-collar workers in the financial services sector of Britain and the Federal Republic of Germany', *Work, Employment and Society* 1, 57–83.
——(1989) *Management and Labour in Europe*, Aldershot: Edward Elgar.
Larson M. S. (1977) *The Rise of Professionalism: A Sociological Analysis*, Berkeley: University of California Press.
Lawrence, P. (1980) *Managers and Management in West Germany*, London: Croom Helm.
——(1981) *Technische Intelligenz und Soziale Theorie*, Munich: Saur GmbH.
Lawrence, P. and Spybey, T. (1986) *Management and Society in Sweden*, London: Routledge & Kegan Paul.
Layton, E. T. Jr. (1986) *The Revolt of the Engineers*, Baltimore: Johns Hopkins University Press.
Lazonick, W. (1985) 'Strategy, structure and management development in the US and Britain', mimeo, University of Harvard.
LeBold, W. R. P. and Howland, W. (1966) 'The engineer in industry and government', *Journal of Engineering Education* 56, 237–59.
Lee, G. L. (1988) 'Managerial strategies, information technology and engineers', in D. Knights and H. Willmott. (eds) *New Technology and the Labour Process*, Basingstoke: Macmillan.
——(1989) 'Managing change with CAD and CAD/CAM', *IEEE Transactions on Engineering and Management*, 38 (3), August, 227–33.

References 213

——(1990) 'Competence based management education and development: a challenge for the 1990s', Queen's University School of Business Research Seminar, Queen's University, Kingston, Canada, March.

——(ed.) (1991a) *The Changing Professions: Accountancy and Law*, Centre for the Study of the Professions Workshop Series, Birmingham: Aston Business School.

——(1991b) 'The challenge of CAD/CAM: some experiences of British and Canadian engineering companies', *New Technology, Work and Employment* 8 (2), 100–111.

——(1991c) 'Tradition and change in the Canadian engineering and accountancy professions', paper presented to the British Association for Canadian Studies 1991 Conference, Nottingham, April.

Lee, J. (1990) *Ireland 1912–1985: Politics and Society*, Cambridge: Cambridge University Press.

Légaré, R. and Baignée, A. (1990) 'The national graduate survey', *Indicator*, 2 (4), 9–12.

Littler, C. R. (1982) *The Development of the Labour Process in Capitalist Societies*, London: Heinemann.

Locke, R. R, (1984) *The End of the Practical Man: Entrepreneurship and Higher Education in Germany, France and Great Britain, 1880–1940*, Greenwich, Conn.: Jai Press.

——(1989) *Management and Higher Education since 1940: The Influence of America and Japan on West Germany, Great Britain and France*, Cambridge: Cambridge University Press.

Long, R. J. (1987) *New Office Information Technology: Human and Managerial Implications*, London: Routledge.

Loveridge, R. (1990) 'Incremental innovation and appropriate learning styles in direct services', in R. Loveridge and M. Pitt, *Strategic Management of Technological Innovation*, London: Wiley.

Lynn, R. (1968) 'The Irish brain drain', Paper No. 43, Dublin: Economic and Social Research Institute.

Lyon, D. (1986) 'From "post-industrialism", to "information society": a new social transformation?', *Sociology* 20 (4), 577–88.

——(1987) 'Information technology and information society: a response to Fincham', *Sociology* 21 (3), 467–8.

McCormick, B. (1985) 'The causes of low unemployment in Japan', Occasional Papers in Employment Studies No. 4, University of Buckingham, Employment Research Centre.

McCormick, K. J. (1988a) 'Vocationalism and the Japanese educational system', *Comparative Education* 24 (1), 37–51.

——(1988b) 'Engineering education in Britain and Japan: some reflections on the use of "the best practice" model in international comparison', *Sociology* 22 (4), 583–606.

McKinlay, A. and Smith C. (1988) 'Between capital and craft: technical workers in British engineering, 1887–1939', paper presented to the British Sociological Association Annual Conference, 28–31 March.

McLoughlin, I. (1989) 'CAD – the "Taylorization" of drawing office work?', *New Technology, Work and Employment* 4 (1), 27–39.

McMahon, A. M.(1984) *The Making of a Profession: A Century of Electrical Engineering in America*, New York: IEEE Press.
Management Charter Initiative (1990) *Broadening Responsibility: Diploma Guidelines*, London: MCI.
Mangham, I. L. and Silver, M. S. (1986) *Management Training: Context and Practice*, Bath: University of Bath, School of Management.
Mann, M. (1988) *States, War and Capitalism*, Oxford: Blackwell.
Manning, M. and McDowell, M. (1984) *Electricity supply in Ireland: the History of the ESB*, Dublin: Gill & Macmillan.
Mant, A.D. (1983) *Leaders We Deserve*, Oxford: Martin Roberston.
Marosi, M. (1988) *A szervezés és irányitás nemzetközi fejlödése – magyar gyakorlata* ['International development of the organization and direction – Hungarian practice'], Budapest: Közgazdasági és Jogi Könyvkiadó.
Marquand, D. (1988) *The Unprincipled Society: New Demands and Old Politics*, London: Cape.
Maurice, M., Selier, F. and Silvestre, J. J. (1986) *The Social Foundations of Industrial Power: A Comparison of France and Germany*, Cambridge, Mass.: MIT Press.
May, T. (1979) 'Middle-class unionism', in R. King and N. Nugent (eds) *Respectable Rebels: Middle-Class Campaigns in Britain in the 1970s*, London: Hodder & Stoughton.
Meiksins, P. (1986) 'Professionalism and conflict: the case of the American Association of Engineers', *Journal of Social History* 19, 403-21.
——(1988) 'The revolt of the engineers reconsidered', *Technology and Culture*, 24, 219-46.
——(1989) 'Engineers and managers: an historical perspective on an uneasy relationship', paper presented to the American Sociological Association Meetings, San Francisco.
Meiksins, P. and Smith, C. (1991) 'Why American engineers aren't unionized: a comparative perspective', Centre for the Study of the Professions, Working Paper 2, Birmingham: Aston University.
Meyerson, D. and Martin, J. (1987) 'Cultural change: an integration of three different views', *Journal of Management Studies* 24 (6), 623-47.
Millard, R. J (1988) *The Master Spirit of the Age: Canadian Engineers and the Politics of Professionalism 1887-1992*, London: University of Toronto Press.
Mintzberg, H. (1973) *The Nature of Managerial Work*, New York: Harper & Row.
Morita, A. (1988) 'World economy: the wrong time?', *The Director*, February, 50-2.
Muta, H. (1990) 'Survey Report – Japan' in H. Muta (ed.) *Educated Unemployment in Asia*, Tokyo: Asian Productivity Association.
Nakagawa, K. (ed.) (1977) *Strategy and Structure of Big Business*, Tokyo: University of Tokyo.
National Economic and Social Council (1985) *Manpower Policy in Ireland*, Dublin: NESC.
——(1991) *The Economic and Social Implications of Emigration*, Dublin: NESC.

References 215

Nemes, F. (1990) 'Az egységeülö világgazdaság kihivásai a va' llaltokkal és vezetöikkel szemben' ['Challenges of the world economy in becoming unified against the companies and their managers']. *Kögazdasági Szemle* 9.

Noble, D. (1977) *America by Design*, New York: Knopf.

Northrup, H. (1946) *Unionization of Professional Engineers and Chemists*, New York: Industrial Relations Counsellors.

O'Donnell, M. (1980) 'Engineering manpower for economic development: present and forecast capacity', paper presented to the Conference on Engineering Manpower for Economic Development, Dublin.

O'Malley, E. (1989) *Industry and Economic Development: the Challenge for the Latecomer*, Dublin: Gill & Macmillan.

Office of Educational Research and Improvement (1987) *Japanese Education Today: A Report from the US Study of Education in Japan*, prepared by a special task force of the OERI, Washington DC: US Department of Education.

Okayama, R. (1987) 'Industrial relations in the Japanese automobile industry 1945-70: the case of Toyota', in S. Tolliday and J. Zeitlin (eds) *The Automobile Industry and its Workers: Between Fordism and Flexibility*, Oxford: Polity Press.

Okuda, K. (1983) 'The Role of Engineers in Japanese Industry and Education – An Industrial Sociologist's View', *Journal of Japanese Trade and Industry*, 5, September/October, 23-26.

Olson, M (1982) *The Rise and Decline of Nations*, New Haven: Yale University Press.

Oshima, K. and Yamada, K. (1985) 'Continuing engineering education in Japan', *European Journal of Engineering Education* 10 (3, 4), 217-20.

Patel, K. (1991) 'The course that started an exodus', *The Engineer*, 2 May, 24-5.

Perrucci, R. (1971) 'Engineering: professional servant of power' in E. Freidson (ed.) *The Professions and their Prospects*, Beverly Hills: Sage Publications.

Perrucci, R. and Gerstl, J. (1969) *Profession without Community: Engineers in American Society*, New York: Random House.

Peters, T. J. and Waterman, R. H. Jr (1982) *In Search of Excellence – Lessons from America's Best-Run Companies*, New York: Harper & Row.

Platt, J. W. (1963) Evidence to the Robins committee, part 2, vol. D, p. 1390, in Lord Robins (chairman) *Report of the Committee on Higher Education*, London: HMSO

Pollard, S. (1982) *The Wasting of the British Economy*, London: Croom Helm.

Popper, K. R. and Eccles, J. C. (1977) *The Self and its Brain*, Berlin: Springer.

Pross, H. and Boetticher, K. (1971) *Manager des Kapitalismus*, Frankfurt: Suhrkamp.

Raelin, J.A. (1986) *The Clash of Cultures: Managers and Professionals*, Boston: Harvard Business School.

Rajan, A. (1987) 'Jobs and the service sector: a down-to-earth look at a promised land', *Personnel Management*, April, 40-44.
Rawle, P. R. (1985) *The Training and Education of Engineers in Japan*, London: General Electric Company.
Robins, Lord (Chairman) (1963) *Report of the Committee on Higher Education*, London: HMSO.
Rose, M. (1985) 'Universalism, culturalism and the Aix Group', *European Sociological Review* 1 (1), 65-83.
Roslender, R. (1983) 'The Engineers' and Managers' Association', *Industrial Relations Journal* 14, 41-51.
Rosovsky, H. (1972) 'What are the "lessons" of Japanese economic history?', in A. J. Youngson (ed.) *Economic Development in the Long Run* London: Allen & Unwin.
Rothstein, W. (1968) 'The American Association of Engineers', *Industrial and Labor Relations Review*, 22, 48-72.
Routh, G. (1980) *Occupation and Pay in Great Britain, 1906-1979*, London: Macmillan.
Sakakibara, K. and Westney, D. E. (1985) 'Comparative study of the training, careers, and organization of engineers in the computer industry in the United States and Japan', *Hitotsubashi Journal of Commerce and Management* 20 (1), 1-20.
Sampson, A. (1981) *The Changing Anatomy of Britain*, London: Hodder & Stoughton.
Sato, H., Imano, K. and Yahata, S. (1987) *Jishu-gijutsu kaihatsu to soshiki jinji senryaku ni kansuru teigen*, ['Organizational and personnel administrative strategies for innovative R & D'], Tokyo: Japan Productivity Centre.
Sato, H., Imano, K., Yahata S. and Davis, S. (1988) *Organization and Administration of R & D Personnel in Japan*, Tokyo: Japan Productivity Centre.
Scott, B. R., Rosenblum, J. W. and Sproat, R. (1980) *Case Studies in Political Economy: Japan 1854-1977*, Boston: Harvard Business School.
Sikora, G. and Tóth, A. (1990) *A mérnöki munka társadalmi elismertsége és a mérnökök jövedelem viszonyai* ['Social recognition of the engineer's labour and the income conditions of engineers'], Miskolc: A Mérnöki Kamara Kiskönyvtára.
Sinclair, B. (1980) *A Centennial History of the American Society of Mechanical Engineers, 1880-1980*, Toronto: University of Toronto Press.
Sisson, K. (ed.) (1988) *Personnel Management*, Oxford: Blackwell.
Slinn, J. (1989) *Engineers in Power: 75 Years of the EPEA*, London: Lawrence & Wishart.
Smith, C. D. (1984) 'Design engineers and the capitalist firm', Work Organization Research Centre Working Paper Series, Birmingham: Aston University, November.
——(1986) 'Engineers, trade unionism and TASS', in Peter Armstrong *et al.* (eds), *White Collar Workers, Trade Unions and Class*, London: Croom Helm.
——(1987) *Technical Workers: Class, Labour and Trade Unionism*, London: Macmillan.

References

——(1989) 'Technical workers: a class and organizational analysis', in S. Clegg (ed.) *Organization Theory and Class Analysis,*' London: De Gruyter.
——(1990) 'How are engineers formed?', *Work, Employment and Society* 4 (3), 451-70.
Smith, C.D., Child, J. and Rowlinson, M. (1990) *Reshaping Work: The Cadbury Experience*, Cambridge: Cambridge University Press.
Smith, C. D. and Meiksins, P. (1991) 'Theories of cross-national organizational analysis: a new theoretical model', Tenth EGOS Colloquium 'Societal Change between Market and Organization', Vienna, 15-17 July.
Smith, P. B. and Peterson, M. F. (1988) *Leadership, Organizations and Culture*, London: Sage Publications.
Snape, E. and Bamber, G. (1989) 'Managerial and professional employees: conceptualizing union strategies and structures', *British Journal of Industrial Relations* 27, 93-110.
Snow, C. P. (1959), 'The two cultures and the scientific revolution', The Reith Lecture.
Solymosi, Zs. and Székelyi, M. (1984) *A mérnökökről* ['About the engineers'], Budapest: A Művelődési Minisztérium Kiadója.
Sorge, A. (1979) 'Engineers in management: a study of the British, French and German traditions', *Journal of General Management* 5, 46-57.
——(1985) 'Culture's consequences', in P. A. Lawrence and K. Elliott (eds) *Introducing Management*, London: Penguin.
——(1991) 'Strategic fit and the societal effect: interpreting cross-national comparisons of technology, organization and human resources', *Organization Studies* 12 (2), 161-90.
Sorge, A. and Warner, M. (1986) *Comparative Factory Management: An Anglo-German Comparison of Manufacturing Management and Manpower*, Aldershot: Gower.
SPEE (Society for the Promotion of Engineering Education) (1930) *Report of the Investigation of Engineering Education, 1923-29*, Pittsburgh: University of Pittsburgh Press.
Stewart, R. (1982) *Choices for the Manager*, Maidenhead: McGraw-Hill
Sturmthal, A. (ed.) (1967) *White Collar Trade Unions*, Urbana: University of Illinois Press.
Susánszky, J. (1985) *Tanulmányok a szervezésről és a vezetésről* ['Studies on organization and management'] Budapest: Akadémiai Kiadó.
Swidler, A. (1986) 'Culture in action: symbols and strategies', *American Sociological Review* 51, 273-86.
Swords-Isherwood, N. (1979) 'British management compared', in K. Pavitt (ed.) *Technical Innovation and British Economic Performance*, London: Science Policy Research Unit, University of Sussex/Macmillan.
Tanaka, H. (1980) 'How Japan prepares its graduates for future management', *Journal of College Placement*, summer, 37-41.
Tari, E. (1988) *Iparvállalatok belső irányítási szervete* ['Internal direction organization of the industrial companies'], Budapest: Közgazdasági és Jogi Könyvkiadó.
Taylor, F. W. (1947) *Scientific Management*, New York: Harper & Bros.

Thackray, J. (1986) 'The corporate culture rage', *Management Today*, February, 67-9, 114.
Touraine, A. (1971) *The Post-Industrial Society*, New York: Random House.
Training Agency (1989) 'Some engineering graduates go into accountancy', *Skills Bulletin*, 14. Sheffield: Training Agency, 10 autumn.
Tse, K. K. (1985) *Marks & Spencer: Anatomy of Britain's Most Efficiently Managed Company*, Oxford: Pergamon.
Tyson, S. (1987) 'The management of the personnel function', *Journal of Management Studies* 24 (5), 523-32.
Universities Central Council on Admissions (1983) *Twentieth Report 1981-82*, Cheltenham: UCCA.
——(1991) *Twenty-Eighth Report 1989-90*, Cheltenham: UCCA.
University of Toronto Career Centre (1989, 1990) *On-Campus Recruitment Programme Salary Survey 1988-89*, also *1990*, Toronto: University of Toronto.
Urwick, L. F. (1963) 'Development of industrial engineering', in H. B. Maynard (ed.) *Industrial Engineering Handbook*, New York: McGraw-Hill, 2nd edn.
——(1964) *Is Management a Profession?*, London: Urwick, Orr & Partners.
Veal, A.J. (1987) *Leisure and the Future*, London: Allen & Unwin.
Veblen, T. (1921) *The Engineers and the Price System*, New York: Viking.
Walton, R. (1961) *The Impact of the Professional Engineering Union*, Boston: Division of Research, Harvard Business School.
Warner M. (1987) Book review, *Journal of General Management* 12 (4), 105-8.
Watson, H. B. (1975) 'Organizational bases of professional status: a comparative study of engineering professions', Ph.D. dissertation, University of London.
Weiner, M. (1981) *English Culture and the Decline of the Industrial Spirit, 1850-1980*, Cambridge: Cambridge University Press.
Wersky, G. (1987) *Training for Innovation: How Japanese Companies Develop their Elite Engineers*, London: General Electric Company.
Whalley, P. (1986) *The Social Production of Technical Work: The Case of British Engineers*, London: Macmillan.
Whitley, R., Thomas, A. and Marceau, J. (1981) *Masters of Business? Business Schools and Business Graduates in Britain and France*, London: Tavistock Publications.
Whittington, R. (1991) 'The fragmentation of industrial R & D', in A. Pollert (ed.) *Farewell to Flexibility?*, Oxford: Blackwell.
Wickham, J. (1988) 'Trends in employment and skill in the Irish electronics industry', paper presented to the Labour Process Conference, Aston University.
——(1989) 'The over-educated engineer?', *Irish Business and Administrative Research* 10, 19-33.
Wickham, J. and Murray, P. (1987) *Women in the Irish Electronics Industry*, Dublin, Employment Equality Agency.

References

Wild, R. (1986) Discussion, the British Academy of Management First Annual Conference, Warwick University.
Williams, K., Williams, J. and Thomas, D. (1983) *Why Are the British Bad at Manufacturing?* London: Routledge & Kegan Paul.
Wilson, A. H. (1990) 'The public's awareness of engineering', *Indicator* 2 (4), February, 16–17.
Winch, G. (1989) 'The implementation of integrating innovations: the case of CAD/CAM', paper presented to the British Academy of Management Third Annual Conference, Manchester, September.
Women's Engineering Society (1990) 'WES matters', *The Woman Engineer* 14 (II), autumn, 15–18.
Wood, W. J. (1991a) 'Who is running British manufacturing?', School of Business Strategy and Development Working Paper, Kingston-upon-Thames: Kingston Business School.
——(1991b) 'The Influence of directors' "qualifications" on profitability in UK manufacturing companies', in D. Bennett and C. Lewis (eds) *Achieving Competitive Edge: Getting Ahead through Technology and People*, London: Springer-Verlag.
Wrigley, C. (1986) 'Technical education and industry in the nineteenth century', in B. Elbaum and W. Lazonick (eds) *The Decline of the British Economy*, Oxford: Clarendon Press.
Yonekawa, S. (1984) 'University graduates in Japanese enterprises before the Second World War', *Business History* xxvi (2), July, 193–218.
Zapf, W. (1965) 'Die deutschen Manager – Sozialprofil und Karriereweg', in W. Zapf (ed.) *Beiträge zur Analyse der deutschen Oberschicht*, Munich: Piper, 2nd edn.
Zussman, R (1985) *Mechanics of the Middle Class: Work and Politics among American Engineers*, London: University of California Press.

Index

Abernathy, W.J., 29, 51
Adler, G., 195
Ahlström, G., 23, 155
Aldington, Lord, 39
Alford, B.W.E., 39, 40
Allaire, Y., 27-8
American Association of Engineers (AAE), 155
Amsden, A., 16
Aoki, M., 61
apprenticeship systems: in Britain, 91; in Germany, 91-2
Armstrong, M., 29
Armstrong, P.J., 22, 45, 52, 57, 148
Ascher, K., 43, 49
Association of Professional Scientists and Technologists (APST), 153
Association of Scientific, Technical and Managerial Staffs (ASTMS), 144, 145, 146, 153
Association of Supervisory and Executive Engineers (ASEE), 146, 153

Baignee, A., 126, 130
Bain, G.S., 160
Balaton, K., 108
Bamber, G., 145, 146
Bannock, G., 202
Barnard, C., 90
Barnett, C., 22, 32
Barsoux, J.-L., 98
Bayer, H., 86, 87

Bell, D., 23, 32, 33, 35
Bendix, R., 156
Berkó, I., 102
Berthoud, R., 43
Bessant, J., 31
Bhasavanich, D., 65
Birman, E., 102
Blackburn, P., 37
Boetticher, K., 84-5
Boltanski, L., 7
Boltho, A., 55
Booz, Allen and Hamilton, 93, 94-7
Branyiczky, I., 110
Brinkmann, G., 86
Britain: 18, 21-2, 57, 65, 66, 118, 184-6, 202-3; apprenticeship systems, 91; education and training of engineers, 10, 22-3, 62, 63, 64, 66, 123-4, 157-8, 193-5, 196, 197; engineering unionism, 65, 142, 143-7, 149, 152, 153-4, 159, 160, 161, 202; industrialization, 21; management education and training, 188-91; *see also* management education movement; organizational structures, 3-4; professional associations, 140-1, 149, 152-4, 193; *see also* Engineering Council; recruitment of engineers, 197-9; research and development, 128-9; salaries, 74; status of engineers, 9-10,

123-4, 126, 141-2, 146-7, 155, 157-8, 197, 200; women engineers, 125-6, 198-9
British National Committee for International Engineering Affairs (BNCIEA), 196
Bryant, C.G.A., 30
Budde, A., 27

CAD/CAM systems, 186, 187
Calvert, M., 139, 156
Canada: 117-36, 202; career structures for engineers, 130-1, 133-4; chemical engineers, 128, 130; civil engineers, 127, 128, 130; education and training of engineers, 118, 120-1, 202; electrical engineers, 127, 128, 130; employment opportunities for engineers, 127-8, 129-30, 134-5; engineering unionism, 118; licensing of engineers, 11, 12, 119, 120, 121; mechanical engineers, 128, 130; professional associations, 118, 120, 135-6; recruitment of engineers, 130-3; status of engineers, 11-12, 119, 121-3, 126, 135; supply of engineers, 125; women engineers, 125, 126
Canadian Council of Civil Engineers (CSCE), 118
Canadian Council of Professional Engineers (CCPE), 120
Canadian Engineering Accreditation Board (CEAB), 120
Canadian Engineering Manpower Board, 128
Capital, 81-2
career strategies, 3
career structures for engineers: in Canada: 130-1, 133-4; in Ireland, 178-82
Carter, R., 160, 161, 199
Chandler, A.C., 155
Chandler, A.D., 60
chemical engineers, 128, 130
Child, J., 4, 5, 22, 31, 187

Chokki, T., 59
civil engineers, 127, 128, 130
Clancy, P., 163, 164
Clark, K.B., 29
Clegg, H., 143
Cohen, S.S., 34, 39
Constable, J., 49, 189
Cool, K.O., 30
Coombs, P., 37
corporatist forms of organization, 7
Council of Engineering Institutions (CEI), 153, 154
craft forms of organization, 6
Crawford, S., 8, 37
credentialism, professional, 139, 140, 148
Crompton, R., 199
culturalism, 5

Dalton, M., 3
design and development engineers in Hungary, 102-4
Dickens, L., 145
Dobák, M., 108
Dobson, S., 3
Dore, R., 61, 63, 173
Dougall, J.R., 125
Draughtman's and Allied Technician's Association (DATA), 144
Drucker, P., 29, 46
Dunn, J., 198

Eaton, J., 145
Eccles, J.C., 26
economic benefits of management education, 52
education and training: 31, 173; of engineers, *see* engineering education; in Germany, 74-80; management, *see* management education
Elbaum, B., 155
Electrical, Electronic, Telecommunications and Plumbing Union (EETPU), 146, 154

222 Index

electrical engineers, 127, 128, 130
Electrical Power Engineers' Association (EPEA), 145, 153
Electrician's Trade Union (ETU), 153
Electricity Supply Board (ESB) (Ireland), 163
electronics engineers, 163, 164, 165–6, 167–73, 178–82
emigration, 166, 181–2, 201
employment: in manufacturing, 33–4, 35–6, 39, 167–73, 185–8, 191; in service sector, 33, 34, 35, 36, 37, 38, 39
Engineering Council, 118, 119, 123, 124, 128, 154, 191–5, 198, 199, 203
engineering education and training: 195–7; in Britain, 10, 22–3, 62, 63, 64, 66, 123–4, 193–5, 196, 197; in Canada, 118, 120–1; in Germany, 76, 78, 79–80, 86–7; in Hungary, 101, 113–16; in Ireland, 163–5, 173–8; in Japan, 62–4, 65
engineering professionalism, 139–41, 147–50, 152, 202
engineering unionism, *see* trade unionism
Engineers' Guild, 144–5, 152–3
Engineers' and Managers' Association (EMA), 145, 146, 153, 154
Engineers and Scientists of America (ESA), 143
EPEA (Electrical Power Engineers' Association), 145, 153
estate forms of organization, 7
Ettlie, J.I., 28
European Community, professional qualifications and, 195–7
Evans, F., 39
expert knowledge and post-industrial theory, 35

Farkasné Déri, K., 110
Fayol, H., 44, 45

Fédération Européene d'Association Nationales d'Ingénieurs (FEANI), 195, 196
Feilden, G.B.R., 49, 52
Fincham, R., 23
Finniston, Sir M., 18, 23, 41, 42, 49, 55, 123, 128, 185, 193
Firsirotu, M.E., 27–8
Fores, M., 21, 23, 26, 35, 36, 49, 74
Forrester, P.G., 42, 49
France, 7, 8, 97–8
Frankel, B., 36
Franks, Lord, 50
Fraser, A., 151
Freeman, C., 56, 60, 61
Fukuda, K.J., 30
Fülöp, Gy., 105
functional management, 3–4

Gallagher, C.C., 36
Germany: 7, 8, 51, 72–99, 200–1; apprenticeships systems, 91–2; education and training of engineers, 76, 78, 79–80, 86–7; educational background of managers, 80–6; management education, 76–80; management theory, influence of, 108; status of engineers, 12–13, 73–4, 164, 200
Gershunny, J.I., 34
Gerstl, J.E., 43, 72, 140, 152
Giddens, A., 33
Gill, C., 145
Gispen, K., 12
Glover, I.A., 18, 22, 24, 25, 26, 31, 35, 39, 49, 51, 145
Godley, W., 38
Goldner, F., 149
Goldstein, B., 138, 155
Golzen, G., 28
Goodwin, B., 199
Gouldner, A.W., 29
Graham, I., 30
Green, K., 37
Griffiths, B., 53
Grunt, M., 31
Guardian, 18

Gunz, H., 28

Halberstam, D., 60
Handy, C., 3, 31, 42, 49, 51, 189
Hanlon, G., 167
Hardie, C.J.M., 55
Harsanyi, I., 100, 112
Hartmann, H., 81, 83–4
Harvey-Jones, Sir J., 39, 40
Hayes, R.H., 51
Heidenreich, M., 7–8
Hickson, D., 32
Hirschorn, L., 37
Holme, P., 199
Horovitz, J., 97
hours of work, 64–5
Howland, W., 141
human resource management, 28–30
Human Resources Revolution, The (Kravetz), 29
Hungary: 100–16, 201; design and development engineers, 102–4; education and training of engineers, 101, 113–16; management theory, application of, 108–10; organizational structures, 105–8; privatization, 107; production engineers, 104; research and development, 101, 102–3, 106; sales and marketing activities by engineers, 105; status of engineers in, 14–16, 112–13
Huntford, R., 32
Hurst, D.K., 51
Huszar, T., 100, 112
Hutton, S.P., 43, 72, 73, 74, 87, 140, 152, 164

Imano, K., 68
Ince, M., 129
information society, notion of, 36–7
information technology, 8, 37, 186–8
Institute of Mechanical Engineers, 152

Institution of Electrical Engineers (IEE), 153, 193
Institution of Manufacturing Engineers, 193
Institution of Mechanical Engineers, 193
Institution of Production Engineers, 193
institutionalism, 5–7
Ireland: 162–83, 201; career structures for engineers, 178–82; education and training of engineers, 163–5, 173–8; electronics engineers, 163, 164, 165–6, 167–73, 178–82; emigration, 166, 181–2, 201; industrialization policy, 162–3; manufacturing industry, 167–73; production engineers, 171–2, 175–6, 177; research and development, 169, 170, 172–3, 176, 177, 182; status of engineers, 16–17, 164, 201; women engineers, 180
Italy, 8
Iwata, R., 58

Jaeger, A.M., 30–1
Japan: 7, 30, 51, 54–71, 200; corporate development, 57–61; education and training of engineers, 62–4, 65; engineering unionism, 65–6; Irish based firms, 178; joint stock company system, 57–8; management theory, influence of, 109–10; research and development, 67–9; status of engineers, 13–14, 200
Johnson, T., 139
joint stock company system, 57–8
Joseph, Sir K., 41

Kantrow, A.M., 29
Kaplan, R.S., 51
Kassalow, E.M., 143
Kelly, M.P., 18, 25, 39, 145
Kempner, T., 31
Kennedy, P., 38

Killeen, M., 165
Kirkup, G., 199
Kleingartner, A., 138, 143, 155
Kogon, E., 73
Koike, K., 67
Koontz, H., 44, 46
Korea, 16
Kotter, J.P., 48
Kozma, F., 110, 113
Kravetz, D.J., 29
Kruk, M., 84, 85–6
Kuhn, J., 142, 143
Kumar, K., 23, 35, 36

labour, divisions of, 24–5, 31
labour unions, *see* trade unionism
Ladó, L., 113
Lane, C., 5–6
Larson, M.S., 139, 141
Lawrence, P., 26, 32, 51, 73, 74, 86, 87, 98, 164
Layton, E.T., 139, 148, 151
Lazonick, W., 155, 158
LeBold, W.R.P., 141
Lee, G.L., 186
Lee, G.L., 186, 187, 189, 202
Lee, J., 164
Legare, R., 130
Lengnick-Hall, C.A., 30
licensing of engineers: in Canada, 11, 12, 119, 120, 121; in the USA, 139
Littler, C.R., 32
Locke, R.R., 31
Loveridge, R., 187
Lynn, R., 166
Lyon, D., 23, 36

McCormick, R., 10, 50, 55, 63, 152, 189
McDowell, M., 163
McGregor, D., 29
McLoughlin, I., 186, 187
McMahon, A.M., 151
McMillan, C., 32
Management Charter Initiative (MCI), 189–90
management education movement (MEM), 41–53, 188

management education and training: in Britain, 188–91; *see also* management education movement; in Germany, 76–80; in Hungary, 113–16
managerial forms of organization, 6–7
Mangham, I.L., 49, 52
Mann, M., 24
Manning, M., 163
Mant, A.D., 23
manufacturing: arguments for, 37–40; employment in, 33–4, 35–6, 39, 167–73, 185–8, 191
Manufacturing, Science and Finance (MSF), 146
Marceau, J., 42
Marks & Spencer, 25
Marosi, M., 105
Marquand, D., 24
Martin, J., 28
May, T., 154
mechanical engineers, 128, 130
Meiksins, P., 5, 6, 9, 139, 148, 149, 151
Meyerson, D., 28
Miles, I.D., 34
Millard, R.J., 11, 118
Mintzberg, H., 47–8
Mitsubishi Electric, 64
Morita, A., 39
Morris, R.S., 145
Murray, H., 53, 180
Muta, H., 63

Nakagawa, K., 57
National Economic and Social Council (NESC) (Ireland), 166
Neighbourhood Engineers Scheme, 198
Noble, D., 11, 139, 157
Northrup, H., 143

O'Donnell, C., 44, 46
O'Donnell, M., 167
Okayama, R., 59
Okuda, K. 61
Olson, M., 24

O'Malley, E., 162
organizational culture, 23, 24–32, 188
organizational structures: in Britain, 3–4; in Hungary, 105–8

Parnaby, J., 49
Patel, K., 197
Perrucci, R., 140, 141
Peters, T.J., 31
Peterson, M.F., 65
Platt, J.W., 43
Pollard, S., 38
Popper, K.R., 26
post-industrialism, 21, 23, 32–7
privatization, 107
production engineers: in Hungary, 104; in Ireland, 171–2, 175–6, 177
professional associations: in Britain, 118, 140–1, 149, 152–4, 193; see also Engineering Council; in Canada, 118, 120, 135–6; in United States, 139, 140–1, 149, 150–2
professional credentialism, 139, 140, 148
professional qualifications: recognition within European Community, 195–7; see also engineering education and training
professionalism: engineering, 139–41, 147–50, 152, 202; and unionism, 137–8, 149–55
project management, 4, 65
Pross, H., 84–5

qualifications, see professional qualifications

Raelin, J.A., 29
Rajan, A., 37
Rawle, P.R., 63
recruitment of engineers: in Britain, 197–9; in Canada, 130–3
research and development: 23; in Britain, 128–9; in Canada, 128; in Hungary, 101, 102–3, 106; in Ireland, 169, 170, 172–3, 176, 177, 182; in Japan, 67–9
reverse engineering, 60–1
Ritti, R.R., 149
Rosenblum, J.W., 60
Roslender, R., 145
Rosovsky, H., 58
Rowlinson, M., 4

salaries: 74, 131–2, 136
Sampson, A., 41
Sanderson, K., 199
Sato, H., 68
Scott, B.R., 59
self-service economy, 34, 38–9
service sector, employment in, 33, 34, 35, 36, 37, 38, 39
Sikora, G., 112
Silver, M.S., 49, 52
Sinclair, B., 151
Sisson, K., 29
Slinn, J., 153
Smith, C.D., 4, 5, 6, 7, 8, 9, 123, 139, 144, 145, 158
Smith, D.J., 43
Smith, J.H., 73, 74, 87
Smith, P.B., 65
Snape, E., 145, 146
Snow, C.P., 87–8
social division of labour, 24–5, 31
Solymosi, Zs., 112
Sorge, A., 23, 26–7, 28, 30, 31, 33, 49
Soviet management theory, 109
sponsorship, industrial, 197–8
Sproat, R., 60
Spybey, T., 32
status of engineers: 9–17, 121–4, 155–8, 201; in Britain, 9–10, 123–4, 126, 141–2, 146–7, 155, 157–8, 197, 200; in Canada, 11–12, 119, 121–3, 126, 135; in Germany, 12–13, 73–4, 164, 200; in Hungary, 14–16, 112–13; in Ireland, 16–17, 164, 201; in Japan, 13–14, 200; in United States, 11, 141–2, 155–7, 158

Steel Industry Staff Association (SIMA), 146
Stewart, R., 3, 48
strategic management, 51
Sturmthal, A., 138, 155
Susanszky, J., 110
Sweden, 7
Swidler, A., 32
Swords-Isherwood, N., 31
Szekelyi, M., 112

Taft-Hartley Act (1947), 143
Tanaka, H., 64
Tari, E., 105
TASS, 144, 145, 146, 153
Taylor, F.W., 44
technical division of labour, 24–5, 31
technical expertise: relevance to management functions, 44–5, 46–7, 48–9, 52, 53
Technik, German notion of, 87–91
technocracy, 33
technology: in Hungarian industry, 104; see also information technology
Thackray, J., 25–6
Thomas, A., 42
Thomas, D., 44
Tóth, A., 112
Touraine, A., 32, 33, 35
trade unionism, 137–8, 141–7, 202; in Britain, 65, 118–19, 142, 143–7, 149, 152, 153–4, 159, 160, 161, 202; in Canada, 118; in Japan, 65–6; in United States, 142–3, 149, 150, 154–5, 159, 160, 161
Training Agency, 129
Tse, K.K., 25
Tyson, S., 29

unionism, *see* trade unionism
United Kingdom Association of Professional Engineers (UKAPE), 145, 146, 153
United States: 7, 121, 202; engineering unionism, 142–3, 149, 150, 154–5, 159, 160, 161; licensing of engineers, 139; management theory, influence of, 108–9; professional associations, 139, 140–1, 149, 150–2; status of engineers, 11, 141–2, 155–7, 158; women engineers, 125
Urwick, L.F., 45

Veal, A.J., 36
Veblen, T., 21

Walton, R., 142, 143, 149
Warner, M., 26–7, 28, 30, 31, 33
Waterman, R.H., 31
Watson, H.B., 140
Weiner, M., 158
Wersky, G., 61
Whalley, P., 9, 17, 37, 141, 148, 158
Whitley, R., 28, 43
Whittington, R., 4
Wickham, J., 163, 165, 168, 180
Wienold, H., 83–4
Wild, R., 43
Williams, J., 44
Williams, K., 44
Wilson, A.H., 124–5
Winch, G., 187
women engineers, 125–6, 180, 198–9
Women in Science and Engineering Programme (WISE), 125, 198–9
Wood, W.J., 185, 190
Wrigley, C., 157

Yahata, S., 68
Yonekawa, S., 58

zaibatsu groups, 58–9, 60
Zapf, W., 82–3
Zussman, R., 11, 37, 138, 139, 155
Zysman, J., 34, 39